T0406531

Border Masculinities

Amit Thakkar • Brian Baker • Chris Harris
Editors

Border Masculinities

Literary and Visual Representations

Editors
Amit Thakkar
School of Global Affairs
Lancaster University
Lancaster, UK

Brian Baker
Department of English Literature and
Creative Writing
Lancaster University
Lancaster, UK

Chris Harris
School of Global Affairs
Lancaster University
Lancaster, UK

ISBN 978-3-031-68049-6   ISBN 978-3-031-68050-2   (eBook)
https://doi.org/10.1007/978-3-031-68050-2

© The Editor(s) (if applicable) and The Author(s), under exclusive license to Springer Nature
Switzerland AG 2024

This work is subject to copyright. All rights are solely and exclusively licensed by the
Publisher, whether the whole or part of the material is concerned, specifically the rights of
translation, reprinting, reuse of illustrations, recitation, broadcasting, reproduction on
microfilms or in any other physical way, and transmission or information storage and retrieval,
electronic adaptation, computer software, or by similar or dissimilar methodology now
known or hereafter developed.
The use of general descriptive names, registered names, trademarks, service marks, etc. in this
publication does not imply, even in the absence of a specific statement, that such names are
exempt from the relevant protective laws and regulations and therefore free for general use.
The publisher, the authors and the editors are safe to assume that the advice and information
in this book are believed to be true and accurate at the date of publication. Neither the
publisher nor the authors or the editors give a warranty, expressed or implied, with respect to
the material contained herein or for any errors or omissions that may have been made. The
publisher remains neutral with regard to jurisdictional claims in published maps and
institutional affiliations.

This Palgrave Macmillan imprint is published by the registered company Springer Nature
Switzerland AG.
The registered company address is: Gewerbestrasse 11, 6330 Cham, Switzerland

If disposing of this product, please recycle the paper.

Dedicated to Sebastian Pelayo (1994–2023)

ACKNOWLEDGEMENTS

We would like to thank Palgrave Macmillan for their patience with this project. It was delayed several times by illnesses, setbacks and tragedies affecting the children of the editors, most recently the death of a beloved stepson in 2023, at the age of twenty-nine, after a long battle with brain cancer. Throughout, Palgrave Macmillan have been flexible, compassionate and accommodating. We would also like to thank our contributors for their understanding and for staying with the project throughout these events and delays. We are honoured to have their work in this volume. Their impressive scholarship and insights have been a joy to read and learn from. We would also like to thank our families for their loving support of the project, and indeed we thank each other, as editors, for the solidarity and collaborative spirit required to complete this volume.

CONTENTS

1 Border Masculinities: Spatial and Affective Borders
Across the Planet   1
Amit Thakkar, Brian Baker, and Chris Harris

2 Working-Class Masculinities in Postsocialist Chinese
Television: Mediating (Im)potency and Reproducing
Transnational and Localised Inequalities   21
How Wee Ng

3 Crossing Borders in Two Francophone Texts: Ying
Chen's *Les Lettres chinoises* and Ananda Devi's
Les Hommes qui me parlent   45
Ashwiny Kistnareddy

4 On the Road to Y Wladfa: Mobility and Masculinities in
Separado!, Patagonia and *American Interior*   67
Brian Baker

5 Liminal Bodies: Disability and the Making of a
Masculinity in J. M. Coetzee's *Slow Man*   87
Svetlana Stefanova

6   Paul Auster's *The New York Trilogy*: Writing/
    Fatherhood/Borderlands   109
    Chris Harris

7   Gendered Borders/Bordered Genders in Maryse
    Condé's *Les Derniers Rois mages*   129
    Laura McGinnis

8   A Very English Caciquismo?: Land, Badlands and
    Habitus in Fiona Mozley's *Elmet*   149
    Amit Thakkar

9   Superheroes, Spectacles and Hoods: 'Dances of Identity'
    in Uncommon Spaces   171
    Saul Pandelakis

10 Reconfiguring Masculinities: Generic Hybridisation,
    Postfeminist Fatherhood and Queer Readings in *Les
    Misérables*   191
    Eleonora Sammartino

11 Feminicidal Masculinities: Cultural Contestations of
    Gender Violence in Ciudad Juárez   213
    Joey Whitfield

Index   235

NOTES ON CONTRIBUTORS

Brian Baker is Senior Lecturer in English and Creative Writing at Lancaster University, UK. He has published books and articles on masculinities, science fiction and science fiction cinema, Iain Sinclair, literature and science and in a critical/creative mode. *Contemporary Masculinities in Fiction, Film and Television* was published by Bloomsbury Academic in 2015. Two books of visual poetry (*Argo-0*, Steel Incisors 2022 and *An Invention*, Trickhouse Press, 2023) have been recently published, both of which rework texts by H.G. Wells. He has recently published on masculinities in *Star Wars* and is working on a project that considers masculinities, radical abjection and counterculture.

Chris Harris is now semi-retired and holds a part-time senior teaching associate role at Lancaster University. Together with Amit Thakkar (Lancaster), he has previously co-edited a special issue of the *Bulletin of Hispanic Studies* on cultural representations of masculinities and violence in Latin America as well as the volume *Men, Power and Liberation: Readings of Masculinities in Spanish American Literatures* (Routledge). His interests have long centred around Mexico, Mexican literature and gendered readings of post-Revolutionary fiction with various publications on Mariano Azuela, Elena Poniatowska, Juan Rulfo, Luis González de Alba, Agustín Yáñez, Rosario Castellanos and Rius.

Ashwiny Kistnareddy is a Leverhulme Early Career Fellow, Sir William Golding Fellow at Brasenose College and Lecturer in French at Christ Church College at the University of Oxford. She has a long-standing interest in contemporary women's writing. Her PhD at the University of

Cambridge focused on 'Masculinities in Immigrant Women's Writing in France and Canada' and was published with Palgrave Macmillan under the title *Migrant Masculinities in Women's Writing: (In)hospitality, Community, Vulnerability* (2021). She has published a monograph on Ananda Devi's works, *Locating Hybridity* (2015), and has also published articles on Kim Thúy's, Fatou Diome's, Léonora Miano's and Malika Mokeddem's texts. Her monograph *Refugee Afterlives: Home, Haunting, and Hunger* will be out in August 2024. She is currently working on a monograph on refugee life narratives and documentaries.

Laura McGinnis completed her PhD in twentieth- and twenty-first-century Antillean literature and visual culture in 2017. Her primary research interests are contemporary French and francophone literature and visual culture, as well as postcolonial, post-plantation and post-slavery theory, and gender studies. She has authored two articles focused on portrayals of gender in French Caribbean memorialisation: 'Mother, Daughter, Slave, (Re)sist(e)r? The Female Body in Antillean Visual Commemoration' (2019) and 'Memorializing Male Heroism? Gendering the Iconography of French Colonialism and Anti-colonial Resistance in Martinique and Guadeloupe' (2022). She is currently working as a Learning Development Tutor at Queen's University Belfast.

How Wee Ng is a lecturer at the School of Humanities, University of Westminster and co-founder of the Association for Curators and Programmers of Asian Cinemas (ACPAC). Research interests include Sinophone theatre, cinema, television, literature and, broadly, the exclusionary politics of representation related to ethnicity, gender, sexuality and class in visual culture. His new monograph *Worrying About the Audience in Postsocialist China: The Censorship Discourse on Chinese Television* will be published in 2025/2026.

Saul Pandelakis is an illustrator, design researcher, teacher and science-fiction author based at the University of Toulouse–Jean Jaurès (France). He is a former student of the École Normale Supérieure de Cachan. His current research aims at mapping feminist and queer empowerment in the kitchen. Aside from this main project, Saul works on the potential of sexbots (with researcher Anthony Masure) and the overlap between cinema and design (in the CinéDesign project). His film studies dissertation (Paris III-Sorbonne Nouvelle) was entitled 'Hindered Heroism, or the Male Body in American Cinema, 1978–2006' and supervised by Jean-Loup

Bourget. His first science-fiction novel (*La Séquence Aardtman*) was published in 2021 by Goater Éditions, followed by the novella *Les Hygialogues de Ty Petersen* in 2023.

Eleonora Sammartino is a Teaching Fellow in Film Studies at the University of Southampton. She holds a PhD from King's College London (2018) with a thesis on the relationship between gender representation and contemporary American film musicals. She has published on musicals and gender representation in the *European Journal of American Studies* and the collections *Musicals at the Margins* (eds. Lobalzo Wright and Shearer 2021) and *Working Women on Screen: Paid Labour and Fourth Wave Feminism* (eds. Tomsett, Weidhase and Wilde 2024). She has also contributed to the *Journal of Italian Cinema and Media Studies* and has co-edited with Alice Guilluy a special issue of *Celebrity Studies* on Hugh Grant's celebrity persona.

Svetlana Stefanova is Professor of English at the Universidad Internacional de La Rioja (Spain). She holds a PhD in English. Her doctoral thesis is a comparative study of the fiction of Caryl Phillips and J.M. Coetzee. Her primary research interests include postcolonial and gender studies. She has published articles and book chapters on the fiction of Caryl Phillips, J.M. Coetzee, Zoë Wicomb, Nnedi Okorafor, Namwali Serpell and Chimamanda Ngozi Adichie, among others. She is currently working on the representation of space and place in Phillips's works, with a special interest in gendered spaces.

Amit Thakkar is a senior lecturer at Lancaster University in the School of Global Affairs. He researches the fictional and photographic work of the Mexican writer Juan Rulfo, on whom he has published a monograph (Tamesis, 2012). With Professor Chris Harris (Lancaster), he has co-edited a special issue (*Bulletin of Hispanic Studies*, 2010) on cultural representations of masculinities and violence in Latin America, as well as the volume *Men, Power and Liberation: Readings of Masculinities in Spanish American Literatures* (Routledge 2015). His articles and chapters on Spanish American film deal with the traumatic effects of historical and national ruptures on the lives of individuals. He has also developed the concept of *cine de choque*, a specifically Hispanic aesthetic related to the traumatic resonance of car crashes. He co-edited, with Nick Hodgin (Cardiff University), *Scars and Wounds: Legacies of Trauma on Film* (2017), with Palgrave Macmillan.

Joey Whitfield is Senior Lecturer in Hispanic Studies at Cardiff University where he works on the relationship between culture, crime and punishment. He is the author of *Prison Writing of Latin America* (Bloomsbury 2018), a study of Latin America which compares texts written by 'political' and 'criminal' prisoners from Cuba, Peru, Mexico, Costa Rica, Bolivia and Brazil. He is now working on a second book, on the cultural politics of the War on Drugs. He is involved in teaching in prisons as well as universities. Working with grassroots Mexican organisations such as the Colectiva Editorial Hermanas en la Sombra, Viento Cartonero and La Rueda Cartonera he has supported the publication of writing by imprisoned and formerly imprisoned people and by the families of the disappeared.

CHAPTER 1

Border Masculinities: Spatial and Affective Borders Across the Planet

Amit Thakkar, Brian Baker, and Chris Harris

Since the Second World War, there has been a radical rethinking of global space after the independence of various regions formerly colonised by European powers, the fall of the Berlin Wall and of the Soviet Union and the further integration of the European Union in the 1990s. According to Walter Mignolo, writing in the year 2000, 'history, and particularly the past twenty years, is transforming national geopolitical configurations built mainly during the nineteenth century at the intersection of nations that were empires' (p. 218). The rethinking of borders matured in subsequent years but only more than a decade later did we see workable theorisations. Sandro Mezzadra and Brett Neilson propose 'border as method', a questioning of defined visible borders in which 'spatial thinking [...] identifies fields of relation rather than discontinuous points and lines'

A. Thakkar (✉) • C. Harris
School of Global Affairs, University of Lancaster, Lancaster, UK
e-mail: a.thakkar@lancaster.ac.uk; c.harris7@lancaster.ac.uk

B. Baker
Department of English Literature and Creative Writing, Lancaster University, Lancaster, UK
e-mail: b.baker@lancaster.ac.uk

© The Author(s), under exclusive license to Springer Nature Switzerland AG 2024
A. Thakkar et al. (eds.), *Border Masculinities*,
https://doi.org/10.1007/978-3-031-68050-2_1

characteristic of traditional topography (2012, p. 60). The mere disappearance of a physical wall, in this approach, does not entail the disappearance of the bordering tendencies that that wall represents.

As Wendy Brown, prefacing a new edition of her 2010 work *Walled States, Waning Sovereignties*, asserts: '[Physical walls] rarely succeed at interdiction. Nor do they pose an economical, effective technical response to the most menacing kinds of contemporary powers flowing across borders or threatening political communities' (2017, p. 8). Indeed, returning to Mezzadra and Neilson, we may find, in an increasingly borderless world, not fewer borders but more: 'the proliferation or multiplication of walls and borders of various kinds, not merely to mark the distinction between internal and external spaces, but also within the space and time of global capital and the borders of differential inclusion' (p. 71). Mezzadra and Neilson refer specifically to migration and its effects on the citizen-worker dyad. They rightly insist on the need to rethink borders as borderscapes, rather than lines on a map, in which the key is simultaneous inclusion and exclusion, or 'differential inclusion' (p. 67). Political subjectivities and activist potentialities, their main concern, continue to proliferate as a result of continued migrations since the publication of their work.[1] This model of simultaneous border collapse/proliferation, while helpful to us, need not be the only potential approach.

The term 'borderity', developed by Anne-Laure Amilhat Szary and Frédéric Giraut (2015), demands that we 'throw off a tautological relationship between territory, state and borders' (p. 4) so that the conception of border becomes one imbricated with mobility where migration and technology are key. We are now subject to 'a multitude of adapted technologies that not only distinguish between persons, goods, capital and information, but also between those flows that are desirable and those that are not' (pp. 5–6). Such 'flows' had been imagined in more positive terms, of course. Particularly inventive in this regard is Gustavo Pérez Firmat's *Life on the Hyphen: The Cuban-American Way* (1995), which looks at the lives of Cuban-American immigrants, who 'fall somewhere between the first and second immigrant generations' (p. 3), in a way that celebrates the hyphen in their identity as a process of constant negotiation:

> Hyphenation can mean different things: having American-born children; marrying an American man or woman; using the English language. But fundamentally it names a spiritual bilocation, the sense of being in two places at once, of living in one while residing in another. (1995 [2012], p. xi)

Thus, just as the field of border studies expands and develops in an ever less, ever more bordered world, so too the study of subjectivities, within this paradox, demands sophisticated analyses of their resulting configurations. It is in this spirit that the current volume offers a snapshot of configurations of specifically masculine subjectivities, in literary and visual cultural forms, that transcend national contexts. The analyses offered here demonstrate that modern masculinities are often both nation-contingent, sometimes nationalism-contingent, *and* spun into a vortex of unpredictable, infinite variations created by spatial borders in flux. This flux inevitably creates a to-and-fro of collapse and proliferation as a contradictory constant. Whilst the renegotiation of the border paradigm undoubtedly involves migration, new mobilities and technologies, it is also true that the complex cathectic relations created by such spatial and affective flux, with attendant transformations in power and production relations, find expression in literary and visual products. These cultural products have been revealing the contradictions, tragedies and joys of this ongoing process for much longer than the last couple of decades of increased migration and geopolitical upheaval, and they continue to do so. To an extent, we agree with Mezzadra and Neilson that the border offers 'an epistemological viewpoint that allows an acute critical analysis not only of how relations of domination and exploitation are being redefined at the present time but also of the struggles that take shape around these changing relations' (pp. 66–67). We insist, and indeed they might agree, that literary and visual cultural products can chart collapsing/proliferating spatial and affective borders—and resulting modes of connectedness between individuals—in a way that few traditional cartographers could venture to attempt. As Terry Eagleton puts it, 'no cognitive form is more adroit at mapping the complexities of the heart than artistic culture' (2000, p. 50).

A very recent contribution to that mapping can be found in Claudia Capancioni, Mariaconcetta Costantini and Mara Mattoscio's *Rethinking Identities Across Boundaries: Genders/Genres/Genera* (2023), which invites us to 'reinvent theoretical and pragmatic approaches to existing categories and cartographies, in order to envision alternative epistemologies' (p. 18). Their volume covers a range of cultural products which challenge borders at the level of gender and genre, mobilising the ambivalence of the Italian word *genere* ('gender', 'genre' and 'genus' simultaneously') with chapters that 'reflect on the enclosing typological nature of borders and border imagery, and on the significance and potentialities of crossover phenomena taking place in borderlands' (p. 7). This intervention is correspondingly scaffolded with chapters that analyse a range of specifically cultural products and producers in precisely that spirit of Mezzadra and Neilson's 'border as method', but there is no attempted focus on masculinities. Working simultaneously but separately, the editors of the present volume made a call for contributions that would identify the effects of borders on specifically *masculine* subjectivities caught up in the various ramifications of border flux. This volume is centred around the specific impacts on masculinities of an explosion in spatial border-crossing phenomena, always overlapping with conceptual borders based on gender, Self and Other, writer and reader, private and public, and many others. Throughout, collapsing/proliferating spatial borders remain central. We turn to these first before discussing concepts that deal with their affective impacts.

The Importance of Place; The Importance of Concept

There have been insightful nation-focused works on masculinities by, for example, the contributors to Carolina Rocha's *Modern Argentine Masculinities* (2013), and Derek Hird and Geng Song's edited volume *The Cosmopolitan Dream: Transnational Chinese Masculinities in a Global Age* (2018), as well as the monograph of Lawrence R. Schehr, *French Postmodern Masculinities* (2009). Hird's is most relevant to the current volume in its consideration of 'transnational' masculinities, and tellingly the most recent, but each of these works examines, at points, the impact of currents in their respective countries of study that are not just national but emanate from places beyond (Africa and Southern Europe for Rocha; Germany and Japan in Hird and Song's volume; North America for Schehr).[2] Indeed, for Gloria Anzaldúa, the notion of borderlands has never been anchored exclusively or particularly in one space: 'In fact, the Borderlands are physically present *wherever* two or more cultures edge each other, where people of different races occupy the same territory, where under, lower, middle and upper classes touch, where the space between two individuals shrinks with intimacy.' (1987, p. 9, emphasis added). Her use of the word 'intimacy' recalls Eagleton's 'mapping the complexities of the heart', mentioned above, and reaffirms our insistence on affect in the discussion of spatial borders. The project involves representations of masculinities not necessarily confined to single nations, though these remain central to most discussions. It envisions an epistemology of planetary borderlessness, where the nation-state is a framework that runs side-by-side with global considerations, even if the terms 'planetary' and 'global' must be de-conflated and our conclusion to this essay will attempt a reckoning with this task.

This epistemology of planetary borderlessness emerges out of the embracing of a range of widely applicable heuristic tools for analysing not just spatial borders but conceptual connections across those borders which help us to scrutinise the affective flux created by modern border volatility (their absence/presence, disappearance/multiplication). Such concepts include not just the classic borders of Self and Other, etc. mentioned above, but more complex borders such as feminist and postfeminist (Eleonora Sammartino), hegemonic and sub-hegemonic masculinities (How Wee Ng), or the liminal space of rites (Svetlana Stefanova). Whilst working within classic paradigms of nation, class and race, then, the chapters also mobilise conceptual frameworks which illuminate restless spatial borders, for example, femicide and feminicide in the US/Mexican borderlands (Joey Whitfield), rhizomatic mobilities across Africa, the Caribbean and the United States (Laura McGinnis) or the localised form of power known as *caciquismo* from Spanish America to England (Amit Thakkar). Other conceptual prisms in this volume for the border trope, that could easily be applied beyond the locations in which they are studied here, include diasporic communities versus migrant transnationalism (Brian Baker), superheroic versus vigilante spaces (Saul Pandelakis), the writerly present self/future self dyad (Chris Harris) and Anzaldúa's highly portable concept of *la facultad* (Ashwiny Kistnareddy).

In Chris Haywood and Máirtín Mac an Ghaill's *Men and Masculinities* (2003), there is a call for further study of the extent to which 'academic concepts developed and used in [British, American and Australian] contexts have limited purchase in different social and cultural arenas', especially in developing countries (p. 149). The study of border masculinities focuses on concepts that therefore transcend geographical and spatial boundaries, making conceptual and affective connections across those increasingly mercurial boundaries. This approach to gender and borders draws—like that of Capancioni et al.—from a wide range of fields and theories including, but not limited to, literary studies, film studies, politics, religion, geography, history, sociology and psychology. With consideration of texts from geographies as diverse as Patagonia (Brian Baker) and New York (Chris Harris), and considering genres ranging from detective novels (Joey Whitfield) to epistolary forms (Ashwiny Kistnareddy) to music and musicals (Baker, again, and Eleonora Sammartino), it is in that specific interest of initiating dialogue—between forms, regions, theories, languages and fields of academic study—that this volume has been conceived. The resulting volume is a set of global subject material that deploys the diverse concepts stated above, according to the cases of each particular chapter. But all the material also coheres more generally around the concept of unstable spatial and affective borders, the ways in which the former give birth to the latter, and—crucially—around the use of specific media to express them.

For example, how does independent filmmaking, specifically, convey a Welsh hard labourer masculinity in the colonising project of a nascent Argentina? What do we learn from a work of literary fiction, a novel, about an African Caribbean masculinity marginalised within a feminised domestic space in the United States, or a novel about an English rural strongman who behaves much like a Spanish American rural strongman, or a novel about a sudden disability and its effect on an Australian's manhood rites? How does a trilogy of New York-set novels help us to chart the maturation of an iconic writer from literary son to literary father? How are nineteenth-century French masculinities refracted through the international commercial prism of a twenty-first-century Hollywood adaptation? How differently do Hollywood films and Netflix series help us to interrogate the evolving use of props such as spectacles and hoods in the conceptual borderland between big-screen superheroes and box-set vigilantes? How is a French-Mauritian model of masculinity challenged through autofiction? How do historic Confucian models of masculinity play out in state-sponsored, Beijing-centric television? What do a detective novel and a feature film reveal about a female masculinity, a Mexican lesbian, who behaves like a classic (male) hard-boiled film noir detective? With such an array of different forms and genres, the chapters in this volume underline, through cultural production, John MacInnes' assertion (2005) that 'masculinity', singular, can never be ascertained as an essence, and that there are, instead, as many masculinities as there are men; perhaps, as the last example above suggests, as many as there are individuals.

BORDER MASCULINITIES

The volume therefore examines literary and screened representations of what the editors term 'border masculinities'. This collection contains a range of theoretically informed responses to varying representations of masculinities in contexts that are European, North and South American, Afro-Caribbean, Australasian and Asian. It does not seek to intervene in debates about 'world literature' or 'world film' but, instead, to understand masculine subjectivities, through fiction and screen, within a complex global arena of relationships and fluid movements across multiple boundaries within that arena. Despite the resurgence of strongly defended national borders of both water (the English Channel) and land (Schengen, Palestine, Mexico), as well as those created temporarily by the coronavirus pandemic (interestingly dissolved by the virus itself), increased mobilities have, as noted, been a defining feature of our times. The global scenario is fast-moving and impossible to capture in a single project but this volume is informed by the identity-morphing nature of such traffic, related to class, gender and ethnicities, as well as other theoretical parameters which cut across porous spatial boundaries. For this introduction, various terms were considered for representing masculinities most implicated with borders, both spatial and conceptual. How should such subjectivities be considered as a whole? Masculine borderhood? Bordered masculinities? We wondered what contribution to the debate might be brought about by neologisms we could have created such as 'borderality' or 'borderedness'. What about 'borderless masculinities'? It is true that spatial boundaries ebb and flow, become weaker and stronger (see Brown, 2017). But the affective borders that conceptually exist on this almost skittish hyphen, like Self-Other, Afro-Caribbean, son-father, are precisely those that continue to help us to think about our identities, shape them and form connections across any specifically spatial barriers, whether the latter are weak or strong. In the end we eschewed the academic fashion to invent a word in the hope that it might somehow embrace such an array of subjective possibilities. By pairing the word 'border' with 'masculinities', the volume encapsulates both the spatial borders affecting such subjectivities *and* the affective space of a *process* of hyphenation, where there is often a defiance of spatial and temporal boundaries.,

In an epoch where the full range of masculinities is often collapsed into the term 'toxic masculinity', this volume insists therefore on the heterogeneity and plurality of masculine subjectivities, including Connell's now classic quartet hegemonic/complicity/subordinate/marginalised (1995) but also embracing less-discussed manifestations such as postfeminist, sub-hegemonic and female masculinities. Connell argues also that '[i]deas about gender-appropriate behaviour are constantly being circulated' but that '[b]eing a man or woman is not a pre-determined state. It is a *becoming*, a condition actively under construction' (1995 [2005], p. 5; italics those of Connell). In the process of becoming, the subjects analysed in this volume find themselves on historical, emotional and intellectual borders, and very often at the nexus of all of these, overlaid with the classic paradigms mentioned above. How to negotiate the proliferation of borders in a supposedly less bordered world is a question that does concern us. For example, it is self-evident that such processes of becoming are not uniform and that they do not always pertain to groups of specifically resistant masculinities. The lack of an identikit model of resistance is not in itself a reason to discontinue analysis since there is much to learn from why certain masculinities resist and others do not, as Connell insists: 'a concept of generalized instability [does not] give any grip on why some people would want to change gendered arrangements, while others would resist' (Connell 1995 [2005], p. 90). Conversely, patriarchal masculinities do not sit still but themselves evolve to meet the challenges presented by those masculinities which resist. It is unsurprising, indeed, that 'new structures of dominance', new hegemonic masculinities, constantly emerge (p. 91), as we see in many of the chapters of this volume.

Whilst the geographical range of border masculinities that constitute the base matter for our contributors is broad in reach, then, no less so is the range of theoretical responses to the process of masculinities constantly 'becoming', the space of a hyphen which need not be divisive but based on constant negotiation and renegotiation. The contributions are thus varied not just in geographical focus but also in theories deployed, in this way reflecting the myriad nature of becoming. Major themes cut across and link individual pieces, such as sacrifice, fatherhood, borders between genres, liminality, Confucianism, queerness, and the patriarchal dividend, revealing both manifest and less manifest boundaries which might configure such subjectivities. These themes represent the kinds of research questions which the editors urged contributors to address, and they have used a variety of contemporary materials to do this. We will now run through exactly how they achieve this before concluding with a steer towards Gayatri Spivak's conceptualisation of 'planetarity' (2015) for future directions in border studies.

WAYS OF BECOMING: CHAPTER SUMMARIES

The chapter that follows this Introduction illustrates the ways in which a masculine subjectivity's becoming is indeed one of constant reshaping and is subject to shifting hegemonies. With the mobilisation of Christine Beasley's category of 'sub-hegemonic' masculinities (2008), which nuances Connell's of hegemonic masculinities, How Wee Ng argues that Damin, the star of the acclaimed hit Chinese television series *Garrulous Zhang Damin's Happy Life* (*Pinzui Zhang Damin de xingfu shenghuo*, Haofang Shen 2000), carves out a position of dominance between the hegemonic patriarchal structures around him, including the postsocialist Chinese state, and his own subordinate position as a working-class urban worker. He manages this by a series of manipulations of familial and work relations spurred on by a wit, more urban than urbane, which protects him from all sorts of threats to the hegemonic status he has within his private gender regime. Thus, for example, whilst his love rival travels to the United States, ostensibly to improve himself, Damin woos the woman he leaves behind in China, Yunfang. This type of triumph needs to be assessed in terms of Connell's notion of the 'reproductive arena' (1995) and Foucault's biopolitics (1976). As Ng states: 'Damin thus metaphorically prevents this territorial incursion into China and potentially into Yunfang's body, and thus secures the integrity of the body of the nation (symbolised by Yunfang) and the borders of China from "foreign men"'. In another example, although Damin is himself laid off, and has to work for the woman he once saw as his *tudi* (disciple), he manufactures her matrimony with his younger brother Daguo, thus reasserting his hegemony within the terms of his 'everyday' private life even if, within the wider public gender order, Ng asserts, Damin always remains subordinate. The deployment of comedy for these machinations by the witty Damin merely underscores his ability to juggle various masculine identities ultimately to his benefit, essentially making his sub-hegemonic positionality, on the border between hegemonic and subordinate, a positive one for his own subjectivity, but a demeaning one for those immediately around him. The 'gift of the gab' may seem to empower the working-class man with agency to challenge his social marginalisation, but this is ethically problematic as it involves discrimination against and domination of others, fuelled by Beijing-centrism and a panoptic patriarchy rooted in a traditional Chinese family structure.

In Chap. 3 of the volume, the private family structure, even when progressive, becomes an oppressive framework. Departing from Anzaldúa's notion of the border as a space which releases a 'constant state of transition', Ashwiny Kistnareddy writes of the borderland as a realm in which there is significant 'emotional and affective bearing on the individual psyche', such that it can be disempowering as easily as it can be empowering. Kistnareddy explores two French-language novels, the autofictional

Les Hommes qui me parlent (2011) by Ananda Devi, and *Les Lettres chinoises* (1996) by Ying Chen, the first of which demonstrates the impact of an Indo-Mauritian family's move from Mauritius to France on their second son. The parents' successful creativity becomes a source of release, the mother a writer and the father a photographer, but it is the son, having suffered bullying in the host country, due to his physical difference, who suffers the greatest psychological burden. It leaves him in a space which is indeed that of a 'constant state of transition' while the parents have successfully 'transitioned', reversing the usual expectations around adjustment where it is assumed children will adapt more readily to their host country. Ironically, the son seems to suffer from a *lack* of borders. A heavily bordered, 'tribal', almost nationalist masculinity helps the father to define himself whilst the son responds to his lack of interest in tribal borders by creating a more general border 'between himself and the world'. Ultimately, Yuan, the Chinese protagonist of the second work examined by Kistnareddy, suffers a similar fate during a period of stay in Canada. Caught between two cultures, traditional Confucianist and modern Western, and between his fiancée in China and his lover in Canada, he finds himself muddled and unable to successfully navigate towards his desired modern, Western self without the guilt of sacrificing his Chinese origins. On the surface, both Yuan and Devi's son have an empowering foot in the camps of two cultures. In reality, they are stranded between them in different ways, leading to a sense of helplessness despite the fact that they both objectively possess Anzaldúa's powerful sense of *facultad*. Kistnareddy argues that Amin Maalouf's notion of 'diverse belongings' (1998), rather than a kind of 'crossroads' identity, as proposed by Anzaldúa, seems more capable of explicating the experiences of the two male protagonists.

More positively, such crossroads can be a powerful source of solidarity across time and space, as demonstrated in Chap. 4 by Brian Baker, who considers the condition of contemporary Welsh masculinities through an examination of passage across significant borders. Through an initial analysis of Raymond Williams' *Border Country* (1960) and the television series *Y Gwyll/Hinterland* (2013–2016), which examine the construction of masculinities through a generational lens and the crossing of the border between Wales and England, Baker suggests that Welsh masculinities are currently in a period of decomposition and realignment. Traditional models of stoicism and physical strength, born of the conditions of hard labour in industry and agriculture, have declined along with the economic centrality of those industries to Wales and the UK more generally. Challenging the conventional Welsh feeling of loss and melancholia denoted by the word 'hiraeth', Baker suggests that, particularly in the work of the musician Gruff Rhys, transnational mobilities offer the opportunity to reconfigure masculinities through hybridisation and collectivity. Baker uses the history of Welsh settlement in Patagonia, Y Wladfa ('The Colony'), and in particular Rhys' road movie *Separado!* (2010), in which he tours small towns in Patagonia in a quixotic search for his cousin, the Welsh Gaucho singer René Griffiths, to rethink Welsh masculinities and narratives of return. The chapter turns to thinking about music and digital transmission channels to elucidate potentials for 'post-national' Welsh masculinities which demonstrate diverse and fluid inheritances, allegiances and forms of expression.

Borders can be crossed via such formal and geographic mobilities, of course, but they can also be traversed via immobility and a single form. The concept of liminality, and its relationship with cultural and social codes, is marshalled by Svetlana Stefanova in her assessment of the disability and masculinities in J.M. Coetzee's novel *Slow Man* (2005), in which the protagonist Paul Rayment has a leg amputated after an accident. Liminality is contrasted with marginality which, as Stefanova states, 'implies discrimination, exclusion, and inferiority with relation to a dominant centre, while liminality implies a transition, a crossover from one state to another'. Set in Australia, the 'crossover' in this novel is marked by borders related to exterior versus interior spaces, the public and the private, as well as the sexual ramifications of a transition from uncomplicated capability and interest to a perceived incapability and lack of interest. The key to unlocking the crossover, the gate on the other side of the bridge, as it were, is not held by Marijana, the Croatian care nurse who Rayment admires (and whose son Drago he would like to be a kind of father to), but by Elizabeth Costello, the protagonist of Coetzee's eponymous novel, published in 2003. In an attempt to help Rayment heal, Costello encourages a sexual encounter with another disabled person, Marianna, pronounced in the same ways as Marijana, thereby letting him confront the fear of his own otherness and overcome it within a ritualistic space similar to that which exists between boyhood and manhood, and in which 'manhood acts' can take place (Michael Schwalbe 2014). It is through this crossover that Rayment becomes able to understand his own masculinity, which is Coetzee's main concern according to Stefanova, rather than align

12   A. THAKKAR ET AL.

with any specific category of masculinity, such as hegemonic, subordinate or marginalised (Connell 1995).

In Chap. 6 of the collection, metafictional concerns also help Chris Harris to question categories, this time those of author/narrator, writer/reader and ultimately father/son. Harris reads Paul Auster's *The New York Trilogy* (1987) as 'a complex and creative account of what it means to be an American writer, on the one hand, and what it means to be a contemporary father, on the other, with myriad overlaps, or border-crossings, within and between these two literary and autobiographical meditations'. Overall, this reading brings into focus four of Auster's characteristic preoccupations relating to borders and literary masculinities. Firstly, Auster's writing is shown to dwell reflectively and philosophically in the conceptual borderlands between, *inter alia*, literary tradition/innovation, popular/high-brow literary genres, and masculine writerly identity/otherness. Secondly, Harris suggests that Auster's postmodern style makes *The New York Trilogy* a literary borderland in itself through an elaborate network of artistic border-crossings that include a deconstruction of generic conventions and ratiocination in mystery novels, and multiple intertextual references and allusions that embrace Cervantes and Borges as well as nineteenth-century American writers like Hawthorne, Poe and Thoreau. Thirdly, Auster's writing is presented as an exploration of the affective borderlands between notions of failure and success in the self-understanding of both male writers and fathers, and these borderlands are explored through the lives of characters who are all writers and fathers, or father-figures: Daniel Quinn in *City of Glass*, Blue in *Ghosts*, and the unnamed narrator of *The Locked Room*. Auster's trilogy thus enables a meditation on 'chance' that stands out as another, fourth, characteristic feature of his writing linked directly to borders and masculinities. As Harris shows, in each narrative Auster explores parallel realities: the reality of a male character's life as it is being lived, compared to the reality of what that life might have been like if, when faced with a Borgesian forking path, each one had made a different life decision. Harris concludes by insisting that at the end of *The Locked Room* Auster moves beyond the many oscillations between fiction and autobiography to articulate self-consciously and presciently his moment of arrival as a successful American writer, as well as his self-identification as a proud, engaged father.

In a manner less metafictional, but just as complex, it is also the form of the novel through which Laura McGinnis analyses borders, here 'the intersection of geographical, political, spatial, sexual, racial, and cultural borders' in Maryse Condé's *Les Derniers rois mages* (1992) in the context of Édouard Glissant's concept of 'Relation' (1990) and Aimé Césaire's of *Négritude* (1956). McGinnis scrutinises the male Antillean characters of Condé's novel, and their relationship with their African heritage, in a way that makes clear that the trope of the rhizome inherent in Relation, here connecting Africa to the Caribbean (specifically, Guadeloupe and Martinique) to the United States, is far more relevant than the singular 'identité-racine' (root identity) of *Négritude*. The latter reduces these characters to a patrilineal line, one which is tied to the discovery of male African ancestors and their relevance, rather than to a more feminised present in the Caribbean, and the United States, where the protagonist and narrator Spéro moves with his wife Debbie to live in what is ultimately a matrifocal domestic home environment. As Spéro's migration and his career as an artist flounder, this domestic space evokes for McGinnis Glissant's idea of the slave ship as an entity between the borders of life and death, a 'womb-abyss', a generative environment but also one in which people perish. McGinnis advocates Glissant's Relation, then, due to the 'complexity produced by the non-hierarchical and multifarious contact between cultures, and [the fact that it] privileges connectedness, favouring an all-encompassing vision of identity such that borders and boundaries become irrelevant'. She makes clear that it is not only male but female characters, like Debbie, who can become obsessed with restrictive notions of identity favoured by the *Négritude* movement.

This dissolution of borders and boundaries characterises Fiona Mozley's *Elmet* (2017), discussed in Chap. 8 by Amit Thakkar. Of indigenous origins, the word 'cacique' was originally used to refer to a local leader who would liaise and negotiate between the Spanish colonialists and his own community. From the nineteenth century, the post-independence Spanish American cacique has evolved and survived various attempts to curb his power (Thakkar 2012). This chapter explores the extent to which forms of behaviour associated with this cacique, termed *caciquismo* or local bossism, can be observed beyond Spain and Spanish America. It does so by analysing a novel described as a 'Yorkshire western', one which crosses generic borders by borrowing from gangster, cowboy and myth genres, among others. The landowning villain Mr Price, the 'very English cacique' of the chapter's title, is analysed within the framework of certain features of Spanish American *caciquismo*, exercising local economic power, if not cultural legitimacy, in much the way caciques of Spanish American novels do, for example, in the manner of Juan Rulfo's *Pedro Páramo* (1955).

Depending on spatially contingent power relations, then, there is a very local, private regime dominated by one man. The behaviour is discussed in connection with patterns which are hegemonic, sub-hegemonic (Beasley 2008), subordinate and complicit, thus defying (bordered) categorisation. The defiance of borders leads to an analysis of the relevance of Bourdieu's habitus and the ways in which a destructive, capitalist habitus can be countered by Price's nemesis, the novel's 'hero', John Smythe, the father of the family who occupies Price's land. He builds an alternative lifestyle of gentle, planet-friendly animal and land husbandry, where gender boundaries are diffuse for his children if not for him, personally. Ultimately, the chapter enquires whether Smythe's family's defiance of the English cacique's borders, and the acquiescent habitus on which they parasitically depend, can serve as an inspiration to defy all human borders in favour of a greater awareness of our precariously incidental existence on a planet (Spivak 2015).

In Chap. 9, borders are defied quite differently, through visual cinematic and televisual props. In fact, rarely do props receive the kind of methodical attention that Saul Pandelakis gives to glasses and hoods in a piece that shines a much-needed light on the in-between space occupied by filmic superheroes and their 'normal', everyday counterparts. The Superman trilogy and its offshoots provide the framework for a discussion on the nature of seeing through glasses. The difference between male and female uses of this prop demonstrates that, while the female deployment of glasses establishes an obvious boundary between (perceived) beauty and non-beauty, the male use of them is not dissimilar. Superman's alter ego Clarke Kent's spectacles, for example, are a prop to signify aesthetics, on the one hand, and function, on the other, but they also represent the power of a gaze that is coded as masculine, and that therefore should, according to the famous theory of Laura Mulvey (1975), manifest the power of the male wearer and indeed that of the masculinised, narcissistic viewer. Pandelakis demonstrates how this is not actually the case and how, with the use of spectacles, as with costumes, 'the male superhero incidentally defuses the masculinity embodied by his superpowers […] building one's masculine power leads to deconstructing it'. The argument evolves, via M. Night Shyamalan's *Unbreakable* (2000), and the Netflix television series *Dexter* (2006–2013), with a nod to the French series *Lupin* (2021–), among an array of other screen products, to examine the trope of the hooded hero as one which evokes a seamlessness between identities, rather than boundaries. In the cases of both hood and spectacles, a border characterised by duality is framed not as binary but highly sophisticated in its nuance, since 'to be dual, one has to accept discontinuity, in terms of body and space'.

Also concerned with the power of visual transformations, Eleonora Sammartino examines the protagonists of the Hollywood version of Victor Hugo's *Les misérables* (1862 [2009]), Valjean and Javert, within a multi-layered framework informed by homosocial bonding (Eve Kosofsky Sedgwick 1985), the slash fiction eroticisation of their adversarial on-screen relationship and the borders between public and private spheres of the display of masculinities. The resulting analysis, which includes very close readings of the historical epic musical directed by Tom Hooper in 2012, allows Sammartino to posit that the relationship between the two men, read and understood from a queer perspective as one of voyeuristic narcissism, can be ascertained from the 'insistence of the camera on Valjean's body [, which] recalls Christological iconography, while a staging [...] favours a collective performance and wider perspective'. Sammartino thus places the nexus of the physical-private border at the site of the body, where Javert's gaze often falls on that of Valjean, but also situates the film generically within the interstices of various representations of the original work by Hugo, as she guides us through the literary, theatrical and filmic manifestations of the original work. She concludes with a brief analysis of the queer slash-fiction perspective that destabilises any perceived unreconstructed masculinisation of the robust, muscular epic heroic national figure that is Valjean. Throughout, Sammartino argues that Valjean, through his paternal relationship with Cosette and even more markedly with Marius, also evokes a contemporary American, specifically post-9/11 postfeminist fatherhood, as discussed by Hannah Hamad (2014), highlighting the opposition of that model of masculinity to the 'angry white male' figure represented by Javert (Michael Kimmel 2013).

In the final chapter, we return to the now archetypal borderland between Mexico and the United States. The 'angry white male' is as relevant here as the 'angry Mexican lesbian detective'. Joey Whitfield examines, through film and literature, masculinities involved in the hundreds of murders in the border city of Ciudad Juárez. These masculinities are both femicidal, in the sense that they represent men murdering women, and feminicidal, more broadly understood to be linked to a category of masculinity within which structural institutions, factors and attitudes are at play in such murders, including the state, especially in the form of the police. A 'continuum of misogyny' is identified where femicide and feminicide on the Ciudad Juárez/El Paso border between Mexico and the

United States is 'at the extreme end of the extreme end'. The obvious link between men and physical gender violence is questioned via cultural products which, through a process of 'affective theorising', bring into sharper relief those structural, rather than individual, factors, without ever downplaying the latter. For Whitfield, two works which successfully perform this task are Alicia Gaspar de Alba's detective novel *Desert Blood: the Juárez Murders* (2005) and Carlos Carrera's film *El traspatio/Backyard* (2010). The violence perpetrated by the male characters in each of these works is analysed in terms of its relationship both to individual circumstances, all different in themselves but related in their connections to the physical border of the United States and Mexico, and to the conceptual border of femicidal/feminicidal. Whilst the male characters prove categorically that the term 'feminicidal' is more appropriate for the analysis of their behaviour, emerging as the most compelling border character is the female masculinity represented by Ivon, the hard-boiled, anti-patriarchal lesbian detective in *Desert Blood*, whose own violent tendencies are not ignored in that novel. The chapter helps not just to nuance the now well-known taxonomy of Connell (1995), based on hegemonic, complicit, marginalised and subordinate masculinities, but also to advance an understanding of masculinities that dissolves such (potentially) rigid borders into the more protean 'affective theorising' supplied by cultural products.

Conclusion: Collapsing Spatial Borders with 'Planetarity'

Parenthetically, we mentioned the coronavirus pandemic earlier in this Introduction. Fuelled by the ever-increasing carbon-heavy mobility of human beings, the pandemic revealed that borders are created by humans but easily traversed by nature, in this case by the virus itself. The masks designed to protect us from, arguably, the revenge of nature also betrayed the very anti-nature quality of humanity. Borders are the means by which humans—usually men, but not always—construct and reconstruct the planet but they are contingent entirely on the extent to which the planet will tolerate them. We are ultimately bound by the laws of physics rather than anything we create, which is always fleeting in comparison. Need this be something negative, though? Given the climate emergency, there is some urgency in the consideration for planetarity (Gayatri Spivak 2015) to replace an apprehension of the world like globalisation, increasingly fixated as that term is on global (human) economics, the defence of national identities against globalising forces and trade barriers, a limited understanding perhaps propelled by interests which benefit from such a worldview. Instead, as Spivak argues, we could see the planet as 'an undivided "natural" space rather than a differentiated political space' (p. 290), without ever, of course, allowing this to become an excuse for 'good imperialism' (p. 291) to continue with its guilt assuaged.

Rightly rejecting Richard Dawkins' 'dogmatic' DNA-based notion of what drives the planet, Spivak insists on the alterity of our planet, much like that of others not known to us, arguing that it is reasonable to accept that we cannot apprehend the planet just because we live on it:

> If we think critically - via Kant again - only in reference to our cognitive faculties and consequently bound to the subjective conditions of envisioning planetarity, without undertaking to decide anything about its object, we discover that planetarity is not susceptible to the subject's grasp. (p. 291)

Traditional and current epistemologies, especially any based on borders, including our own here, do not start with the alterity of the planet. Could future studies incorporate planetary disinterest in borders as a starting point in their analyses of cultures and histories? To think in an expressly ambitious fashion, could a new border epistemology be one of 'borderlessness as method', or at least 'borderlessness' as both starting point and ethical objective, to turn the apprehension of 'border as method' on its head? Our sense is that the answer is in the affirmative. After all, the planet does not recognise nor ever create borders. Land runs under the sea and the sea runs into land, just as our invented spatial or conceptual borders, as the chapters within this volume demonstrate, are constantly traversed, eroded, dissolved and reformed. In this respect, Mezzadra and Neilson's 'discontinuous points and lines' (topographical borders) are all too human rather than cosmic, all too global rather than planetary; they are the points and lines we live by, and that prevent us from understanding the planet and the cosmos. Merely accepting this fact might be the start: to transgress, to do 'borderlessness as method' or at least to find a way to think beyond borders in a way that is enabling and empowering. Leaving the last loose ends to Spivak, the planet is best apprehended as alterity and, thus,

> to think of it is already to transgress, for, in spite of our forays into what we render through metaphor, differently, as outer and inner space, it remains

that what is above and beyond our own reach is not continuous with us as it is not, indeed, specifically discontinuous. (p. 292)

After all, the planet we live on, according to Spivak is one we 'inhabit on loan' (2015, p. 291). This very understanding of our cosmic ephemerality can itself contribute to our ability to concentrate on those affective borders that help build us, rather than on those spatial borders that only divide us, that are arbitrary, irrelevant to the cosmos, and far more likely to collapse, or at least slowly vanish even as they ebb and flow.

NOTES

1. Of interest to those investigating such political subjectivites, particularly, is *The Ashgate Research Companion to Border Studies* (2011), and other contributions to the same volume. These form an excellent basis not only for the study of individual border regions but also for the consideration of different ways to 'think borders'. Anssi Paasi's introductory essay for that volume does not shy from linguistic considerations, such as the implications of the multiple grammatical uses of the word 'border' as verb, adjective and noun, or the emergence of terms such as 'cross-border regions' as well as processes such as 'de-bordering' and 're-bordering'. There are other very interesting discussions of, for example, symbolic cross-border 'encounters' between presidents on the US-Mexican border and the smuggling of people, bodies, between North and South Korea. The focus is spatial but such work demonstrates that there is scope for dialogues between cultural studies and other fields in the humanities if only such terms become part of a more fluid exchange. Cultural products can be effective vectors of such an exchange, of course, as we argue here.
2. There are useful and interesting isolated studies concerning 'border masculinities', either anchored in very defined spatial borderscapes (Elsa Tyszler 2019 on the Spanish-Moroccan border), or in both spatial and affective tensions in cultural products. See Katherine Anne Roberts (2017), for example, on a novel set on the Canadian-American border around Niagara and Katherine Sugg (2001), on literature and film on the Mexican-US border.

WORKS CITED

Amilhat Szary, Anne-Laure, and Frédéric Giraut. 2015. Borderities: The Politics of Contemporary Mobile Borders. In *Borderities and the Politics of Contemporary Mobile Borders*, ed. Anne-Laure Amilhat Szary and Frédéric Giraut, 1–19. London: Palgrave Macmillan.

Anzaldúa, Gloria. 1987. *Borderlands/La Frontera: The New Mestiza*. San Francisco: Aunt Lute Books.

Auster, Paul. 1987. *The New York Trilogy*. London: Faber and Faber.

BBC/S4C. 2013–2016. *Y Gwyll/ Hinterland*.

Beasley, Christine. 2008. Rethinking Hegemonic Masculinity in a Globalizing World. *Men and Masculinities* 11 (1): 86–103.

Brown, Wendy. 2010 [2017]. *Walled States, Waning Sovereignties*. Princeton University Press.

Capancioni, Claudia, Mariaconcetta Costantini, and Mara Mattoscio, eds. 2023. *Rethinking Identities Across Boundaries: Genders/Genres/Genera*. London: Palgrave Macmillan.

Carrera González, Carlos. 2010. *El Traspatio [Backyard]*. Maya Entertainment.

Césaire, Aimé. 1956. *Cahier d'un retour au pays natal*. Paris: Présence africaine.

Chen, Ying. 1996. *Lettres Chinoises*. Paris: Babelio.

Coetzee, J.M. 2005. *Slow Man*. New York: Viking.

Condé, Maryse. 1992. *Les Derniers rois mages*. Paris: Mercure de France.

Connell, Raewyn. 1995 [2005]. *Masculinities*. Berkeley: University of California.

de Alba, Alicia Gaspar. 2005. *Desert Blood: The Juárez Murders*. Houston: Arte Público Press.

Devi, Ananda. 2011. *Les hommes qui me parlent*. Paris: Gallimard.

Eagleton, Terry. 2000. *The Idea of Culture*. Oxford: John Wiley & Sons.

Foucault, Michel. 1976 [1979]. *The History of Sexuality Vol. 1: An Introduction*. London: Allen Lane.

Glissant, Édouard. 1990. *Poétique de la Relation (Poétique III)*. Paris: Gallimard.

Goch, Dylan, and Gruff Rhys, Directors. 2010. *Separado!* Ie Ie Productions.

Hamad, Hannah. 2014. *Postfeminism and Paternity in Contemporary U.S. Film: Framing Fatherhood*. New York/London: Routledge.

Haofang, Shen, Director. 2000. *Pinzui Zhang Damin de xingfu shenghuo* 贫嘴张大民的幸福生活 (The Happy Life of the Garrulous Zhang Damin).

Haywood, Chris, and Máirtín Mac an Ghaill. 2003. *Men and Masculinities: Theory, Research and Social Practice*. Buckingham: Open University.

Hird, Derek, and Geng Song, eds. 2018. *The Cosmopolitan Dream: Transnational Chinese Masculinities in a Global Age*. Hong Kong University Press.

Hooper, Tom, Director. 2012. *Les Misérables*. Universal Pictures.

Hugo, Victor. 2009. *Les Misérables*. Trans. Julie Rose. London: Vintage.

Kimmel, Michael. 2013. *Angry White Men: American Masculinity at the End of an Era*. New York: Nation Books.

Maalouf, Amin. 1998. *Identités meurtrières*. Paris: Grasset.

MacInnes, J. 2005. The Crisis of Masculinity and the Politics of Identity. In *The Masculinities Reader*, ed. S.M. Whitehead and F.J. Barrett, 311–329. Cambridge: Polity.

Manos, James, Jr. 2006–2013. *Dexter*. Netflix Series.

Mezzadra, Sandro, and Brett Neilson. 2012. Between Inclusion and Exclusion: On the Topology of Global Space and Borders. *Theory, Culture and Society* 29 (4/5): 58–75.

Mignolo, Walter. 2000. *Local Histories/Global Designs: Coloniality, Subaltern Knowledges and Border Thinking.* Princeton University Press.

Mozley, Fiona. 2017. *Elmet.* London: John Murray.

Mulvey, Laura. 1975. Visual Pleasure and Narrative Cinema. *Screen* 16: 6–18.

Paasi, Anssi. 2011. A Border Theory: An Unattainable Dream or a Realistic Aim for Border Studies Scholars? In *The Ashgate Research Companion to Border Studies*, ed. Doris Wastl-Water, 11–32. London/New York: Routledge.

Pérez Firmat, Gustavo. 1995 [2012]. *Life on the Hyphen: The Cuban-American Way.* Austin: University of Texas Press.

Roberts, Katherine Anne. 2017. 'The Taste of Wet Steel', Bordertown Masculinities in Craig Davidson's *Cataract City. Studies in Canadian Literature/Études en littérature canadienne* 42 (2): 66–90.

Rocha, Carolina, ed. 2013. *Modern Argentine Masculinities.* Bristol: NBN International.

Rulfo, Juan. 1955 [1989]. *Pedro Páramo.* Madrid: Cátedra.

Schehr, Lawrence. 2009. *French Post-modern Masculinities: From Neuromatrices to Seropositivity.* Liverpool University Press.

Schwalbe, Michael. 2014. *Manhood Acts: Gender and the Practices of Domination.* Boulder and London: Paradigm Publishers.

Sedgwick, Eve Kosofsky. 1985. *Between Men: English Literature and Male Homosocial Desire.* New York: Columbia University Press.

Shyamalan, M. Night, Director. 2000. *Unbreakable.* Buena Vista Pictures,

Spivak, Chakravorty Gayatri. 2015. Planetarity. In 'Translation and the Untranslatable', July 2015. *Paragraph* 38 (2): 290–292.

Sugg, Katherine. 2001. Multicultural Masculinities and the Border Romance in John Sayles's *Lone Star* and Cormac McCarthy s Border Trilogy. *CR: The New Centennial Review* 1 (3): 117–115.

Thakkar, Amit. 2012. *The Fiction of Juan Rulfo: Irony, Revolution and Postcolonialism.* Woodbridge: Tamesis.

Tyszler, Elsa. 2019. The Performative Effects of the European War on Migrants. Masculinities and Femininities at the Moroccan-Spanish Border. *Gender a výzkum / Gender and Research* 20 (1): 40–66.

Wastl-Water, Doris, ed. 2011. *The Ashgate Research Companion to Border Studies.* London/New York: Routledge.

Williams, Raymond. 1960 [1964]. *Border Country.* London: Penguin.

CHAPTER 2

Working-Class Masculinities in Postsocialist Chinese Television: Mediating (Im)potency and Reproducing Transnational and Localised Inequalities

How Wee Ng

This chapter offers a critical reading of the popularly acclaimed twenty-episode television series, *Garrulous Zhang Damin's Happy Life* (*Pinzui Zhang Damin de xingfu shenghuo*, Haofang Shen 2000), adapted from Liu Heng's eponymous novella. Alongside high ratings, especially in Beijing and Northern China, the soap opera has won official accolades from the Ministry of Propaganda (Kong 2008, p. 81). The programme has also been understood as belonging to a popular television production trend in the 1990s that is seen to represent the 'everyday life' of 'ordinary people braving life's vicissitudes' and how 'a better tomorrow' can be achieved through 'love, patience and perseverance' (Zhu et al. 2008, p. 9). Critics also assert that Zhang Damin epitomises the 'daily grim life structures of destitute urban social groups' marginalised by economic growth (Cai

H. W. Ng (✉)
University of Westminster, London, UK
e-mail: H.Ng@westminster.ac.uk

© The Author(s), under exclusive license to Springer Nature Switzerland AG 2024
A. Thakkar et al. (eds.), *Border Masculinities*,
https://doi.org/10.1007/978-3-031-68050-2_2

21

2016, p. 7), through the use of witty dialogue, for the purpose of 'coming to terms with the difficulties and trivial dilemmas of their life situation' (Kong 2008, pp. 81–82). But what is so 'ordinary' and 'everyday' about the mediated reality of a Beijing working-class man like Zhang Damin? If comic effect is deployed as a 'psychological painkiller in its efforts to appease the agitated and dejected mood of the economically and socially underprivileged social cohorts', as Cai (2016, p. 7) claims, to what detriment would this be of even more marginalised groups such as women and men from other cities and provinces? How do interactions between Damin and others reveal a patriarchal Beijing-centric discourse?

To answer these questions, I begin by turning to Kam Louie's (2002) study of Chinese masculinities. His seminal conceptualisation of the *wen-wu* dyad has become the most referenced framework for scholars across different fields, including literature and popular culture. *Wen* embodies qualities of cultural attainment and literary achievements while *wu* represents martial valour. The most ideal Chinese masculinity, according to Louie, would be an amalgamation of *wen* and *wu* characteristics (2002, 2015), and he sees the dyad as shifting according to global conditions and interacting with other East Asian and Western cultures to enrich itself (2015). Additionally, the paradigm is perceived to be cross-culturally enduring 'because it has proven to be a powerful tool for ordering human relationships, whether they be between people, classes or nations' (Louie 2015, p. 6). Indeed, recent literature has acknowledged its importance as a 'powerful analytical tool' as it 'invites more historically specific scrutiny of a variety of discursive constructions of masculinity' (Song and Hird 2014, p. 4). On the other hand, scholars have also interrogated the assumptions underlying the *wen-wu* model for being ahistorical and overlooking the diversity of masculinities during the imperial period (Lean 2003, p. 834; Sommer 2015), as well as for lacking empiricism and sidestepping regional and transnational differences in more contemporary contexts (Yao 2002). Given that academia has undergone a poststructuralist shift towards problematising grand narratives, an all-encompassing and transhistorical framework for theorising Chinese masculinities can be questionable. Although the *wen-wu* dichotomy has worked for scholars examining male characters in Ming-Qing classical novels (Louie 2002; Song 2004; Huang 2006; Sommer 2015), Foucault's (1976 [1979]) biopower and R. W. Connell's work on masculinities (1995) would allow for a more nuanced reading of the paradoxes, power relations and complexities in the intersectionality of mediated Chinese working-class masculinities, including Damin's, in postsocialist and regional settings.

Foucault emphasises how the physical body is appraised according to 'its usefulness and its docility, its integration into systems of efficient and economic controls', and as a vehicle for perpetuating the social body, which 'serv[es] as the basis of the biological processes: propagation, births and mortality, the level of health, life expectancy and longevity [...]' (Foucault 1976 [1979], p. 139). The interplay between different masculinities in the series follows a Foucauldian biopolitics in which bodies are hierarchised for ensuring the survival of the social body, a premise closely related to Connell's 'reproductive arena' in which the 'everyday conduct of life' is 'defined by the bodily structures and processes of human reproduction', which includes 'sexual arousal and intercourse, childbirth and infant care, bodily sex difference and similarity' (Connell 1995, p. 71). In *Garrulous Zhang Damin*, the preoccupations of the protagonist revolve around 'biological processes'. Damin lives with his mother, two sisters and brother in a claustrophobic one-storey house situated in a *hutong* (alley). Being the eldest son underscores his patriarchal masculinity in a typical Confucian family model where the eldest son is vested with more responsibilities and power compared to his siblings. This is especially so after the demise of his father when Damin had to take care of the family during his childhood. Following marriage, other than shouldering the burden of supporting his own family, he has also been caring for his ailing mother, a Confucian responsibility which the eldest son is expected to assume. His masculinity can be examined through his many subjectivities: as head of household, surrogate father, son, husband, father, eldest brother, brother-in-law and worker. As I shall demonstrate, Damin's masculinity is predicated upon the inequalities of locality within China for establishing the libidinal superiority of the Beijing man over his counterparts from other provinces and cities, all of which resonates with the notions of 'biological processes' and 'reproductive arena'. While the series appears to allow for positive representations of the working-class man, it ironically denies Damin any actual agency as social injustices are contained through the fabrication of a private fantasy world in which women's bodies are mediation sites for conflicts between men and the recuperation of injured heterosexual working-class masculinities.

My reading situates the series in the lineage of the Chinese television dramas on the family during the 1990s and early 2000s, which have been commonly examined as an allegory of the nation-state where national and

24   H. W. NG

regional identities are continuously recreated through categories of gender, class and locality as they are constituted in popular narratives. One such example is *Yearnings* (*Kewang*, Lu Xiaowei 1990), a highly successful melodrama,[1] which became a nationwide controversy because it allegorises post-Tiananmen dilemmas of national identity in relation to socialism and to the diverse class and gender positionings of the characters as well as the viewers (Rofel 1994, p. 700). In other series such as *A Beijinger in New York* (1993) and *Sunset at Long Chao Li* (1995), scholars have argued that a remasculinisation of the Chinese man is achieved through the conquest of the foreign white woman (Barmé 1995; Lu 2000; Erwin 1999), or through Chinese victory over Japanese villains in dramas depicting the Sino-Japanese war (Song 2010, 2016). These readings highlight China's growing political and economic influence in the global arena and decentre the West as the producer of global modernising discourses through the triumph of Chinese masculinity over white and Japanese masculinities. However, a more critical approach is necessary for understanding the complex dynamics of locational and political inequalities reproduced on Chinese television (Erwin 1999, p. 235). This includes the study of the televisual representations of Chinese working-class men, which remains relatively unexplored.

During the Maoist period, workers, peasants, and soldiers were upheld as positive role models in everyday life by the Chinese Communist Party. Sheldon Lu suggests that these models have now become unattractive since economic reforms began in 1978, and 'men must search for suitable new subjectivities' (Lu 2016, p. 174). The post-Mao era sees the emergence of the *yinsheng yangshuai* discourse, driven by a conservative backlash against women's gains in socioeconomic opportunities and rights, often understood as a zero-sum game in which any progress in gender equality comes at the expense of losses for men (Zhang 2011). The concept suggests the growing prominence of women's standing above that of men (Zhong 2000, pp. 49–50), articulating a 'disappointment with Chinese men as compared with Western and Japanese men and anxiety over the virility of China as a nation in the globalizing world' (Song 2010, p. 407). The liberation and reassertion of individuality-cum-masculinity was a major concern in Chinese public culture. 'The search for Chinese masculinity' (Song 2010) was a predominant theme in intellectual discourse, literary production, and popular culture; the articulation of masculinity was used not only as a device for critiquing state discourse, but also as an allegory of China's quest for modernity and self-affirmation of national power (Rofel 1994; Zhong 2000; Song 2010, 2016).

Throughout the 1980s and 1990s, the aforementioned trope of *yinsheng yangshuai* found manifestations in many films and television series, including *Garrulous Zhang Damin*. This was also a period of economic restructuring policies when many state-owned factory workers were laid off, contributing to widespread unemployment. Under the fear of disrupting social order and challenging the legitimacy of the Party-state, their struggles are often underrepresented in mass media. Jie Yang (2010) suggests that China's integration into the global market has contributed to the reshaping of the working-class, which was previously the pillar of a socialist planned economy, into a source of labour for market exploitation. What results is not only the loss of livelihood of male workers but also their sense of virility associated with lifelong employment (Yang 2010, p. 558).[2] Running parallel with the anxiety of joblessness and the emasculated masculinity of the working-class is the rise of the nouveau riche in postsocialist society. With increasing images of successful businessmen and white-collar workers in popular media, wealth has become one of the successful indicators of Chinese masculinity (Hird 2016; Song 2010, p. 410; Hird and Song 2014, pp. 1–27). A working-class character like Damin would now be positioned at the social borders of Beijing, although this is also a position that is still higher than those of migrant workers and peasants from other provinces. An examination of the intersectionality of Damin's working-class background with his privileged position as eldest son in the family and native Beijinger will, in fact, demonstrate how locality inequalities and gender discrimination are not only used for comic effect to entrench his hegemonic masculinity, but that they also mitigate his undesirable class status in a post-reform era. The series also glosses over injustices of unemployment and social inequalities as Chinese society transitions from a command economy to a neoliberal 'socialist' market economy and suggests that the individual, through channelling energies to the domestic realm and with self-determination, can overcome socioeconomic hardship. In Damin's case, he achieves this with his talent of garrulousness. In other words, the televisual representations of working-class masculinity *reproduce* rather than critique state discourse on neoliberal inequalities.

To nuance the representation of underprivileged social groups and not simply see them as representative of the 'shared' and 'everyday' experiences of 'ordinary Chinese', Lisa Rofel invites us to learn from

26 H. W. NG

'postcolonial scholars, anthropologists and those in cultural studies' by approaching culture not as

> a set of shared meanings found in a bounded space, but rather as ongoing discursive practices with sedimented histories that mark relations of power. Thus, it becomes important to attend to how, by whom, and in what context, 'Chinese culture', for example, is invoked—that is, to the discursive effects of Chinese culture as an object of knowledge in (neo)orientalist geopolitics as well as in specific power-saturated contexts within China. Additionally, it becomes crucial to examine how people live out these imagined invocations of culture—how they are pulled into normalising practices that establish hegemonic cultural logics kept in place by ongoing iterations even as these logics reveal traces of displacements, instabilities, and engaged resistances. (Rofel 2007, p. 93)

Though the vicissitudes of a family belonging to Beijing's lower strata of society featured in *Garrulous Zhang Damin* might fall under a national allegory reading (Jameson 1986), I would go further to examine how it mediates Chinese masculinities by *reproducing* inequalities in locality, gender and class, contributing to the normalisation and entrenchment of hegemonic cultural logics, following Rofel. Three groups of men-men relationships are examined, namely those between Zhang Damin and his love rival Xu Wanjun, his brother-in-law Li Mushao, and his younger brother Zhang Daguo. I will demonstrate how Damin's masculinity is aggrandised through his assertion of libidinal superiority at the expense of discrimination towards the Shanghai male Other, belittling the Shandong rural male Other, and a panoptic assertion of patriarchy over women and men in the domestic realm. In other words, the series can be read as a national allegory which reproduces class and gender inequalities in postsocialist China.

EMASCULATING THE TRANSNATIONAL SHANGHAI MAN

When considering the intersections of Damin's familial roles and socioeconomic circumstances, his masculinity is *sub-hegemonic*, a concept suggesting that hegemonic discourses can be simultaneously legitimated by dominant ideals and by politically subjugated hypermasculinities stemming from working-class ideals (Beasley 2008; Coates 2018, p. 129). As a patriarchal figure, Damin frequently asserts his authority over other men and women and assumes a hegemonic masculinity with attendant sub-hegemonic, or at least not strictly dominant-class political or socioeconomic features, including garrulousness, social connections and resource mobilisation, all of which contribute to what Connell might term 'the hegemonic position in a given pattern of gender relations, a position always contestable' (Connell 1995, p. 77). His 'hegemonic' masculinity is thus enhanced by the assumption of other roles, such as playing conflict mediator for his siblings, as mentor to a woman subordinate at his factory, matchmaker for his brother and even problem-solver for his brother-in-law's impotence. Despite the sub-hegemonic capital he builds up, Damin is also politically subjugated as he is a worker of a state-owned vacuum-flask manufacturing factory where his father was an ex-employee. His class, plump and plain-looking appearance define him as the Chinese 'everyman' figure and symbolise the downtrodden collective of the working-class, highlighting the increasing disparity between the rich and poor in postsocialist China. In addition, his physical attributes and economic status also compromise his marriage eligibility in a consumerist postsocialist China where looks and wealth are increasingly privileged. These circumstances situate him at the 'border' of Chinese masculinities: between a hegemonic, sub-hegemonic and subjugated masculinity. Damin's sub-hegemonic masculinity not only is driven by negotiations and assertions of his power over others within the domestic realm, but also involves marginalising other men within a specific, private gender regime. As Connell states, after all, between groups of men, 'there are specific gender relations of dominance and subordination' (1995, p. 78), and in the reproductive arena of a local gender regime, 'there will always be a hegemonic masculinity which attempts to exclude, or at least marginalise, all others' (Thakkar 2013, p. 442). However, his subjugated masculinity in the wider gender order, as China undergoes transformation to a postsocialist market economy, suggests that his sub-hegemonic masculinity is at best a precarious one.

As a means of coping with day-to-day struggles, and as an expression of his masculinity, Damin compensates with a sharp tongue, arguably associated with a Beijing humour and wit that allows him to win arguments and resolve conflicts. In fact, I would argue that his gift of the gab symbolises his virility which he uses to successfully court a woman, Li Yunfang, who was initially engaged to a Shanghainese, Xu Wanjun, who goes to the United States. Hird and Song (2018) have emphasised the growing importance of studying Chinese masculinities just as Chinese men

28 H. W. NG

themselves are 'increasingly part of transnational circulations of people, ideas, images, and objects' (Hird and Song 2018, p. 1), a phenomenon which is evident in Ashwiny Kistnareddy's discussion of Ying Chen's *Lettres chinoises* in Chap. 3 of the present volume. There is a growing number of positive representations of the transnational, white-collar Chinese man, depicted as superior to his global counterparts of other nationalities and ethnicities (Song 2018). While such self-affirming tropes can be understood as an expression of China's newfound confidence (and anxieties) as a nascent superpower aspiring to global acceptance, the tensions between Damin and Wanjun highlight similar anxieties in China's imagined self-redemption in its confrontation with other countries and, in particular, the United States. Yet, as I shall demonstrate, Damin and Wanjun's interactions are also driven by a more regional rivalry and a nationalism that affords the working-class man a tantalising self-rehabilitation in a neoliberal capitalist China.

As one of the metropolises that first opened up to Western capitalism and spearheaded China's economic development, Shanghai lays claim to Chinese modernity in a way that no other mainland city does. Its cosmopolitan lifestyle and advanced infrastructure after the early twentieth century have accorded Shanghainese with a unique sense of identity and sense of superiority (Lu 1999). This has resulted in envy, resentment, and rivalry from other cities, including Beijing, the nation's capital. The political, economic, and cultural competition between these two metropolises is well-known and is sometimes represented in Chinese popular media.[3] Additionally, Shanghainese characters are often ridiculed and portrayed negatively, and their masculinities are often depicted as weak, questionable, and effeminate. (Rofel 1994) These tropes are part of an entrenched discourse of differences between northerners, including Beijing men, who are assumed to be bigger, tough, straightforward and generous, while southerners, including Shanghai men, are perceived to be smaller in stature, meek, calculating and stingy (Song 2010; Song and Hird 2014, p. 39). When Shanghainese Wanjun leaves for the United States, he abandons Yunfang (also a Beijinger), leaving her heartbroken. Opportunistically, the Beijinger Damin provides her with moral support, eventually winning her heart.[4] At the end of the series, when Wanjun (having a newly acquired American citizen status), returns to Beijing from the States for a vacation, Damin meets up with him. He makes sarcastic remarks at Wanjun to reaffirm his own achievement of having won the woman over. While bidding Xu farewell, Damin says that their meeting was a great pleasure, as he 'has never met an American in his entire life'. The conflict between Damin and Wanjun calls to mind the love rivalry over Liu Huifang between Wang Husheng, a Shanghai intellectual who looks down upon workers including his competitor, and Song Dacheng, a Beijing factory worker, in *Yearnings*. Damin's interactions with Wanjun may also be read as a recurring transnational Chinese masculine trope from earlier series such as *A Beijinger in New York* (1993) and *Sunset at Long Chao Li* (1995).[5] Tensions between Damin and Wanjun reveal the complex dynamics of locational and political inequalities within China, as, in the series, the device of transnational masculinisation is once again evoked.

The aggrandisement of the Chinese male ego is multifold: it accommodates the Beijing working-class man's fantasy of asserting libidinal superiority over the middle-class man from Shanghai, alluding to the rivalry between Beijing and Shanghai. Secondly, the Mainland Chinese man triumphs by ensuring that the native woman stays on Chinese soil and does not run away with the diasporic Chinese man, thus parochially preserving the masculinity and national integrity of China.[6] Lastly, a victorious Beijing masculinity is further boosted by defeating the Shanghai urban middle-class man who has symbolically turned 'white' via his migration to America, and even by stopping the native woman from turning 'white', evoking the xenophobic and nationalistic undertones of a post-Mao era.[7] After the 1989 Tiananmen incident, attempts have been reformulated to reinforce the authority of the Party-state through patriotic propaganda and 'state-of-the-nation education' (*guoqing jiaoyu*), specifically targeted at workers and the young (Barmé 1995, p. 212). In this context, Damin's victory over his love rival Wanjun, an American citizen, supplements the long list of Chinese men recuperating their lost masculinities in a postsocialist era. This is a deeply rooted Chinese male anxiety which Geng Song and Derek Hird refer to as a fear entwined with the supposed threat to Chinese masculinities, especially as tens of thousands of Chinese women, many of whom are young and highly educated, have married foreigners since economic reforms (2014, p. 11).

As a working-class man positioned at the borders of society, Damin has limited social and transnational mobility compared to his foreign white-collar competitors. His love victory is hence a triumph for the nation, which may also be understood to be what Geremie Barmé describes as 'the coming of age of Chinese narcissism', which 'bespeaks a desire for revenge for all the real and perceived slights of the past century' (Barmé 1995, p. 210). As aptly put by Todd Reeser, 'a nation that has suffered, or fears suffering, military defeat may use images of masculinity to revitalise or revirilise itself' (2010, p.189), which suggests that the body of a transnational Chinese man, Wanjun, like the woman's body of Yunfang, becomes a vehicle for glorifying the masculinity of a jingoistic China. Pivotal to the Party-state's legitimacy (and by association, the virility of 'tough' leaders like Mao Zedong and present Xi Jinping) is sovereignty, which is to protect China's borders from foreign transgressions, ending the 'century of humiliation' of imperialist domination of China. State propaganda often entails stoking fears of foreign aggression on China's sovereignty and foreign influence over Chinese society. In this climate, Damin's 'triumph' in preventing Yunfang from turning 'white' is a national triumph of resisting and overcoming foreign influence, the latter symbolised through the traitorous behaviour of Wanjun, who has betrayed China by becoming an American. Damin thus metaphorically prevents this territorial incursion into China and potentially into Yunfang's body, and thus secures the integrity of the body of the nation (symbolised by Yunfang) and the borders of China from 'foreign men'. In doing so, Damin asserts Beijing and working-class men as the true patriots and defenders of the nation, vis-à-vis the suspect Shanghai middle-class who collude with foreigners and allow them access to the nation and its women. It is through this manoeuvre that Damin recuperates his subjugated masculinity—that is, his disadvantaged status as a reform-era working-class man—by mapping it onto the power centre of the nation and, to some extent, reinforcing therefore the sub-hegemonic status he enjoys within his gender regime. Amid all this contestation between men, Yunfang is relatively passive and lacking agency, her body a cypher through which masculinities are constructed and geopolitical powerplays are carried out. In these terms, the television series could be said to function as national allegory.

'Terror' and 'violence', Connell claims, can be 'means of drawing boundaries and making exclusions' and 'asserting masculinity in group struggles' (1995, p. 83). While Damin's sub-hegemonic masculinity is subordinate insofar as he struggles socioeconomically due to being working-class, it is also dominant in that it is predicated upon the comedic Othering, that is, the violence of ridiculing men from other cities and provinces for self-revitalisation. Deep-seated in his triumph is his fear of losing his love interest to the transnational, white-collar Shanghai man. Entwined with this implicit inferiority complex is his sense of superiority over his rural-class brother-in-law from the countryside whom he perceives as backward and uncouth. In sum, Damin's masculinity is constituted by the intersections of power (hegemonic-sub-hegemonic/ subordinate), within borders that are both national (xenophobic) and regional (Shanghai/Beijing/countryside).

EMASCULATING AND EMPOWERING THE IMPOTENT SHANDONG MAN

The libidinal supremacy of the Beijing man over men of other provinces is reinforced by the portrayal of male impotence. Male (im)potency has been featured in some films produced in the post-Mao era and is usually read as a national allegory of China's struggle for world recognition (Lu 1997), or the emasculation of the social body during the post-Mao period (Zhong 2000). In the post-Mao era, since the 1980s, there has also been an emergence in China of *nanke* (men's medicine), which is primarily used for impotence, and this is seen as the signalling of 'a new moral code that produces desire-centred subjectivity' (Zhang 2007). In the series, Damin's potency is symbolised by his eloquence in courting Yunfang which enables him to beat his Shanghainese love rival, and his powers of wit and humour in ridiculing his peasant brother-in-law whom he perceives as uncouth and backward. The transnational patriarchal politics inherent in his 'triumph' over the former, which defines his masculinity, is underscored by the localised patriarchal politics in his interactions with the latter. In other words, the trope of (im)potency in the allegory serves both to entrench and *reproduce* localised inequalities through legitimising the marginalisation of the Shandong rural male Other within a Beijing-centric discourse.

The husband of Zhang Dayu (Damin's second sister) is Li Mushao, a pig farmer from Shandong, a coastal province in eastern China. Damin derisively calls Mushao by the nickname of 'Shandong lü' (donkey) in his absence to highlight the latter's peasant background and to ridicule his supposed lower intelligence and cultural backwardness. Notably, Mushao's name literally means 'wooden spoon' and highlights his peasant status which never rises above the concern of subsistence. This is apparently a stereotypical name to clearly distinguish the character's peasant background from the Zhangs' urban working-class status. Thick, black-rimmed glasses, ill-matching baggy western suits and a heavy Shandong accent further worsen the unflattering stereotype of this 'country bumpkin'. The comical representation of Mushao's impoverished masculinity is only one example of the frequent Othering of people from provinces outside

Beijing, which clearly demonstrates Beijing-centrism. It is deeply rooted in the patriarchal state discourse which posits Beijing as the legitimate political, cultural and economic centre of China, as symbolised by the masculinity of Damin.

Mushao's obsession in the series is closely intertwined with Connell's concept of the 'reproductive arena' (1995, p. 71–73) in which 'complex, historically changing social structures' are relevant to how our 'reproductive capacity is deployed and transformed' (Connell 2009, p. 68). He desires a child badly and fails despite multiple attempts, causing the couple to fight constantly. To escape the physical abuse of Mushao, Dayu returns to the Zhang family and this is the first time Damin and Mushao meet. Interestingly, Damin also evokes stereotypes of peasants when he tells Mushao off for abusing his wife. In Damin's own words, 'The poor and lower-middle peasants (*pinxiazhong nong*) love to beat their wives. This we know, but you dare come to the house of the working-class and do this! How can this be condoned?' This not only places the urban working-class on a higher moral ground in the political pyramid of postsocialist China, but also dismisses peasants as culturally backward and violent. Damin questions Mushao for the harm inflicted on his sister, but when it is revealed that the cause of their problem lies with their inability to have a child, the focus of the narrative shifts to the issue of men's infertility, brushing aside and condoning issues of male aggression and domestic violence.[8] The urban/rural divide in modern China has been and remains prominent—rural farmers and villagers have been stigmatised since the 1950s through the *hukou* (household registration) system,[9] which discriminates against them vis-à-vis city dwellers. The notion that domestic violence is endemic in the countryside and rare in cities is deeply embedded, despite data that proves otherwise (Cao et al. 2006).

When Mushao confides in Damin about his anxiety at being childless, the latter immediately asks if Mushao had brought his wife to see a doctor, demonstrating a male chauvinism which presupposes infertility to be inherently a woman's problem. Indeed Mushao reveals that they have been to three clinics and found nothing wrong with her, to which Damin suggests that the root of the problem then lies with Mushao and he needs to seek medical assistance. However, Mushao tries to absolve himself of the responsibility for fear of facing the truth about his own infertility. Thus, the two men are guilty of male bigotry by shifting the blame to the woman, for the shame and fear associated with impotence bespeaks the supposed erosion of masculinity. Additionally, Damin's supposed virility is also expressed through frequent boasting of his ability to have a son in front of Mushao, thereby symbolically emasculating the latter while deepening his sense of inferiority. Nevertheless, Damin's skills of persuasion commit Mushao to a visit at the male fertility clinic in Damin's company. The diagnosis shows Mushao's sperm count to be low and with Damin's compelling encouragement, he starts on a fertility treatment regime. Incidentally, it is through resolving the issue of male impotence together that Damin and Mushao forge a close brotherly bond that transcends class and regional borders. In fact, there are several times when Mushao stays for the night and Damin arranges for Yunfang to sleep with his sister so that Mushao can share his matrimonial bed. The triangular relationship between the two men and Yunfang/Dayu calls to mind Eve Sedgwick's conceptualisation of homosociality: 'men's heterosexual relationships … have as their raison d'être an ultimate bonding between men; and … this bonding, if successfully achieved, is not detrimental to 'masculinity' but definitive of it' (1985, p. 50). The heterosexual couple's bedroom becomes, in fact, an intimate homosocial space which allows the two men to strengthen their kinship, and with Damin's intervention, Mushao and Dayu eventually reap the fruit of their yearning. While homosocial bonding in the bed of the Beijing man symbolically cures the Shandong rural man of his infertility, it is insufficient to give him a male heir, much to his disappointment. His lamentation is filled with envy towards Damin who is father to a boy, which is indicative of the continuing patriarchal attitude that values sons above daughters.

Mushao's sense of inadequacy reinforces Damin's perceived superior virility of being able to produce a male heir. His sexual potency is also symbolically acknowledged when Mushao often praises him for his *hao zui* (literally good mouth, meaning eloquence), not forgetting that this was the same mouth that garners him respect, wins the hand of Yunfang and humiliates Wanjun. More importantly, the male bonding is successfully forged through the sexual empowerment of the impotent Shandong man by the virile Beijing man. Disregarding and condoning male-inflicted domestic violence, the latter helps Mushao to impregnate Dayu, relegating her subjectivity to the status of a reproductive tool. In this respect, the woman's body is once again reduced to a site for the rehabilitation of Chinese masculinity. To express gratitude to Damin for helping him to overcome his impotence, Mushao virtually kowtows to him and even presents a pair of gold rings and a bracelet as gratitude, only to be rejected by Damin initially. He dismisses Mushao's overt gesture, and he asserts that they are 'now in Beijing, not the Jiao County of Shandong'. He even ridicules him for behaving like a culturally backward nouveau riche, even though he somewhat reluctantly accepts the gift in the end, again demonstrating the stereotypical perception of Shandong people informed by a Beijing-centric sub-hegemonic masculinity. The representations of the masculinities of Wanjun, Mushao and Damin demonstrate that there is a complex geopolitics and politics of locality at play in their televisual constructions.

The White-Collar Woman's Body: Mediating Class Conflict and Brotherly Dispute Between Men

Damin is a hardworking and committed employee of a state-owned factory, but he is one of the first to be laid off when the state-owned factory undergoes restructuring, just because he is perceived by his superior as being 'less likely to seek revenge'. This implies that workers reticent about their oppression are subjected to greater social injustice in a postsocialist China. Instead of using his eloquence to protest the management's decision to lay off workers, Damin eventually accepts his joblessness, which then invokes the state's liability for this condition—represented in official discourse as *daigang*, that is, an unemployed status euphemised as a condition of waiting to be called back for work. This is part of the vocabulary of terms to cope, or contain, rather, the inequalities caused by market reforms in attempts to label the unemployed, alluding to the socialist commitment of full employment by the Chinese government, something held up to distinguish socialism from capitalism (Rofel 2007, p. 35). The series touches on the social reality of the difficulties workers have to struggle with, such as lack of housing, the rising cost of living, unemployment, difficulty in applying for financial assistance, all reinforced by Damin's helplessness as he loiters in the city after being laid off. For Damin, losing his job would imply an erosion of his patriarchal status in the household as husband, father and eldest brother and, more importantly, a perceived weakening of his masculinity, which is already subordinate to the nascent middle-class and educated man. In other words, he now occupies a position of social marginality, a masculinity on the border of working and unemployed. However, the fact that he does not use his prowess of persuasion to resist on behalf of the collective alludes to the shift towards self-preservation in an increasingly neoliberal, postsocialist-capitalist China.

With the help of his former colleague Xiaotong, Damin now becomes a janitor at a hotel in which she is manager. This suggests that his personal connections have been crucial in ensuring job security in a post-reform area, which absolves the state of tackling unemployment. Xiaotong is presented as a young, beautiful woman who was mentored and supervised by Damin while they were colleagues at the factory. She had addressed Damin there by the deferential term *shifu* (mentor or master) and the latter referred to her as *tudi* (disciple) in reciprocation. The term *shifu* relates to a patriarchal Confucianist discourse. As the *shifu* imparts skills and knowledge to the *tudi*, the latter is required to act deferentially to the *shifu* at all times, as if it were a relationship between a child and a parent in a traditional Chinese family. The privileging of knowledge as a prized possession accorded teachers and mentors with great respect and power, permitting them to dominate their students and disciples. With Damin's present status as janitor and Xiaotong his manager, whom he now must address by the formal title of *jingli* (manager), the masculinity of Damin is challenged as he must accept his former woman *tudi* as his superior. The subversion of their previously unequal gender and power relations in the new workplace seems to confirm the patriarchal fear underlying the *yinsheng yangshuai* discourse: in the post-reform era, women are perceivably advancing socioeconomically to the supposed detriment of men's interests. However, what follows in the series is, in fact, a reactionary patriarchy attempting to mitigate this fear. When Damin tries to matchmake Xiaotong with his youngest brother, Daguo, she becomes the object which contributes to the successful mediation of the long-standing disputes between these two brothers. As prospective wife to Damin's younger brother, her superior position at the workplace would eventually be compromised by being placed lower in relation to Damin in the hierarchy of a traditional Confucian family. In other words, Damin's attempts at reshaping his power relations with Xiaotong can be read in terms of evoking the *yinsheng yangshuai* discourse, exemplified here in a masculinity now occupying the borders of society, due to his unemployment, yet seeking to contain the new socioeconomic power enjoyed by women.

Meanwhile, in this Confucian household, father-son relations are pivotal. Damin has been playing surrogate father to his siblings after the demise of their father. However, this has caused tensions to surface after Daguo graduated from university. His contempt for Damin lies in the patriarchy embodied by the latter, as he has been in charge of the household since they were young. In one episode, Daguo expresses scorn at his brother for his low educational qualifications and his profession. Therefore, Daguo's multiple attempts to obtain a degree may be perceived not only as a struggle to break free from his working-class background, but also as resistance to Damin's domination. Daguo later becomes a civil servant and is seen aspiring to climb the political ladder. This increasingly strains the relationship between the brothers and alludes to the tension between the masses represented by working-class Damin and the Party-state represented by Daguo in an increasingly neoliberal society where educational qualifications pave the route to wealth and status. Whilst the contrasting language of the two brothers has been examined as an illustration of class conflict and a critique of Party-state discourse (Liu 2013, pp. 63–64), I would argue that the mediation of sibling tensions does not critique state power, but instead merely reproduces it by employing the woman's body as an instrument of arbitration. When Daguo is of marriageable age, Damin encourages Xiaotong to court him, but Daguo repeatedly rejects her advances. Eventually, when Xiaotong is on the verge of giving up and gives Daguo the cold shoulder, Daguo panics and is at a total loss. Xiaotong regrets her hostility towards him and confides in Damin for advice. Damin instructs her to play up her femininity by tilting her head with blinking eyes in a ladylike manner when she sees Daguo.

Xiaotong's 'emphasised femininity', which Connell defines as 'oriented to accommodating the interests and desires of [heterosexual] men' (Connell 1987, p. 183), relegates her to a subordinate position. In her attempt to seduce Daguo, Xiaotong becomes complicit with heterosexual-masculinism and is sexually objectified, culminating in a reversion to unequal power relations between her and Damin, as I shall illustrate. Humbled by Xiaotong's rejection, Daguo visits Damin at his workplace, the men's lavatory of the hotel. In a space where physiological needs are relieved, the toilet is an intimate homosocial sphere in which occasional trivialities and private conversations between men can be exchanged. In this scene, the toilet serves as a highly charged masculine site that not only demarcates Damin's inferior class position as a janitor but also allows his masculinity to convalesce by reclaiming the lost respect from Daguo who is of a higher social status. After Damin dishes out love advice to his brother, the latter feels enlightened and encouraged to court Xiaotong. In the end, the couple finally embrace and declare their feelings for each other. The sibling rivalry is resolved and, should the couple marry eventually, Damin's patriarchal position in the Confucianist family will be reinforced as he regains respect from Daguo as his elder brother-cum-patriarch, and as Xiaotong's prospective elder brother-in-law.

Further reinforcing the masculinity of Damin is the panoptic gaze which he holds over Daguo and Xiaotong. Two pivotal scenes where the couple's actions fall under his surveillance demonstrate this. When the two brothers are napping on the benches at the hospital to keep their cancer-stricken sister Daxue company, Xiaotong pays a visit and discovers the two of them asleep. She gets physically close to the sleeping Daguo and admires his physical features and is caught in the act by a secretly gazing Damin. On another occasion, when the couple are kissing and hugging secretly at a stairway in Daguo's workplace, they are coincidentally caught red-handed by Damin who advises them to 'choose a better spot'. As a civil servant and the only member who has been elevated from working-class status in the Zhang family, Daguo represents the same state power driving economic restructuring and layoffs from formerly state-owned factories where Damin used to work. The two scenes illustrating Damin's omni-scient presence in the domestic realm to which Daguo belongs, are a self-soothing attempt to mitigate the state violence on laid-off workers. On a metaphorical level, the working-class Damin achieves a symbolic victory over his brother by using the woman's body as an instrument and through panoptic knowledge of their intimacies. This may seem to offer comic relief, yet it sidesteps the tensions and any possibility of head-on conflict in the narrative that might occur between ruling-class Daguo and working-class Damin. What results is a further entrenchment of gender inequalities and neoliberal state power, all of which affords Damin the agency to just about offset the injustice suffered by laid-off workers, but only by making a regressive turn towards the domestic realm for revitalisation and conso-lation of the injured but narcissistic male ego.

Conclusion

As demonstrated above, there exists a complex geopolitics and politics in this televisual construction of Chinese masculinities. In the series, Damin's interactions with other men and women can be read as an allegory of how certain bodies are privileged over others in a postsocialist China replete with gender and regional inequalities. The intersectionality of his social class and multiple familial roles informs the subordinate and hegemonic categories which are traversed in the in-betweenness of his sub-hegemonic masculinity, the televisual construction of which is contingent upon the varying contexts of love life, family and workplace. The old Maoist hegemonic structure of Chinese masculinity with workers positioned at the social apex has given way to a new postsocialist neoliberal model in which working-class Damin can only self-recuperate through the assertion of his power relationships with other men, all of which position the women's body as a tool of mediation and self-aggrandisement of the male ego. The perceived libidinal superiority complex of the Beijing man over the Shanghai urban middle-class man and Shandong rural man is predicated on the symbolic reinforcement of patriarchy and centrism of Beijing as the political, cultural and economic capital of China.

A comparison between the working-class male Zhang Damin and the character of Ah Q in Modern Chinese Literature would further highlight the dimensions of the former's supposed potency. The latter is an itinerant peasant-class odd-job labourer of early twentieth-century China, a marginalised male figure known for achieving 'spiritual victories' when humiliated by upper-class men. He psychologically persuades himself that he is spiritually 'superior' to his oppressors even as he lies powerless to their tyranny and bullying. Whereas Ah Q talks to himself for self-consolation, and compromises by accepting his lowly existence, Damin proactively engages in dialogue with others to resolve conflicts and issues. An attempt to see a gift of the gab that empowers the working-class man in overcoming social silencing might invite us to read this as agency, but it would be a most precarious and ethically questionable one as it involves discrimination against and domination of others, fuelled by Beijing-centrism and panoptic patriarchy rooted in a traditional Chinese family structure.

On the other hand, the masculinities of Ah Q and Zhang Damin might appear similar insofar as they depend on speech to overcome adversity in life and therefore on aggrandising their own masculinities by asserting their dominance over women, albeit to widely different degrees and success. Differences in historical and social conditions aside, what further distinguishes Damin from Ah Q is not only the former's more fortunate socioeconomic circumstances, but also his fulfilling family life, defined by the traditional family unit of a loving wife and obedient son. More importantly, whilst both male figures are of a lower class, Damin's privileged status lies in his being a native resident of the nation's capital, Beijing, the symbolic power of which lends him perceived legitimacy to avow his superiority over men from other provinces and cities. With growing research examining social tensions arising from encounters between subjects of different classes, regions and cities in relation to Chinese masculinities (Lin

2013; Choi and Peng 2016; Lin 2019), this chapter highlights the significance of studying masculinity through the lenses of transnational and localised inequalities in China, as epitomised by the popular culture figure of Zhang Damin.

NOTES

1. The fifty-episode *Yearnings* premiered in late 1990 and was produced by Beijing Television Arts Centre, the first mainland Chinese state-owned television production company established in 1982. The story background spans from the 1960s to the 1980s and revolves around the lives and struggles of the Wangs, a family of intellectuals and the Lius, a family of workers. Featuring the female protagonist Liu Huifang entrapped in a loveless marriage with intellectual Wang Husheng, the former is portrayed as a long-suffering and selfless character.
2. It is crucial to note that the widespread retrenchment of factory workers following Chinese economic reforms is a gendered process that affected older women disproportionately. See Liu (2007).
3. While some comparisons have been made on the culture and societies of these two cities, Western research on this area is still rather lacking. See Yang (2006) for a full-length comparative study of the urban culture between Beijing and Shanghai.
4. Damin's wife, Li Yunfang is a reproduction of the television soap stereotype of the virtuous and loyal wife, Liu Huifang from the earlier *Yearnings* (*Kewang* 1990). It is by no means a coincidence that the two characters share very similar names, especially the Chinese character 'fang' (芳). This character is used to signify 'fragrance' or to describe someone with a good reputation or a virtuous person, and due to its feminine connotations, it is often a popular choice for women's names. In the contexts of both series, 'fang' emphasises the virtuousness of the two women and symbolises their domesticity as mothers and housewives in a patriarchal family. In the last few episodes, Yunfang's domesticity is further enhanced by frequently appearing in an apron and because she is always seen involved in household chores and taking care of her mother-in-law. We seldom see her at work, even though she has a full-time job. Her femininity and virtuousness not only bolsters Damin's masculinity, but also adds to the typology of the 'virtuous and loyal wife', which has been promoted as a role model for women to emulate for millennia, and also mass-produced for popular televisual consumption. See Rofel (1994) for a more detailed analysis of *Yearnings*.
5. The popular serial, *Beijinger in New York* a 21-episode serial drama, captivated the attention of the entire nation. It was the first Chinese television

40   H. W. NG

drama shot entirely outside China. Transnational Chinese masculinity is expressed in that series through the protagonist, a Beijing man who struggles to become a successful entrepreneur in the United States. See Lu 2000 for a more detailed analysis. *Sunset at Long Chao Li* is a highly popular television movie set in Shanghai that addresses the rapid transformation of the city in the 1990s. See Erwin (1999) for a detailed analysis.

6. Kathleen Erwin's analysis of the Shanghai television drama, *Sunset at Long Chao Li*, explores the trafficking, or loss, of women to overseas Chinese and foreign men (which dovetails with concerns about China's dominance in the transnational capitalist sphere), and provides insights on the cultural salience of contemporary Chinese society (Erwin 1999, p. 233).

7. Jingoistic and parochial overtones can be found in the television series, *Beijinger in New York*. The protagonist Wang Qiming and his wife Guo Yan seek better life opportunities in America. Guo falls for an American white entrepreneur and divorces Wang, symbolising masculine anxiety over Chinese women leaving the country and marrying foreigners. Eventually Wang scores a nationalistic victory by acquiring the American factory after the latter has gone bankrupt.

8. While Dayu retaliates by hitting Mushao back, I would argue that the latter has caused her greater distress and abuse through his incessant demands for a baby boy.

9. The *hukou* system is the household registration system which determines an individual's residency status in China. Closely linked to public services, it has been a major source of social inequality since its establishment in 1949 as the availability and quality of services provided by the government can differ greatly for individuals, depending on whether they hold a rural or urban residential status.

WORKS CITED

Barmé, Geremie R. 1995. To Screw Foreigners is Patriotic: China's Avant-garde Nationalists. *The China Journal* 34: 209–234.

Beasley, Christine. 2008. Rethinking Hegemonic Masculinity in a Globalizing World. *Men and Masculinities* 11 (1): 86–103.

Cai, Shenshen. 2016. *Television Drama in Contemporary China: Political, Social and Cultural Phenomena*. London: Routledge.

Cao, Yu-ping, Ya-lin Zhang, and Doris F. Chang. 2006. A Comparison Study of Domestic Violence in Hunan, China. *The Yale-China Health Journal* 4: 27–43.

Choi, Susanne Yuk-Ping, and Yinni Peng. 2016. *Masculine Compromise: Migration, Family and Gender in China*. Berkeley: University of California Press.

Coates, Jamie. 2018. Persona, Politics, and Chinese Masculinity in Japan. In *The Cosmopolitan Dream: Transnational Chinese Masculinities in a Global Age*, ed.

Derek Hird and Geng Song, 127–148. Hong Kong: Hong Kong University Press.

Connell, R.W. 1987. *Gender and Power: Society, the Person and Sexual Politics.* Cambridge: Polity.

———. 1995. *Masculinities.* Cambridge: Blackwell.

Connell, R. 2009. *Short Introductions: Gender.* Polity: Cambridge.

Erwin, Kathleen. 1999. White Women, Male Desires: A Televisual Fantasy of the Transnational Chinese Family. In *Spaces of Their Own: Women's Public Sphere in Transnational China*, ed. Mayfair Mei-hui Yang, 232–257. Minneapolis: University of Minnesota Press.

Foucault, Michel. 1976 [1979]. *The History of Sexuality Vol. 1: An Introduction.* London: Allen Lane.

Hird, Derek. 2016. Making Class and Gender: White-collar Men in Postsocialist China. In *Changing Chinese Masculinities: From Imperial Pillars of State to Global Real Men*, ed. Kam Louie, 137–156. Hong Kong: Hong Kong University Press.

Hird, Derek, and Geng Song. 2014. Introduction: Chinese Masculinity - Is There Such a Thing? In Men and Masculinities in Contemporary China, ed. Derek Hird and Geng Song, 1–17. Leiden: Brill.

Hird, Derek, and Geng Song. 2018. Introduction: Transnational Chinese Masculinities in a Global Age. In *The Cosmopolitan Dream Transnational Chinese Masculinities in a Global Age*, ed. Derek Hird and Geng Song, 1–24. Hong Kong: Hong Kong University Press.

Huang, Martin W. 2006. *Negotiating Masculinities in Late Imperial China.* Honolulu: University of Hawaii Press.

Jameson, Frederic. 1986. Third-World Literature in the Era of Multinational Capitalism. *Social Text* 15: 65–88.

Kong, Shuyu. 2008. Family Matters: Reconstructing the Family on the Chinese Television Screen. In *TV Drama in China*, ed. Ying Zhu, Michael Keane, and Ruoyun Bai, 75–88. Hong Kong: Hong Kong University Press.

Lean, Eugenia. 2003. Theorising Chinese Masculinity: Society and Gender in China. By Kam Louie. [Cambridge: Cambridge University Press, 2002. 239 pp. ISBN 0-521-80621-6.]. *The China Quarterly*, Vol 175, 832–834.

Lin, Xiaodong. 2013. *Gender, Modernity and Male Migrant Workers in China: Becoming a 'Modern' Man.* New York: Routledge.

———. 2019. Young Rural–urban Migrant Fathers in China: Everyday 'China dream' and the Negotiation of Masculinity. *NORMA* 14 (3): 168–182.

Liu, Jieyu. 2007. Gender Dynamics and Redundancy in Urban China. *Feminist Economics* 13 (3–4): 125–158.

Liu, Jin. 2013. *Signifying the Local: Media Productions Rendered in Local Languages in Mainland China in the New Millennium.* Leiden: Brill NV.

42   H. W. NG

Louie, Kam. 2002. *Theorising Chinese Masculinity*. Cambridge: Cambridge University Press.

———. 2015. *Chinese Masculinities in a Globalizing World*. New York: Routledge.

Lu, Sheldon Hsiao-peng. 1997. National Cinema, Cultural Critique, Transnational Capital, the Films of Zhang Yimou. In *Transnational Chinese Cinemas: Identity, Nationhood, Gender*, ed. Lu Sheldon Hsiao-peng, 105–136. Honolulu: University of Hawai'i Press.

Lu, Hanchao. 1999. *Beyond the Neon Lights: Everyday Shanghai in the early twentieth century*. Berkeley and Los Angeles: University of California Press.

Lu, Sheldon Hsiao-peng. 2000. 'Soap Opera in China: The Transnational Politics of Visuality, Sexuality, and Masculinity. *Cinema Journal* 40 (1): 25–47.

———. 2016. The Postsocialist Working Class: Male Heroes in Jia Zhangke's Films. In *Changing Chinese Masculinities: From Imperial Pillars of State to Global Real Men*, ed. Kam Louie, 173–185. Hong Kong: Hong Kong University Press.

Lu, Xiaowei. Director. 1990. *Kewang* 渴望 (Yearnings)

Reeser, Todd W. 2010. *Masculinities in Theory: An Introduction*. Chichester: Wiley-Blackwell.

Rofel, Lisa. 1994. *Yearnings*: Televisual Love and Melodramatic Politics in Contemporary China. *American Ethnologist* 21 (4): 700–722.

———. 2007. *Desiring China: Experiments in Neoliberalism, Sexuality, and Public Culture*. Durham and London: Duke University Press.

Sedgwick, Eve Kosofsky. 1985. *Between Men: English Literature and Male Homosocial Desire*. New York: Columbia University Press.

Shen, Haofang. Director. 2000. *Pinzui Zhang Damin de xingfu shenghuo* 贫嘴张大民的幸福生活 (The Happy Life of the Garrulous Zhang Damin).

Sommer, Matthew H. 2015. Review Essay: What Does it Mean to be a Man in China? *Cross-Currents: East Asian History and Culture Review E-journal* 16. https://cross-currents.berkeley.edu/e-journal/issue-16/hinsch-song-hird. Accessed 27 December 2019.

Song, Geng. 2004. *The Fragile Scholar: Power and Masculinity in Chinese Culture*. Hong Kong: Hong Kong University Press.

———. 2010. Chinese Masculinities Revisited: Male Images in Contemporary Television Drama Serials. *Modern China* 36 (4): 404–434.

———. 2016. All Dogs Deserve to Be Beaten: Negotiating Manhood and Nationhood in Chinese TV Dramas. In *Changing Chinese Masculinities: From Imperial Pillars of State to Global Real Men*, ed. Kam Louie, 204–219. Hong Kong: Hong Kong University Press.

———. 2018. Cosmopolitanism with Chinese Characteristics: Transnational Male Images in Chinese TV Dramas. In *The Cosmopolitan Dream: Transnational Chinese Masculinities in a Global Age*, ed. Derek Hird and Geng Song, 27–39. Hong Kong: Hong Kong University Press.

Song, Geng, and Derek Hird. 2014. *Men and Masculinities in Contemporary China*. Leiden and Boston: Brill.

Thakkar, Amit. 2013. Latency, Biopolitics and the Reproductive Arena: An Alternative Masculinity in Ricardo Larraín's *La frontera*. *Bulletin of Latin American Research* 32 (4): 438–450.

Yang, Dongping 楊東平. 2006. *Chengshi jifeng: Beijing he Shanghai de wenhua jingshen (xiuding ban)* 城市季風:北京與上海的文化精神　修訂版 (City Monsoon: The Cultural Spirit of Beijing and Shanghai). Rev. ed. Beijing: Xinxing chubanshe.

Yang, Jie. 2010. The Crisis of Masculinity: Class, Gender and Kindly Power in Post-Mao China. *American Ethnologist* 37 (3): 550–562.

Zhang, Everett. 2007. The Birth of *nanke* (Men's Medicine) in China: The Making of the Subject of Desire. *American Ethnologist* 34 (3): 491–508.

Zhang, Xingkui. 2011. Masculinities in Crisis? An Emerging Debate on Men and Boys in Contemporary China. In *Men and Masculinities Around the World: Global Masculinities*, ed. Elisabetta Ruspini, Jeff Hearn, Bob Pease, and Keith Pringle, 191–203. New York: Palgrave Macmillan.

Zhong, Xueping. 2000. *Masculinity Besieged?: Issues of Modernity and Male Subjectivity in Chinese Literature of the Late Twentieth Century*. Durham: Duke University Press.

Zhu, Ying, Michael Keane, and Ruoyun Bai. 2008. Introduction. In *TV Drama in China*, ed. Ying Zhu, Michael Keane and Ruoyun Bai, 1–17. Hong Kong: Hong Kong University Press.

Yao, Souchou. 2002. Review of Kam Louie's *Theorizing Chinese Masculinity: Society and Gender in China*. *Australian Humanities Review* Issue 27. http://australianhumanitiesreview.org/2002/09/01/1877/(accessed 11 December, 2019).

CHAPTER 3

Crossing Borders in Two Francophone Texts: Ying Chen's *Les Lettres chinoises* and Ananda Devi's *Les Hommes qui me parlent*

Ashwiny Kistnareddy

The term 'border crossings', in the sense of the intersections of such crossings with race, gender and geography, was first extensively discussed by Gloria Anzaldúa (1987). While Anzaldúa's main purpose was to situate her own mixed race and physical traversing of the US border in the context of Chicana literature, the notion of crossing borders has become intrinsic to postcolonial studies as a means of debunking accepted, fixed notions of identities, as well as those to do with monolithic theories and concepts. According to Anzaldúa,

> borders are set up to define the places that are safe and unsafe, to distinguish *us* from *them*. A border is a dividing line, a narrow strip along a steep edge. A borderland is a vague and undetermined place created by the emotional residue of an unnatural boundary. It is in a constant state of transition. (1987, p. 3)

A. Kistnareddy (✉)
University of Oxford, Oxford, UK
e-mail: ashwiny.kistnareddy@qeh.ox.ac.uk

© The Author(s), under exclusive license to Springer Nature
Switzerland AG 2024
A. Thakkar et al. (eds.), *Border Masculinities*,
https://doi.org/10.1007/978-3-031-68050-2_3

45

46   A. KISTNAREDDY

Thus, while borders are physical spaces that have been created in order to establish national boundaries for states and nations, the concomitant notion of a 'borderland' is an emotional and affective one that has bearing on the individual's psyche. The individual who crosses a national border incurs a form of emotional instability due to the state of transition in which they find themselves. Anzaldúa specifically defines the individual in question as female, and a *mestiza*, given her own positioning as a lesbian chicana of mixed origins. Her concept of a 'new consciousness' is formulated with the *mestiza* in mind (1987, p. 80), yet she does not fail to highlight that other individuals, including men, may be located in the same borderland: 'the females, the homosexuals of all races, the darkskinned [sic], the outcast, the persecuted, the marginalized, the foreign' (1987, p. 38).

For Anzaldúa, it is crucial to understand that inhabitants of the borderland are endowed with an ability she names '*la facultad*': '*La facultad* is the capacity to see in surface phenomena the meaning of deeper realities, to see the deep structure below the surface. […] Those who do not feel psychologically or physically safe in the world are more apt to develop this sense' (1987, p. 38). It is with the idea of Anzaldúa's empowering borderland in mind that I propose a reading of two Francophone texts, Ying Chen's *Les Lettres chinoises* (1996) and Ananda Devi's *Les Hommes qui me parlent* (2011), which feature, respectively, a 'darkskinned', 'persecuted', 'marginalized' man who was born to immigrant parents on the Franco-Swiss border and a Chinese migrant in Canada, 'the foreign' man. In so doing, I will gauge whether Anzaldúa's 'border consciousness' can be applied to men meeting the criteria she delineates and how their experiences relate to the notion of '*la facultad*'.

It is important at this point to understand what constitutes 'masculinities'. According to Raewyn Connell,

> [m]asculinities are neither programmed in our genes, nor fixed by social structure, prior to social interaction. They come into existence as people act. They are actively produced, using the resources and strategies available in a given social setting. Masculinities are created in specific historical circumstances, and as those circumstances change, the gender practices can be contested and reconstructed. (2000, pp. 12–13)

Thus, depending on the locality and history of the individual, masculinity is conceived in variegating ways and is a changing concept. Chen is a very well-known, prolific Francophone writer in Canada, who was born in

China, and Devi is a Mauritian writer, also famous, of Indian origin, living on the Franco-Swiss border. Both authors situate their oeuvre in a world of change and mobilities. However, while Chen's *Les Lettres chinoises* is in the epistolary form, Devi's is an autofictional text. Chen's narrative is a three-way exchange between Yuan, a young Chinese immigrant in Canada and his fiancée, Sassa, and between Sassa and her friend Da Li who has also emigrated to Canada. Yuan tries to persuade Sassa to join him in Canada, but she is reluctant to leave her country and her family. Da Li falls in love with Yuan in Canada and the latter almost gives up on his Confucian ideals by cheating on Sassa. However, Da Li resists his embrace and puts an end to their dalliance. Sassa ultimately also repudiates him, leaving Yuan alone in his new life. In Devi's text, the author, A.D.N (Ananda Devi Nirsimooloo) experiences deep agony since her son, who was raised in Ferney-Voltaire, is experiencing depression and questioning his identity in the predominantly white and violent world where she has placed him through immigration.

Both authors look at displacement and identity in different ways. Yet there is a sense of *malaise* that is closely related to the notion of border crossings and living in the borderland. One of the questions that this chapter raises is the repercussions of migration on masculinities and how women writers choose to portray them. Whether Yuan's displacement leads to a fluid and wholesome 'border consciousness' in Anzaldúa's terms is explored in this chapter. As someone who inhabits the border space, both literally and figuratively, the son in Devi's work should be experiencing a fulfilling 'border consciousness', but his liminality and his alterity preclude this. I will also examine the texts through Amin Maalouf's notion of one identity and multiple belongings as developed in his *Les Identités meurtrières* (1998) in order to discuss the authors' positions vis-à-vis shifting (im)migrant masculine identities. Given the two separate contexts (Chinese-Canadian and Franco-Mauritian), and starting with the most recent work first (that of Devi), the chapter proposes to examine the extent to which history, locality and traditional notions of masculinities, that are at odds with the host country, aid in the (de/re) construction of masculinities in the postcolonial world of global mobilities.

48 A. KISTNAREDDY

'At Home a Stranger': Psychological Dislocation in the Borderland

A.D.N's son in *Les Hommes qui me parlent* represents the case of a second-generation immigrant who is at odds in the all-white Franco-Swiss border village where he lives. Second son to a well-known author and a photographer/film-maker, he is the man who launches the first protest against his mother, A.D.N, and spurs her on a journey of self-interrogation and self-discovery. Perhaps as a measure to protect her son's identity and afford him a modicum of privacy, Devi never mentions her son's name. He remains one of 'the men who speak to her' in the text, all of whom are unnamed. However, Devi's son remains one of the most salient and prominent presences in her work given his lucidity and his positioning at the crossroads of identities and cultures. The text opens with the author's shock at her son's accusation that she has been a terrible mother and that she should question her own lucidity vis-à-vis the reality of the world.[1] According to Anzaldúa, 'living in a state of psychic unrest, in a borderland, is what makes poets write and artists create' (1987, p. 73). A.D.N is a poet and an author, who finds an outlet in her creativity. Similarly, her husband is a photographer and a film-maker in Geneva. Both parents have been able to channel their own dislocation as immigrants into creative practices that have allowed them to negotiate a new identity in their host country, in line with Anzaldúa's findings.

By contrast, the nameless son finds himself growing up in a world that rejects him due to his physical alterity as he is dark-skinned. He is in full possession of Anzaldúa's '*la facultad*' insofar as he is able to see beneath the surface and look at his parents as they are: 'with the resentment of the child who used to idealise his parents, and the lucidity of the adult who sees them as they are, my son declares today that he will never forgive us' (Devi 2011, p. 18).[2] As Mauritians who have elected to emigrate to Europe, A.D.N and her husband are part of what Vijay Mishra calls the 'new diaspora', as opposed to the 'old diaspora' which consists of populations that have been forced to migrate due to war, slavery, exodus or other constraints (2007, p. 3). But as I remarked elsewhere (Kistnareddy 2015b), they are twice displaced because they are also part of the Indian diaspora that was created in Mauritius due to indenture under the British rule. As a young man, the son saw his parents as the source of his culture and identity, idealised and given prominence due to their social positions, but with an unshakeable sense of self as Mauritians. However, A.D.N's son is now in the borderland, which Anzaldúa describes in the following way: 'Tension grips the inhabitants of the Borderlands like a virus. Ambivalence and unrest reside there and death is no stranger' (1987, p. 4). I contend that the son suffers because he has no sense of belonging to either Mauritius or Ferney-Voltaire.

According to Amin Maalouf, who is himself 'in the borderland between two countries' (1998, p. 7), in his case somewhere between France and Lebanon, as well as at the intersections of several languages and cultural traditions, it is essential not to occlude one aspect of these different sides that make up one's sense of identity. Maalouf indeed equates it to an amputation, a violent excision of a part of oneself if the choice is made between countries or cultures. For Maalouf 'identity is not compartmentalised' and it is not multiple (Maalouf 1998, p. 8), it is simply made up of different elements that vary from person to person and this constitutes their uniqueness. In this way, personal experiences and circumstances affect the individual's sense of identity. At the peak of his breakdown, A.D.N's son compels his mother to see the world through his eyes. He begins by asking her whether she has experienced the range of social issues that he has faced: 'Do you have any idea of dealers, vagabonds, addicts, liars, of the people who scornfully eye you, mock you and resent you due to your colour or your appearance or because they don't know where you're from?' (Devi 2011, p. 18). Violence has marked the son's life in a homogeneous Franco-Swiss border town, but the most poignant and salient aspect is the fact that he has been made aware of his physical alterity on numerous occasions. Since A.D.N grew up in a multicultural society,[3] she does not understand first-hand the primordial sense of dislocation experienced by someone who is not white in a homogeneously white society.

The people who mock A.D.N's son and resent him are on a par with social miscreants in his mind. Devi thus contextualises the social upbringing that has not prepared him for the hatred and misunderstanding of the society into which he has been transplanted by his parents. Much as Frantz Fanon felt ostracised and dehumanised when his alterity was pointed out publicly in an all-white French society (1952), A.D.N's son feels objectified in his alterity, leading to an interrogation of his belonging or, rather, nonbelonging in the society. Those who then question his belonging in their society spark a self-interrogation, of which his mother is fully unaware, as indicated by his questions of her: 'Do you know what it's like to be without an identity? Not knowing who you are?' (Devi 2011, p. 18).

50   A. KISTNAREDDY

Unlike the parents who have created their own space in their host country, the son experiences mental collapse since he cannot fully comprehend where he fits in and ultimately who he is. To echo Anzaldúa's words, 'In the Borderlands/ You are at home a stranger' (1987, p. 194). Nonetheless, while Anzaldúa's inhabitant of the borderland finds living in two worlds and acquiring a 'border consciousness' (1987, p. 80) deeply empowering, the son fails to attain this enabling space where he can tap from both his parents' culture and the culture where he grew up. In fact, his parents' 'home' country cannot be his home as he cannot identify with Mauritians either. Unlike Maalouf, in the son's case, there is an innate need to identify with one particular setting, which cannot be the society in which he has been brought up as his hypervisibility condemns him to being marginalised. Caught between two cultures, A.D.N's son cannot fathom identity as being made up of Maalouf's different elements either, due to the monolithic sense of identity prevalent both in France and in traditional Indo-Mauritian households, which here is represented by his father.

In Devi's narrative, the father/husband remains the epitome of patriarchal oppression and traditional values. In this way, indubitably, A.D.N's response to her son's depression is to listen to her husband's voice and see his presence in her own life as a deeply oppressive force. The father is thus seen as a man who has a strong sense of what masculinity is: that is, built on the notion that the feminine should be submissive and yet strong enough to support the man. The father/husband's model of masculinity is constructed on a traditional Indian model of masculinity wherein the woman is perennially a secondary human being who plays a set, domestic role. As Rajeev Bhargava has expressed: 'Men are sovereign, free and autonomous, in control of the world they inhabit, the women they rule over and the children they beget. In short, part of their freedom lies in having dominion over others, particularly women and "servants."'[4] For Michael Kimmel, 'masculinity and femininity are relational constructs […]. One cannot exist without the other' (1987, p. 12). From the husband/father's perspective, A.D.N in this respect has failed as a wife, because she has constructed a separate fictional world that separates her from her family, a fact which he constantly reminds her of in the oeuvre.

Moreover, A.D.N is also deemed to have fallen short of expectations in her role as a mother. The son's revelation that he has been forced to defend his mother since he was a five-year-old demonstrates a reversal of the natural order of things, and ultimately this forces him to grow up faster than most children. Due to the husband/father's overpowering presence in her life, the mother attempts to be closer to her children, but instead of supporting them, she treats them as friends. However, this variation on motherhood has had negative repercussions as the son categorically claims: 'You wanted to be our mate. We didn't need a mate, we needed a mother' (Devi 2011, p. 41). In Devi's writing then, the son acts as a catalyst for the mother's realisation that her success as an author is not concomitant with her success as a parent: 'he peels the skins of condescendence and complacency in which I enveloped myself. He puts me face to face with an internal gaze in which I see no "angel" […] but an unripe fruit: barely formed, I withered, despite my youthful veneer' (p. 42). The use of the image of layered skins that have to be unravelled until the truth is revealed is significant here insofar as Devi is aware that A.D.N is creating her own illusions to a certain extent. Even if it does not provoke creative or emotional outlets in this case, it is Anzaldúa's *'facultad'* that enables the son to perceive the deeper realities of both his parents' inadequacies. This *'facultad'* that arises from a marginal position is empowering insofar as it permits a direct confrontation. The son's anger is compounded by the fact that there is no outlet for his emotions. His father has modelled the image of a stoic and firm figure of masculinity for him. A self-made man, A.D.N's husband does not give in to his emotions. The son can only channel his emotions into anger: 'he hides behind a terrifying rage' (p. 47). Significantly, Devi uses the word 'hides' because she is fully aware that her son cannot show other types of emotion save for rage. His own father displays only anger and sarcasm when A.D.N chooses to leave the family home in order to make sense of what is happening to their life.[5]

The choice to write a book on an event that deeply affects one's life is not without consequences. While *Les Hommes qui me parlent* is a situational account of A.D.N's questioning of herself and her choices, and especially how her son's suicide attempts have led her to this moment of truth, Devi plays down the autobiographical elements by casting it as 'autofiction'. Rather than any fiction that features a 'je/I' which simply carries the same name as the author, autofiction is what Serge Doubrovsky explains on the back page of his novel *Fils* in 1977: 'Fiction of strictly real events or facts, if we want, autofiction, of having entrusted the adventure of language with the language of an adventure, outside the wisdom of the traditional or new novel'.[6] Thus, while the events are facts and have prompted a shift in the author's self-perception, she remains in control of the material she presents. I contend that given the harshness of the words uttered to her and against her by the men in her life, Devi literally silences them through her language and her writing, thereby according them a place as speaking subjects only through her own creativity and imagination. According to Shirley Jordan, after all, '[a]utofiction is seen to be linked to promoting individual and social change and to constructing identity in situations of tension' (Jordan 2013, p. 82). Crucially, while the narrative is entitled *Les Hommes qui me parlent*, all conversations are in reported speech and are filtered through A.D.N's own consciousness, repeatedly casting the writer as the centripetal force of the narrative and the men as deflected through her own subjectivity, in a way silencing the men who speak to her by depriving them of a voice unless it is through the prism of her writing, through her own voice. Yet, there is a definite sense that the son's predicament is not silenced since he has brought to the fore a phenomenon that is very much topical in the current world of migration.

In his *The Location of Culture* (1994), Homi K. Bhabha's definition of the third space of hybridity is comparable to that of Anzaldúa's border consciousness. In Bhabha's theory, the hybrid subject is empowered because he can move fluidly between fixed identities. Anthony Easthope debunks this theory by underlining the risks associated with the absence of a fixed notion of identity:

> what is recommended is only too like the state of psychosis. The sad old man muttering to himself on the top of the bus has fallen into the gaps coherent identity would conceal—he indeed inhabits an 'interstitial passage between fixed identifications'. (1998, p. 345)

In A.D.N's son's case, it is evident that the dual consciousness advocated by Anzaldúa and the notion of hybrid identity, as enunciated by Bhabha, are not as positive in practice as they seem empowering in theory. Devi's own words in describing her son ('unbalanced [...] disintegrated' (Devi 2011, p. 46)) reveal a sense of self that is imploding. For Devi 'this text emanates from him, from his interrogation, from his challenge, from his suffering, from his anger [...] he is surrounded by restraints that stop him from living fully and which he cannot rid himself of' (p. 47). Those 'restraints' lead to a grief at not belonging that is palpable, as he alternates between rage, violence and the desire to commit suicide:

> [...] my son sleeps, knocked out by sadness. In front of my desk lies a fan he broke today, in a fit of rage.

> In three years of depression he has broken everything he could break in the house. More than anything he broke his own heart every time without managing to annihilate himself completely. (pp. 78–9)

The 'disease' (p. 113) A.D.N identifies in her son, is symptomatic of a disease experienced by individuals who lose their bearings. And as he is 'full of a destructive energy that devours him from inside [, he] is searching for himself, he is searching for us' (p. 112). As discussed earlier, Connell (2000) argues that masculinities are produced in specific historical circumstances and they are mutable depending on circumstances. I propose that, given the immutable and unshakeable allegiances of his father to his identity as an Indo-Mauritian man, the son has not had a model of masculinity in which change is acceptable. For Maalouf, we should be wary of 'so-called fundamental belonging' (Maalouf 1998, p. 9). Maalouf is careful to point out that there is a hierarchy present in the elements that make up our sense of identity and this hierarchy changes according to circumstances: 'identity is not given once and for all, it is constructed and transforms itself throughout one's existence' (Maalouf 1998, p. 31). Given the father's insistence on his own unshakeable sense of identity,[7] it is not surprising that the son experiences severe difficulties negotiating his identity. As Devi states, speaking of her two sons: 'they became men, but some wounds they inherited since childhood' (Devi 2011, p. 73). The father's resistance to change in the host society leads to the son's inability to adapt to his own circumstances in his specific social and historical setting, thus contributing to his psychological dislocation and instability.

Unwanted Metamorphosis: The Consequences of Border Crossings

While Devi focuses on the aftermath of migration and the consequences of alterity in a host country, France, Chen depicts the initial settlement of Yuan, a Chinese man, in Canada and the transformative process he undergoes. Devi's husband and herself did not experience the level of cultural difference undergone by Yuan, especially since language was not a barrier. The son was set apart by his physical difference, but he, linguistically and culturally, was brought up in the host society, even if his dual cultural heritage leads to his eventual mental collapse. Yuan, on the other hand is completely transplanted into a different world which initially is an empowering locality marked by freedom: 'I am free […] I am a free agent responsible for myself' (Chen 1996, p. 35). Yuan's upbringing in a Confucian, communist society, where behaviour and choices are controlled by the state and traditional mores and values, lead to him appreciating the liberties afforded to an individual in a democratic society.

Yet, Yuan's departure from China is not a completely happy event. He has left behind the woman he loves, his fiancée Sassa. In Chinese society, being engaged is on a par with being married and the man gives equal respect as he would his wife. According to Confucian value systems, individuals are always working towards harmonious relationships for societal stability. Marriage, and the meeting of two families, is seen as a pathway to harmony (Liao and Heaton 1992). Even if Yuan and Sassa have not yet entered matrimony, the fact that their parents have approved their relationship and she is due to join him in Canada means that they are officially considered to be promised to each other and Yuan owes her and her parents the respect of treating her as his wife. This is also in line with the concept of filial piety insofar as Yuan would be guilty of dishonouring his family if he mistreats her in any way (Chen 2013). Yuan is in love with Sassa and recalls that her 'smile […] is imprinted in my memory and will engender agonies that will accompany me on the road to my new life' (Chen 1996: 9). His 'new life' is exciting because it brings about changes that he has wanted for a long time. It allows him to enter a new space where choices are his own and where he can be whoever he wishes to be.

However, his 'vagabond instinct' (Chen 1996, p. 9), which has led to his 'abandoning the soil that has fed [him]' (p. 9), creates a sense of guilt in Yuan. This guilt is conducive to an increased sense of nostalgia for the land that he has left behind: 'it is by leaving this country that I am learning to love it more. […] I feel a profound need to recognise my belonging to my country' (p. 10). Marked by difference, then, he feels the need to reaffirm his allegiance to China; he believes that it is due to Canada being 'civilised' that he has to be categorised: 'in order to live in a civilized country, one must identify oneself' (p. 10). Nevertheless, as James Clifford remarks, displaced individuals are marked by 'the experience of separation and entanglement, of living here and remembering/desiring another place' (Clifford 1994, p. 311). Yuan in many ways is clinging to his roots because he feels uprooted and does not experience a sense of belonging to his host country. His feeling of loss is reinforced by the idea that he feels like a 'newborn': 'you know how lonely newborns are' (p. 15), he writes to Sassa, his choice of the word 'lonely' revealing his inability to belong at first. He is experiencing an intense loss, associated with mourning. For

Yuan, the process is complicated by the fact that he does not want to relinquish memories of China, thus bringing to bear the concept of active remembering or active mourning, which constantly creates anguish (Marrone 1998).

According to Robert Marrone, 'mourning involves a search for meaning in our loss and profound changes in our assumptive world that can last for years and, for some of us, may last until we ourselves die' (Marrone 1998, p. 323). At first, Yuan's perception of his new self as an uprooted individual is quite positive: 'I live as a newborn. Is there anything more interesting than rebirth for us mortals? I would suggest that everyone should become an expatriate' (Chen 1996, p. 17). His suggestion that everyone should experience the rebirth he has undergone is testament to the liberating, empowering and enabling effect that migration has on him. His reaction to Sassa's reticence at joining him in Canada is that of disbelief as Chen's male protagonist thinks of it as simple 'migration, migration which we find in every era of human history and in every living species' (p. 38). The cultural differences are also initially quite enlightening for him: the simple fact that in Canada pets are respected and treated kindly is a source of delight: 'In our country humans eat dogs, here dogs benefit from as much food, care and love as human beings' (p. 34). However, whilst freedom is a state that elated him at first, his interrogation of true freedom reveals a realisation that no individual is ever completely free: 'I have chosen this life and so I am almost feel free. But do you think I am freer here than anywhere else?' (p. 21).

Anzaldúa writes that '[c]ulture forms our belief. We perceive the version of reality that it communicates. Dominant paradigms, predefined concepts that exist as unquestionable, unchallengeable, are transmitted to us through the culture' (1987, p. 16). Yuan still upholds the values with which he was inculcated in China: he is accustomed to a certain amount of directionality given to his life by government edicts and laws. Given the freedom to choose what he wishes to do in the new locality he finds himself in, the protagonist still feels the need to turn to his past and his culture even if the fact that he has to travel to China Town to get a card for Sassa allegorises to an extent his gradual extrication from the Chinese community and Chinese culture. However, as Anzaldúa argues, 'our cultures take away our ability to act' (1987, p. 20), and thus Yuan's distancing himself from his Chinese roots might lead eventually to a more empowering sense of self. Sassa's friend Da Li, who is also in Canada and under Yuan's protection, sees the absence of roots as a positive aspect of migration as it is also the absence of conflict and prejudice. It is obvious from Da Li's exchanges with Sassa that she has fallen in love with Yuan. Examining Yuan's love for Sassa, Da Li equates it to his inability to let go of his culture; talking about Yuan, she claims 'he sees in her [Sassa] his past, his youth, his values, his country' (Chen 1996, p. 73). Yuan's attachment to Sassa is a form of mourning since he idealises his past in China with Sassa, who, for her part, debunks his ideals in her replies precisely by accusing him of romanticising this past. Da Li's comment to Sassa that 'he feels like an orphan because he is a migrant' (p. 81) further reinforces the fact that his sense of loss is overwhelming.

Examining migrant Chinese masculinities in North America, Barbara Voss (2005) declares that at the beginning of Chinese migration there were two types of Chinese masculinities: Eastern/emic/traditional and Western/etic/modern. These two essentialised views of masculinities are problematic insofar as they do not take into account history and locality (Williams 2004). The question that must be posed at this point is whether Yuan belongs to either one of the Chinese masculinities delineated. Having come from China and a traditional background, it is evident from the discussion above that after he arrives in Canada he initially belongs to the first group. Yet masculinities change according to circumstances, as Connell (2000) has argued. The crossing of borders into Canada and a new way of thinking and living leads to a more Westernised Yuan who perceives life differently, as seen above. The shift from Eastern to Western is slow in-operating but, as Anzaldúa states, 'having or living in more than one culture, we get multiple, often opposing messages. The coming together of two self-consistent but habitually incompatible frames of reference causes *un choque*, a cultural collision' (Anzaldúa 1987, p. 78). This shock (both cultural and traumatic) that Anzaldúa describes takes place in Yuan's life as well.

In Spanish, *choque* also means 'clash'. Whilst the clashes that the eponymous Damin tries to resolve in *Garrulous Zhang Damin's Happy Life* are external, as How Wee Ng demonstrates in Chap. 2 of this volume, in Yuan's case the conflict is internal. *Choques* are symptomatic of a paradoxical modernity in which patriarchal hegemony is contested or in some ways ineffective but still required to help resolve conflict, whether internal or external.[8] Such paradoxes have also been explored in Taiwanese screenplays such as Edward Yang's *A Confucian Confusion* where the screenplay writer 'looks for the essence of Chinese tradition in modern life' (Xide, quoted in Yang 1994, p. 143). For Emilie Yeh and Darrell Davis, Yang, in his press statements, 'has repeatedly charged Confucian doctrine with irrelevance to contemporary Chinese realities' (2005, p. 121) but Yuan hankers after Confucian authority despite himself, and in a somewhat muddled way, due to his having had a regimented upbringing, much like that of the husband/father in Devi's text. Indeed, given the proximity of Da Li and her blatant interest in him, Yuan—who has been feeling lonely—decides to take advantage of the opportunity to get close to her. As Confucian principles dictate that he give his fiancée the utmost respect, he never mentions the fact that Da Li and he overstep the boundaries of friendship to Sassa. Instead, he does what he considers to be Western and modern: he tries to spend the night with Da Li. Despite perceiving her as different from Sassa, who wishes to cling to her roots and country and, ultimately, her traditions, Yuan accuses Da Li of being 'traditional' when she asks him if he loves her before having sexual intercourse with her (Chen 1996, p. 112). For Yuan, perhaps, his love for Sassa is aggrandised as his love for his country because he associates the two.[9] By contrast, Da Li, in his mind, is like him, an 'orphan', because she has emigrated and has no roots. However, while Yuan is prepared to give in to what he considers to be his new Western identity, Da Li's 'Asian spirit' resurfaces. Thus, the rediscovery that she is still a traditional Chinese woman with Confucian values makes Yuan's new self a betrayal of those same Confucian values. Yuan leaves because his own identity is called into question in that instant, and in this way, he has been emasculated, stripped of his identity as a Confucian man.

At this point, it would be interesting to compare the notion of the Confucian man to that of the Confucian woman. In Da Li and Sassa's exchanges, Da Li tells the story of her love for Yuan to her best friend without revealing Yuan's name. However, Da Li's letters contain far too many clues for Sassa not to understand that it is Yuan with whom Da Li is in love. Yet Sassa never thinks that her best friend and her fiancé might have betrayed her. This is the first proof of her positioning as a Confucian woman. Her faith in the strength of both Da Li's and Yuan's Confucian values is unshakeable. Moreover, in a country where the Confucian woman remains invisible, Sassa fears that she will become 'too visible in another country [Canada]' were she to emigrate and join Yuan (Chen 1996, p. 37). However, the most interesting instance where Confucian values are evidenced is when Sassa says Da Li is not a 'true Chinese woman' now that she has shared her feelings with the man she loves and who is engaged. She chastises Da Li at length about the Confucian values that she has left behind (p. 86). Ironically, Sassa likes the new 'Americanness' that demonstrates Da Li's ability to act on her impulses (p. 87). Da Li's shift from Confucian values is therefore at once seen as a betrayal to her core identity as a Confucian woman (by Yuan) and as a celebration of the power of the American woman who can act as she pleases (by Sassa).

According to Maalouf, 'in every man one can find multiple belongings which are sometimes opposed to one another and compel him to make heartrending choices' (Maalouf 1998, p. 10). Harnessing both what he calls his non-Confucian American and Confucian Chinese consciousness to express his need for Sassa to forgive him, Yuan fails to obtain forgiveness from Sassa who does not understand why he needs to be forgiven. Yuan cannot be fully honest with Sassa and she cannot understand the change that is operating at his core. While, in her letters to Da Li, Sassa understands that migrants must relax their own principles and values in order to integrate into a world with different values, such a concern does not apply to her own fiancé because she believes in the immutability of his Confucian values. To Da Li she replies that the man will return and his situation is understandable: 'He makes love in Montréal and sends letters to Shanghai since he lives in two worlds and loves in two ways' (p. 130). In theory, Sassa lucidly understands that Da Li's lover is now in between the two worlds he inhabits and he loves two women simultaneously but, in practice, Yuan cannot embrace his two loves, his two worlds. 'How do we forget our past, which in reality is a little our present? (Chen 1996, p. 90) says Sassa; it is this difficulty that Yuan experiences in choosing between two cultures and two sets of values, which in his life are essentially represented by two different women, Da Li and Sassa. Though there is no outright acknowledgement on Sassa's part that she has understood through Da Li's letters that it is Yuan with whom the latter has fallen in love, the fact that she gradually distances herself from him and eventually breaks up with him leads us to think that the truth has prevailed. In her novel, Chen thus reiterates the impossibility of reconciling two different cultures if the migrant does not relinquish control and attachment to the home culture.[10] Therefore, any perceived change is conducive to a shock, or *choque*, which leads to even more resistance. According to Anzaldúa,

> [e]very increment of consciousness, every step forward is a *travesía*, a crossing. […] Knowledge makes me more aware, it makes me more conscious. "Knowing" is painful because after "it" happens I can't stay in the same

place and be comfortable. I am no longer the same person I was before. (1987, p. 48)

In a similar sense, when Yuan becomes aware of the change that has occurred within him, he experiences an extreme sense of loss. According to Yeh and Davis, 'Belonging, especially within family, is to assume the proper place, an act of affiliation, submission, and assent to a Confucian hierarchy. [....] In addition, the major Confucian loyalties governing human relations are husband-wife; elder-younger siblings; friend-friend; and ruler-subject' (2005, p. 179). Since belonging is very important to Yuan, the loss of his values, his relationship with Sassa and the country of his birth leads to his interrogation of his own identity as a Confucian man. When Da Li decides to migrate to France, because she has no future with Yuan, the latter is left to ruminate and attempt a final reconciliation with Sassa. However, Sassa uses her ill-health as a way of ending their relationship that has no future.

In contrast to Devi, who writes autofiction to better understand her own decisions and in the meantime deftly undermines the men who speak to her through denying them direct speech, here Chen writes her novel in the form of letters between three individuals who reveal their inner thoughts at a time when the internet and email is at its inception. The importance of the epistolary form is crucial here as this novel is published at a time when a number of novels are written by women using this form. For Elizabeth Campbell, 'in open epistolary fiction, writing, the attempt to be heard, is more important than working toward an ending, than imposing closure' (Campbell 1995, p. 333). For Campbell, 'women's writing and the epistolary style are generally the responses of those who have been oppressed and silenced. This writing is emotional, angry, radical, and markedly different in style and form from that of the dominant culture' (Campbell 1995, p. 335). Nonetheless, whilst Chen has chosen this form, the content itself is not subversive and, instead, shows a deep concern for those who choose to migrate, and especially the men who cannot let go of their attachments. Other critics believe that 'by choosing the epistolary form, novelists implicitly state their concern for individuals, the nuances of their personal voice, awareness of themselves and other people, as well as their place in the world' (Spacks 2006, pp. 104–105). In a world of change where e-communication and the impersonal digital age make their entry, the epistolary form provides us with perhaps a slower and more introspective form of communication which might reveal more

60 A. KISTNAREDDY

about the writer than the quick email or text message. The slowness implied is also relevant as by the time the letter reaches its destination, the writer and the addressee might also be in a different mindset, adding multiple layers of complexity to the process.[11]

Deprived of both sources of 'home', we learn from the letters that Yuan can fully open his eyes to the transformations that have developed within him, invoking a limited form of Anzaldúa's '*facultad*': 'I know I am undergoing a metamorphosis that will perhaps lead me nowhere. [...] If I don't remain myself firmly, if I don't try to remain Chinese, I will not be anything. But how will I be myself without you?' (Chen 1996, p. 133). Given that Yuan associates his Confucian masculinity with his role as Sassa's fiancé and protector, the loss of Sassa, and ultimately the loss of his identity becomes a reality that he has to face. Contrary to Anzaldúa's notion that straddling two worlds simultaneously leads to empowerment, Yuan, like A.D.N's son, demonstrates that 'border consciousness' is not always enabling but leads to the individual losing his sense of identity and thus mentally collapsing. Yuan's statement that '[i]f I don't try to remain Chinese, I will not be anything' is symptomatic of the loss of cultural identity that operates in the aftermath of migration.

LIVING 'SIN FRONTERAS': ONE IDENTITY, MULTIPLE BELONGINGS

According to Anzaldúa, 'to survive the Borderlands/you must live *sin fronteras*/be a crossroads' (1987, p. 195). A crossroads is by definition a place where two or more roads intersect, and the metaphor is used by Anzaldúa to allegorise the importance of multiple identities and cultures when living in the Borderlands. A.D.N's son lives on a physical border between France and Switzerland. He is of Indian origin, his parents were born in Mauritius, he was born and raised on the Franco-Swiss border. In Anzaldúa's theory he is the perfect example of someone who should be a crossroads. Yet this young man who lives '*sin fronteras*' cannot negotiate the multiple identities he was assigned at birth. While it is evident that he has a rich multicultural background, being bullied on a daily basis due to his physical alterity, his dark skin, precludes his identification with the culture of the host country. Being constantly mocked and seen as different leads to his rejection of the host country's societal values. Instead of being '*sin fronteras*', he actually builds a border between himself and that world, a *frontera*. Moreover, as a descendant of Indians who live in Mauritius, he might have the appearance of an Indian, but his culture is hybridised: his demeanour and the way he perceives the world sets him apart from the rest. In fact, he does not even acknowledge that particular identity when he speaks to his mother about the difficulties he experiences. Having closed off both worlds, it is no wonder that he becomes a recluse and gives in to depression. His wish for his mother to aid him in his suicide is significant as she is the one who gave birth to him and he blames her for his lack of belonging. The father's rigidity and lack of comprehension plunges him further into depression and adds fuel to his rage. A.D.N's son is not a crossroads; he is, in line with Anzaldúa's metaphor, a dead end, a *cul de sac*.

By contrast, Yuan's initial foray into North American soil places him in a perfect position towards becoming a crossroads. He welcomes the freedom he enjoys in his host country and wishes everyone could experience expatriation as he has, because it is a new birth. Unlike A.D.N's son, he was not born in the host country but *reborn* into it and discovers it with the wonder of a child. Nonetheless, the adopted world comes crashing down just as quickly. He experiences the loss of his country and values and understands that he is now an orphan, that his motherland is slowly being taken away from him. To him, the next step is to embrace the North American life and, while he misses his fiancée, Da Li becomes his way of changing his values for a more relaxed, perhaps more Western, way of conceiving his sexuality. His failure to bring that about becomes his failure to harness both worlds simultaneously. Like A.D.N's son, he cannot be a crossroads because he is incapable of giving up the boundaries and borders that were imposed upon him at birth and which he continues to uphold. He is ambivalent about change and whilst he understands that his very presence on American soil and in the midst of American culture is changing him, he clings to his identity as a Chinese man because it is the only one he recognises.

Maalouf asserts that 'the host country is neither a blank page nor a written page, it is a page which is being written' (1998, p. 50). Thus, identity in the host nation is also constantly being constructed and is always mutable. Yet, both A.D.N's son and Yuan perceive identity as something ideally concrete. A.D.N's son is lucid when he calls into question his mother's identity because she has cocooned herself in her fictional world and created an immutable identity for herself. Similarly, his father has resisted change from the beginning and although he should have experienced some degree of cultural erosion by virtue of living in Europe, he seems not to have lost his identity as an Indo-Mauritian man. It is from his liminal position and his own interrogations of identity that the son shatters both parents' illusions and forces them to question their identities. Yuan, meanwhile, sees his slipping Chinese identity as symptomatic of a loss of himself because he will not be anything anymore. Both young men perceive identity as something that can change and can disappear leaving them mentally scarred, or perhaps like the living dead in a world where identity is everything, as Yuan observes.

In the globalised world of mobility where both young men live, identity and belonging can in fact be conceived in many ways. I underlined the problematic concept of hybrid identities earlier insofar as it implies that a subject can fluidly move from one identity to another without a feeling of dislocation. Both Yuan and A.D.N's son are proof that such a conceptualisation of identity is idealistic, almost academic, but will not necessarily work in practice. Anzaldúa's border consciousness and the notion of straddling two worlds at the same time fails in both cases because of the inability of Yuan and A.D.N's son to actually straddle the two worlds simultaneously given their specific circumstances. Perhaps it would be better to conceive of identity in Maaloufian terms. According to Maalouf:

> Each one of us should be encouraged to accept his/her own diversity, to conceive his/her identity as the sum of his/her diverse belongings, instead of confusing it with only one identity erected as a supreme belonging, and as an instrument of exclusion. (1998, p. 183)

If identity remains immutable, 'I am' as Devi herself states in a poem (2003, p. 53), such 'diverse belongings' can change depending on circumstances. While it is difficult to extricate the notion of belonging from identity as they are intimately linked in both texts, it is possible to conceive of identity as a whole which is constituted of a range of elements that vary from person to person. Unfortunately, as these texts demonstrate, tribal modes of belonging persist even in a context of globalisation and it is difficult to fight for one's own personal identity in the face of a collective— whether that collective is French, Mauritian, Indian or Chinese—that defines itself against others, and thus suppresses more singular, affective experiences in which, for example, A.D.N's son would be himself, but would also belong to Ferney-Voltaire, to Mauritius, be his parents' son, be the artist he was, all at the same time. Similarly, Yuan would remain Yuan, but equally belong to China as much as he belongs to North America and his new life there. Ultimately, the question of identity has led to much suffering in both young men's cases. As Devi herself states in her aforementioned poem, 'Why ask the question of identity?'. It would perhaps be best, indeed, if the question of identity did not have to be posed.

NOTES

1. See also my discussion of this in *Migrant Masculinities in Women's Writing* (Kistnareddy 2021).
2. All translations from *Les Identités meurtrières, Les Hommes qui me parlent* and *Les Lettres chinoises* are mine.
3. Although there have been several instances of communal violence as the 1999 riots attest. See my discussion of this in *Locating Hybridity: Creole, Identities and Body Politics in the Novels of Ananda Devi* (2015a).
4. See Bhargava (2019).
5. Theorists such as bell hooks (2005) have often commented on the fact the only emotion acceptable in patriarchal masculinity is anger and violence.
6. See also my recent discussion of migrant masculinities in this text through the lens of intertextuality and community in *Migrant Masculinities in Women's Writing: (In)hospitality, Community, Vulnerability* (2021).
7. The father's notion of identity is akin to that of 'tribal' identity which Maalouf exposes as the root cause of violence and murderous acts based on traditional notions of identity leading to genocides and crimes against humanity. However, as the father is away from his home community, he is not part of such radical violent processes. Rather, the attachment to one's traditional identity is a function of not wishing to let go of 'home' values to embrace, instead, the more progressive values, in terms of gender, of the host society.
8. For more on the notion of 'choque' see Amit Thakkar (2014).
9. There is a strong association between woman and the home country in a number of writings on migration, as it is often men who migrate first. For more on this see Gedalof (2003).
10. See also Yeagar (2004).
11. See Irene Oore's (2004) discussion of epistolarity in this novel. See also Kistnareddy (2021).

WORKS CITED

Anzaldúa, Gloria. 1987. *Borderlands/La Frontera: The New Mestiza*. San Francisco: Aunt Lute Books.
Bhabha, Homi. 1994. *The Location of Culture*. New York: Routledge.

Bhargava, Rajeev. 2019. India's Culture of Toxic Masculinity. https://www. Thehindu.com/opinion/op-ed/indias-culture-of-toxic-masculinity/article29262252.ece. Accessed 19 August 2022.

Campbell, Elizabeth. 1995. Re-Visions, Re-Flections, Re-Creations: Epistolarity in Novels by Contemporary Women. *Twentieth Century Literature* 41 (3): 332–348.

Chen, Ying. 1996. *Les Lettres chinoises.* Paris: Babelio.

Chen, W. 2013. Filial Piety in Confucian Family Values. *Journal of Changchun Education Institute* 29 (3): 69–70.

Clifford, James. 1994. Diasporas. *Cultural Anthropology* 9 (3): 302–338.

Connell, Raewyn. 2000. *The Men and the Boys.* Los Angeles: University of California Press.

Devi, Ananda. 2003. *Le long désir.* Paris: Gallimard.

———. 2011. *Les Hommes qui me parlent.* Paris: Gallimard.

Easthope, Anthony. 1998. Bhabha, Hybridity and Identity. *Textual Practice.* 12 (2): 341–348.

Gedalof, Irene. 2003. Taking (a) Place: Female Embodiment and the Re-grounding of Community. In *Uprootings/Regroundings: Questions of Home and Migration,* ed. Sara Ahmed, Claudia Castada, Anne-Marie Fortier, and Mimi Sheller, 91–114. Oxford: Berg.

hooks, bell. 2005. *The Will to Change: Men, Masculinity, and Love.* New York: Washington Square Press.

Jordan, Shirley. 2013. État Présent: Autofiction in the Feminine. *French Studies* LXVII (1): 76–84.

Kimmel, Michael. 1987. *Changing Men: New Directions in Research on Men and Masculinity.* Newbury Park: Sage.

Kistnareddy, Ashwiny O. 2015a. *Locating Hybridity: Creole, Identities and Body Politics in the Novels of Ananda Devi.* Bern: Peter Lang.

———. 2015b. The Twice-displaced: Mapping Alternative Diasporic Identities in Works by Ananda Devi and Nathacha Appanah. *Journal of South Asian Diaspora* 7 (2): 167–181.

———. 2021. *Migrant Masculinities in Women's Writing: (In)Hospitality, Community, Vulnerability.* Cham: Palgrave Macmillan.

Liao, C., and T.B. Heaton. 1992. Divorce Trends and Differentials in China. *Journal of Comparative Family Studies* 23 (3): 413–429.

Maalouf, Amin. 1998. *Les Identités meurtrières.* Paris: Grasset.

Marrone, Robert (1998). Grieving and mourning: Distinctions in process. *Illness, Crisis, & Loss* 6 (3): 320–332. https://doi.org/10.2190/IL6.3.f

Mishra, Vijay. 2007. *The Literature of the Indian Diaspora: Theorizing the Diasporic Imaginary.* New York: Routledge.

Oore, Irène. 2004. *Les Lettres chinoises* de Ying Chen: un roman épistolaire. *Voix plurielles* 1 (1): 2–7.

Spacks, Patricia Meyer. 2006. *Novel Beginnings: Experiments in Eighteenth-Century English Fiction.* Yale University Press.

Thakkar, Amit. 2014. Crash and Return: *choque,* Allusion and Composite Structure in Alejandro González Iñárritu's *Amores perros* (2000). *Quarterly Review of Film and Video* 31 (1): 11–26.

Voss, Barbara. 2005. The Archeology of Overseas Chinese Communities. *World Archeology* 37 (3): 424–439.

Williams, Bryn. 2004. Chinese Masculinities and Material Culture. *Historical Archeology.* 42 (3): 53–67.

Yang, Edward. 1994. *A Confucian Confusion: Edward Yang's Energetic Comedy.* Taipei: Variety.

Yeagar, Jack. 2004. Bach Mai and Ying Chen: Immigrant Identities in Québec. In *Textualizing the Immigrant Experience in Contemporary Québec,* ed. Susan Ireland and Patrice Proulx, 137–148. Westport: Praeger.

Yeh, Emilie Y., and Darrell W. Davis. 2005. *Taiwan Film Directors: A Treasure Island.* New York: Columbia University Press.

CHAPTER 4

On the Road to Y Wladfa: Mobility and Masculinities in *Separado!*, *Patagonia* and *American Interior*

Brian Baker

In this chapter, I will consider a less visible geographical and political border, the one between Wales and England in the United Kingdom. The relative conditions of economic and political power between these two geographical, cultural and social areas have, over many centuries, determined their relation. From the ring of Norman castles that dominate towns in the North of Wales (from Caernarvon to Chirk); the rebellion of Owain Glyndwr in 1400; the history of forcible repression of the Welsh language (Cymraeg) and the 'Welsh Not'; the attacks on English-owned holiday cottages by the Meibion Glyndwr, the 'Sons of Glyndwr' in the 1980s; to the often strained relations between a Labour-administered Wales and a Conservative Westminster government since political devolution was instituted in 1999, Welsh national feeling has often been characterised by a struggle with its dominant neighbour. How a sense of national

B. Baker (✉)
Department of English Literature and Creative Writing, Lancaster University, Lancaster, UK
e-mail: b.baker@lancaster.ac.uk

© The Author(s), under exclusive license to Springer Nature Switzerland AG 2024
A. Thakkar et al. (eds.), *Border Masculinities*,
https://doi.org/10.1007/978-3-031-68050-2_4

67

belonging in Wales is articulated has long been a major point of political contention, not least because Wales is itself subject to a long history of settlement by the English (particularly in the East) and that many Welsh people are English speaking. In a paper produced for the Welsh Assembly in 2010 by Richard Webber, proposing to analyse the percentage of 'Welsh ancestry' in the English-speaking world through the data mining of Welsh surnames and personal names per population, it was found that only 34% of the population of Wales can be considered, by this mode of classification, to have 'Welsh ancestry', compared to 5% for the United Kingdom as a whole. What constitutes Welshness, culturally and linguistically, and what constitutes 'home', is therefore a complex and contentious issue.

This chapter will consider the work of the popular music artist Gruff Rhys as a contemporary figure whose work attempts to grapple with these issues, and to imagine the place of Wales in global, rather than local, contexts. Throughout British industrial and Imperial history, of course, Wales was a central part of the economic landscape, through coal and steel industries in the South, and the export of slate in the North. Once one of the industrial hearts of the United Kingdom, Wales has also considered itself to be a colonised nation within these political and economic formations. In the twenty-first century, one extractive industry, coal mining, has been closed down; another, slate, is a very minor industry. A third, water, was the focus of the revival of Welsh political nationalism in the 1960s with the flooding of the village of Tryweryn in 1965 to create a reservoir to service the city of Liverpool.

Welsh masculinities were also predominantly defined around the stoicism and physical strength demanded by the hard labour of the heavy industries in South Wales, and also that of farming and fisheries elsewhere (though with a very different political organisation: the coalfields in South and North-East Wales have been the seats of most Welsh Labour MPs, where Conservative, Plaid Cymru and Liberal Democrat vie in Mid- and North-West Wales). Madeleine Gustavsson and Mark Riley, in an article which concentrates on the 'socially dominant' forms of masculinity among contemporary fisherfolk in the Llŷn peninsula in North-West Wales, write, 'Perhaps the most common motif of the fishing man is that of ruggedness and stoicism, demonstrating physical strength and the dominating masculinity of being hard-bodied' (Gustavsson and Riley 2020, pp. 202–3). This sense of a 'hard-bodied' Welsh masculinity is also found in Michael R.M. Ward's *From Labouring to Learning* (2015), in which he notes

[t]hese [working] conditions demanded (and helped produce) a specific form of industrial embodied masculinity based on considerable strength, stamina and skill. Men earned respect for working arduously and 'doing a hard job well and being known for it'. (Ward 2015, p. 28)

Since the decline or closure of these industries, there has been a slow re-organising of both Welsh national feeling and dominant masculinities through economic restructuring, chronic deprivation and hardship in post-industrial communities, and a correlative shrinking of social organs that sustained those masculinities: rugby clubs, worker's education, social clubs and pubs. Migration from the former industrial heartlands, especially the Rhondda, and concurrent migration of English incomers into Welsh towns and villages, has changed the way in which Welshness and Welsh masculinities are experienced and articulated. As Ward noted,

> The coalfield was also an environment in which intense male friendships were formed and one's sense of self developed. As [Michael] Kimmel notes, 'in large parts, it is other men who are important to men. Men … define their masculinity not as much in relation to women, but in relation to each other'. (Ward 2015, p. 29; quoting Kimmel 1996, p. 7)

The closing of the industrial bases of Welsh economic activity, especially in the South and North-East, has consequently removed the communal arenas in which these masculinities were embodied and performed. As I will explore in this chapter, the slow shift away from this socially dominant form, often articulated in generational change, has opened the possibility for a re-articulation of Welsh masculinities, away from the one imposed by the conditions of heavy labour. For all the communal and relational effects of this labour, lost in the closure of industries, some of its negative consequences are not to be lamented: as Ward suggests, 'For those who did not conform to and/or deviated from normal expectations of manhood, by rejecting physical labour, sports and hard drinking, "a mocking sissyhood remained the only fate"' (Ward 2015, p. 30).

The films I will consider in this chapter, then, emerge in a period of cultural and social change in Wales, in which traditional social organisation and performances of gender have decomposed, and emergent forms are under development. The relation between these emergent Welsh subjectivities (gender also articulated through class and ethnicity) and older forms of national feeling and belonging have come under scrutiny. Both of the films I will consider in this chapter that feature Gruff Rhys, *Separado!* (2010) and *American Interior* (2014), narrate journeys in which Rhys travels to Patagonia and the United States to re-trace the steps of Welsh migrants and travellers across the Atlantic. As I will discuss later in this chapter, the negotiation of 'roots'—the Patagonian Welsh settlers' orientation towards Wales—and 'routes'—trans-Atlantic travel undertaken by John Evans to search for a mythic 'lost tribe' of Welsh-speaking Native Americans—in both films bears upon a renegotiation of Welsh national feeling that looks outwards rather than inwards, that seeks not to restore some kind of 'homeland' or 'imagined community' (in Benedict Anderson's well-known phrase) but instead to weave Welsh social and cultural production into global contexts, largely through the making of music. Quite knowingly, both films avoid an articulation of Welshness through the traditions of Cymraeg poetry and song celebrated in local and national Eisteddfods, but instead concentrate on hybrid musical forms, shared experimentation, and music as a practice, played live rather than as product, a moment of communion and community shared by performer and audience.

DIASPORA, COLONY, HOME

Many cultures, many imagined communities, particularly those that have experienced displacement, outward migration or the conditions of diaspora, contain a structure of feeling that is organised around a sense of a lost home, a nostalgia or melancholy. In Wales, this is denoted by the word 'hiraeth'. Its derivation is from 'hir', meaning long, and 'aeth', meaning sorrow. As Lily Crossley-Baxter notes, in a BBC article on the word:

> Hiraeth is often likened to nostalgia in English or saudade in Portuguese and it shares qualities with the German concept of sehnsucht, but none quite match exactly. It combines elements of homesickness, nostalgia and longing. Interlaced, however, is the subtle acknowledgment of an irretrievable loss—a unique blend of place, time and people that can never be recreated. This unreachable nature adds an element of grief, but somehow it is not entirely unwelcome.
>
> "It's a kind of longing for a person, a place or a time that you can't get back to, a kind of unattainable longing," explained Marian Brosschot, a Welsh language officer currently working in Trelew, Patagonia. (Crossley-Baxter 2021)

We will return to Trelew with Gruff Rhys later in the chapter. It is of note that 'hiraeth' is mentioned in relation to Patagonia, because this is the site of now well-known Welsh communities that settled there in 1865. One might expect these Welsh-speaking communities to be oriented back towards Europe, but, as we will find, the relation has become increasingly attenuated. In Meic Stephens' *A New Companion to the Literature of Wales*, the entry on 'hiraeth' suggests the following:

> Hiraeth, a word with more than one meaning in Welsh and perhaps no exact equivalent in English, is used to denote nostalgia for childhood, youth, native district or country, or else a yearning for an ideal spiritual state or emotional experience in the future, usually beyond place and time. (Stephens 1998, p. 317)

'Hiraeth' means then looking backwards *and* looking forwards, rootedness in place yet a yearning for a spiritual experience outside the bounds of time and place. It perhaps identifies a peculiar dynamic within displacement and migration, particularly that of the colonist, in being oriented towards past and future at the same time. It is then little surprise that the entry goes on to suggest that hiraeth 'has been detected in attempts to found a new Wales in America' (Stephens 1998, p. 318). In his 1977 travel book *In Patagonia*, Bruce Chatwin encounters many descendants of the settlers of Y Wladfa, and finds a curious displacement that is encapsulated in his meeting with Alun Powell and his wife:

> Alun Powell was a small man, crinkled by the sun and wind. His wife had shiny cheeks and was always laughing. Their living room was blue and had a Welsh dresser with postcards from Wales on it. Mrs Powell's first cousin had left Patagonia and gone back home to Wales.
> 'He has done well,' she said. 'He is now the Archdruid.'
> Their grandfather came out from Caernarvon but she couldn't say where that was. Caernarvon wasn't marked on her map of Wales.
> 'You can't expect much,' she said, 'when it's printed on a tea towel.'
> I pointed out where Caernarvon should be. She had always wanted to know. (Chatwin 1998, p. 30)

Chatwin's deadpan writing only partially masks the exploitation of Mrs Powell's (rather sweet) ignorance of where Caernarfon is located—Chatwin, rather revealingly, uses the Anglicised version of the town's name—as an index of the Welsh Patagonian's dislocation from Wales.

Elsewhere on his travels, the people of Y Wladfa are a stoic bunch, but seem somewhat beaten down by the harsh life of the region, and their adherence to a Welsh identity—several men he meets have Welsh names but speak not a word of Cymraeg and are likely never to visit Wales in their lives—appears if not outright absurd, then anachronistic and a kind of odd fabrication or illusion. Their relation to Wales seems less *hiraeth* than a kind of habit or, at best, curiosity about a place far way and mainly communicated through family stories or letters.

The dreams of a *Nova Cambria* that Gruff Rhys pursues in both *Separado!* and *American Interior*, a way for Welsh communities to propel themselves out of impoverished lives and domination by England (and that border), are themselves problematic, of course. Neither the North American continent nor Patagonia were *Terra Nullia*, blank spaces on the map. Lucy Taylor, in several works, has investigated the implication of colonialism in the project of Welsh migration to Patagonia, known as Y Wladfa ('The Colony') despite it being presented as a usually benign settlement. Welsh settlers arrived in Patagonia in 1865, after a two-month journey in the *Mimosa*, and travelled to the Chubut Valley region of Patagonia, then a disputed territory between Argentina and Chile. The Argentine government had encouraged inward migration and settlement for territorial reasons, not least to assert political control over the indigenous Tehuelche peoples of the area. Taylor interrogates the presentation of Y Wladfa as an 'anti-colonial colony' in her work, but does argue that the Welsh settlers did arrive at a cordial relationship with the Tehuelche, and because of the barren and parched terrain of the settlement, were initially indebted to their help for survival. Taylor writes:

> far from dominating indigenous inhabitants, the Welsh depended on them, respected their autonomy, and eventually tried to defend them against the Argentine state, which in turn disciplined and suppressed their own struggle for political and cultural autonomy. Clearly, Welsh whiteness and Europeanness endowed them with privileges in global hierarchies and in the Argentine nation-state, whereas indigenous communities suffered the violence and indignity of 'elimination'. However, this colonizer–colonized bifurcation masked complex social relations in the colony. The case study suggests the possible importance of common goals and political affinities between settler and indigenous populations, as well as practices of domination and discipline within the settler state, opening this space as a political and politicized arena. (Taylor 2018, p. 468)

In his *A History of Wales* (1990/2007), John Davies suggests that while '[i]n the history of South America, *Y Wladfa* is of considerable importance', its main significance to the history of Wales itself 'is the evidence it affords of the existence, in the middle of the nineteenth century, of aspirations to Welshness' (Davies 2007, pp.402–3, italics his). As a parallel emanation of Welsh national feeling to advocacy for a national daily newspaper in Cymraeg, or a Welsh national university, made around the same time as the first settlement, Y Wladfa becomes re-scripted into a Welsh national story. Crucial to Taylor's argument about Y Wladfa, however, is that it was not the product of 'linear push and pull factors between home and colony […] nor by a one directional journey from metropole to colony, but rather by a series of interconnected initiatives and dynamics, which spanned the globe' (Taylor 2018, p. 458). The initiative for the Y Wladfa settlement had come from the Reverend Michael D. Jones, who, in Taylor's words, '[w]hile travelling in the USA […] encountered the movement to create a separate, Welsh-only colony, which was driven by the energy and charisma of the American-born Edwyn Roberts. Thus, it was in the USA, not in Wales, that the idea of a Welsh-only colony first emerged' (Taylor 2018, p. 457). Y Wladfa, then, in the mid-nineteenth century, is the result of an already-existing dispersed Welsh community, reliant on extant routes of trade and communication, and bound up with multiple (and perhaps incompatible) political imperatives. Y Wladfa is, in a sense, a kind of secondary reproduction of dreams of a *Nova Cambria*, 'a little Wales beyond Wales', that is generated by already-extant communities of a Welsh 'diaspora'.

I would quickly like to problematise 'diaspora' in relation to Welsh communities through a short consideration of the implications of the words 'diasporic communities' and 'migrant transnationalism'. Thomas Faist, in *Diaspora and Transnationalism: Concepts, Theories and Methods* (2010), proposes a useful distinction between these two terms. Diaspora is constituted by 'religious or national groups living outside an (imagined) homeland'; transnational migration is characterised by 'migrants' durable ties across countries in addition to networks, groups and organisations who are active transnationally (Faist 2010, p. 9). His co-editor of this volume, Rainer Bauböck, suggests that 'diaspora emerges as a special case of transnationalism' (Bauböck 2010, p. 317), and he and Faist assert the development of the concept of diaspora over time, from its earliest association with the dispersal of Jewish communities (and later the Palestinian people) to newer uses which refer to any kind of dispersal, and 'replace return with dense and continuous linkages across borders' (Faist 2010, p. 12).

Bauböck insists upon a *political* reading of diaspora, emphasising collective agency and mobilisation, and quotes R.W. Brubaker approvingly, who argued that 'we should think of diaspora not in substantialist terms as a bounded entity, but rather as an idiom, a stance, a claim' (Bauböck 2010, p. 317). Such a conceptualisation avoids the sense that diasporic groups are only acted upon *by* history, in terms of dispersal and a resistance to assimilation into 'host' societies; the orientation towards a homeland can constitute the mobilisation of political projects to the future of the homeland. Y Wladfa is certainly diasporic in some senses, maintaining Welsh language and culture across generations, and also keeping up lateral ties to Wales, but their continued political mobilisation with regard to Wales itself is attenuated. John Evans' journey in *American Interior* appears to be migrant transnationalism rather than diasporic, but on closer examination, there is an inverted diasporic impulse at work: it is as if the dream of the Welsh Indians would enact a 'return' to an 'imaginary homeland' in North America, as though the people of Wales were themselves diasporic. Gruff Rhys, in both film and book of *American Interior*, refers to the work of the Welsh historian Glyn A. Williams, who previously worked on John Evans and his journey; Williams proposed, in relation to the myth of Prince Madog, 'Myth itself can become an historical operative' (Rhys 2014, p. 277). The dream of 'Nova Cambria', informed by the myth of Madog, as well as expressing a radical (or revolutionary) desire for political, cultural and economic emancipation is also the expression of a people who have already been displaced, who live in border country. This is as much a country of the mind, a structure of feeling, as Raymond Williams would have it, as it is a geographical location. We will see this motif echoed at the end of *Separado!* where the putative search for the 'Welsh Gaucho', René Griffiths, ends where Gruff Rhys now lives, in Cardiff. At the end of the film, Rhys says in voiceover: 'sometimes people go away to find themselves, but the answer is at home'. Home, however, is itself problematic for the (returning) Welsh sons.

Welsh Masculinities: Fathers and Sons

Both *Separado!* and *American Interior* are organised around putative quests for the presence or legacies of family members. *Separado!* begins with a fatal horse race in which one of Rhys' forebears is killed in suspicious circumstances; René Griffiths, the Welsh Gaucho singer who Rhys attempts to track down in Patagonia, is a distant cousin or 'Uncle'. *American Interior*'s quest-subject is John Evans, another of Rhys' forebears, who travelled to the United States in a search for Welsh-speaking indigenous tribes somewhere deep in the North American continent. It is important that neither quest comes to fruition, in the way intended, as this deliberately frustrates the kind of masculine agency embedded in such narratives, which is precisely the concern of Laura McGinnis' piece in this volume on the search for African legacies in a US-French-Caribbean context. Rebecca Solnit, in a 2016 article called 'When the Hero Is the Problem', posits the necessity for communal organisation and action, rather than that of the 'lone hero', to approach social and ecological problems:

> Positive social change results mostly from connecting more deeply to the people around you than rising above them, from coordinated rather than solo action. Among the virtues that matter are those traditionally considered feminine rather than masculine, more nerd than jock: listening, respect, patience, negotiation, strategic planning, storytelling. But we like our lone and exceptional heroes, and the drama of violence and virtue of muscle. (Solnit 2019)

Both *Separado!* and *American Interior* play with the iconography of the West and the Western, with the former in particular referring to the Spaghetti Western in its title sequence and trailer (not without some irony, of course, as these were European re-imaginings of American mythic stories of the West with Italian casts, shot mainly in Spain). Throughout, Rhys is displaced as masculine agent, the achiever of the quest, the winner of the Grail. Both road movies work as a series of encounters with people and landscape, and while there does not seem to be a lot of 'strategic planning', the ethics of both films embody the 'feminine' attributes suggested by Solnit. These are films in which masculinity is negotiated and performed *relationally*, in multiple senses of the word: in terms of social communication, and in terms of family histories and connections. In *Separado!* in particular, the crucial familial figures we see are female.

This is, I suspect, a crucial and deliberate strategy deployed by Rhys and the film-makers. In the book of *American Interior*, Rhys' father is much more central: 'all roads lead back to my father, Ioan' (Rhys 2014, p. 3), he writes on the first page of the Introduction. 'My father was a straight-talking, principled public servant and a dependable man, although further evidence points to a romantic streak that lay pretty close to the surface' (Rhys 2014, p. 4), he continues, and most importantly, 'he argued that the spaces between the mountains, the passes and the gaps where people and cultures meet, were more important and more interesting than the summits, the supposed pinnacles' (Rhys 2014, p. 5). Ioan Rhys' 'proto-anarchist' politics and love for the Welsh landscape—he wrote guidebooks in Cymraeg—place his father as a minoritarian figure, if not feminised then displaced from a central role in patriarchal authority. Ioan moved his family, including the young Gruff, from Cardiff to Bethesda in North Wales, at the edge of Snowdonia and the foot of the Ogwen Valley. Gruff Rhys, who speaks with a North Wales accent but lives in Cardiff, presents a somewhat paradoxical or plural embodiment of Welshness: a first-language speaker of Cymraeg, who works in both this language and English, and does not base his articulation of Welsh cultural feeling strictly in terms of language—although both projects are centrally concerned with the practice and fate of Cymraeg. Gruff Rhys is foremost a kind of internationalist, and an inheritor and operator of multiple musical forms, genres and traditions.

He inhabits, then, a very different generation of Welsh masculinities than that of his father's generation. This is that of Raymond Williams' 1960 novel *Border Country*, which concerns a father and son relationship and the border between England and Wales. It can be taken, in some ways, as a classic articulation of the transition from traditional masculine performances to a new, aspirational one, involving not only the crossing of (and return over) a geographical and political border but also one between classes. The novel narrates in two time frames; the first, contemporary to 1960, concerns London-based university lecturer Matthew Price's return to Glynmawr to visit his ailing father and come to terms with his relationship to the family and to the village before his father's death; and the second story, beginning some 40 years before, is of his father's arrival (with his wife) in Glynmawr to take up the position of railway signalman, as well as Price's birth, childhood and maturation until the point at which he leaves for university. His father had recently retired after the signal box had been closed in the wake of the Beeching cuts, the large-scale closure of many branch lines in Britain that took place in the 1960s. *Border Country* takes place at a historical point at which the shift away from industrialism can be foreshadowed: Morgan Rosser, once a workmate of Price's father, has become an entrepreneur, and his food distribution business and its use of the roads is a crucial marker of the economic future of Wales. The movement from railwayman to university lecturer, in the generational shift between father and son, is also an index of a change in the social fabric.

This is felt as a diminishment. Early in the novel, Harry Price, Matthew's father, is called out during the General Strike of 1926, and despite the opprobrium of some of the middle-class members of the community (the schoolmaster, for instance), Harry is solidly behind the strike. When the strike fails due to what is presented as the weakness of the London union leadership—meaning Price is laid off for a time before eventual reinstatement—the bonds of social collectivity remain strong. Having difficulty paying the rent on the family's cottage, his landlady bids he put the proffered money back in his pocket and use it to keep the family. Homosocial bonds are also crucial between the working men; even the station master, who had doubts about the strike action, comes out in solidarity with his colleagues, though the result is that he is moved to another station as a form of employer punishment. This collectivity stands in stark contrast to Price's 'contained indifference' at the beginning of the novel, his isolation and lack of collective bonds with his workmates. Price's 'indifference' is, however, a kind of self-mutilation, a cutting-off of feeling necessitated by his move away from the village and the taking up of another life in England.

The final 'break' comes with Harry's death, after which Matthew undergoes a kind of dark night of the soul, 'watching his own mind, under a breaking tension', after which he finally comes to an understanding and a rapprochement with his upbringing and with himself. Returned to London, he tells his wife Susan: 'Only now it seems like the end of exile. Not going back, but the feeling of exile ending. For the distance is measured, and that is what matters. By measuring the distance, we come home' (Williams 1964, p. 334); and the novel closes with a scene of Matthew going upstairs to the rooms of his own sleeping sons, where he 'bent and kissed them lightly on the smooth fine skin of their temples' (Williams 1964, p. 334). Measuring the distance at last, Matthew comes home, not to Glynmawr, but to himself.

In an analysis of the BBC/S4C *policier* TV series *Y Gwyll/Hinterland* (2013–2016), Elke Weissmann notes a very similar motif embodied in the journey of the main detective protagonist, Thomas Mathias (Richard Harrington), who returns from elsewhere to a role as DCI at Aberystwyth in Ceredigion. He encounters, as part of a three-series story arc, a conspiracy surrounding child abuse at a former children's home in Devil's Bridge, a village close to Aberystwyth, in which crimes have been covered up by a generation of older men, some of them serving or retired senior police officers. As part of his investigation, with his partner Mared Rhys (Mali Harries), Mathias has to confront the influence and power of this older generation to uncover the crimes and conspiracy. Mathias himself has a troubled history; his wife and daughter have emigrated to Canada without him, and he is seen living a rather miserable life in an isolated caravan, alone. Weissmann suggests:

> second-generation men are often violent or at least marked by the violence of their fathers/predecessors. But there is another group of second-generation men who are perceived as different. These are the returnees who left Wales at unidentified moments in the past to try their luck elsewhere. There, they were confronted with their own capacity for violence which they now try to redress. […] their opposition to dominant forms of masculinity is based on their own failure, which means that they are at once closer and at the same time further distanced from the dominant form of masculinity. (Weissmann 2021, p. 128)

Second Generation, it might be noted, was the title of Raymond Williams' second novel in his Border trilogy. Mathias, in *Υ Gwyll/Hinterland*, is emblematic of this second group, the returnees to Wales who confront not only their own propensities for masculine domination and violence, but who challenge the patriarchal generation above them.

Υ Gwyll/Hinterland is an unusual series in that it was shot, and broadcast, in two different versions: one in Cymraeg, and one in English. In the latter, Mathias is at first presumed by his Aberystwyth co-workers to be an Anglophone Welshman, and they speak Cymraeg in his presence on the understanding that he cannot understand. Only later in the series of *Hinterland* is it revealed that he speaks Cymraeg all too fluently. In *Υ Gwyll*, this dynamic is missing. Although parts of the dialogue are in English, Mathias, like the rest of the cast, speak in Cymraeg. Where the English-language version of the series makes a point about inclusion and isolation through capacity in language, this is unavailable in *Υ Gwyll*. The series is also notable for being a major success in international markets in its Welsh-language version, which is an interesting complement to Weissman's argument about the series representing, in some way, a 'postnational' structure of feeling. Drawing on Anderson's 'imagined community', Weissmann suggests that '"post-national" may then be defined as a fundamental disenchantment with the imagined community' (Weissmann

2021, p. 121), one that is negotiated in the contemporary Wales that *Y Gwyll/Hinterland* represents.

Both versions of *Y Gwyll/Hinterland* show a rather gloomy, even grim picture of inland Ceredigion, the 'hinterland' geographically 'behind' Aberystwyth, which is shown as dotted with isolated villages, half-ruined farms and post-industrial, forgotten waste. Weissmann locates this picture in a gendered reading of the changes to work and environment:

> The programme thus draws on an understanding of Wales's national identity that is marked by a key opposition, namely industrialised, English-speaking and modern urban spaces in which women increasingly participate in the workforce and as a result more generally in public life, and a more traditional rural environment in which Welsh is more dominant, but which also continues to see the effects of depopulation and decline. (Weissmann 2021, p. 123)

This picture resonates with the picture of decomposed, 'socially dominant' Welsh masculinities proposed by Gustavsson and Riley, and by Michael Ward, as we saw above. It is also not dissimilar to the one offered in Raymond Williams' Border trilogy; the third of these, *The Fight for Manod* (1979), involves Price involved in the planning process for a new town in South Wales, which would involve the erasure of local communities, and which is revealed in the end to be motivated by capital acquisition: major institutions are involved in a plan to transfer the land away from the local farming families. Development relies on expropriation and loss of community, but a lack of development threatens depopulation and impoverishment. The world of *Y Gwyll*, some 30 years after *The Fight for Manod*, suggests that the fate of the hinterland is the latter. It is the choice of many to leave, and not to return.

Nova Cambria: *Separado!* and *American Interior*

In the book, album and film *American Interior* (2014), Gruff Rhys retraces the journey undertaken by John Evans, who set out to find a Welsh-speaking Native American tribe (the descendants of Prince Madog, a mythic figure who Welsh antiquarians of the late eighteenth century, such as the poet, collector and forger Iolo Morgannwg, claimed to have sailed to the North American continent in the twelfth century). Evans, who was born in Waunfawr in Snowdonia, moved to London as a young man and joined the Gwyneddigion Society, a literary and cultural society founded in 1770, whose members included Morgannwg and who raised the funds for Evans' expedition in 1792. Gruff Rhys suggests that Evans' journey, in which he ends up a Spanish subject, defending the trading networks of the Spanish crown with the Mandan tribe, in what would become North Dakota, from the incursions of traders and agents of British Canada, is an expression of a utopian dream of finding a 'Nova Cambria'. This would be a new and unsullied land far from the English, where Welsh people lived and prospered in peace. For Rhys, migration—which was always far less marked than in either Ireland or Scotland, and often was to London or Liverpool, across the 'dominant' border—is a direct expression of both a late eighteenth-century revolutionary fervour, a desire to remake social structures and formations and a reaction against the conditions of servitude and marginalisation suffered by the Welsh in Wales, particularly in terms of language and culture.

Rhys is fully aware of the ironies that surround both Evans' journey up the Missouri river and the emigration of Welsh settlers to Patagonia. In the book of *American Interior*, Rhys suggests: 'there is a great contradiction in his role as a Madog enthusiast, as it validates the idea of colonization as a noble exercise when it is, by its very nature, exploitative' (Rhys 2014, p. 277). Evans escaped a colonised Wales, where the English language was taught to monolingual Welsh schoolchildren (the 'Welsh Not') and where Evans' own name is an Anglicised version of his name in Cymraeg, Ieuan ap Ifan; yet, he becomes the agent of a colonising power, whose 'trade' with Native American tribes leads directly to a history of dispossession, expropriation and marginalisation. When Rhys meets Edward Benson, the then-septuagenarian, last native speaker of the Mandan language—some efforts have been made to pass on the language through schools projects—the struggle to ensure the survival of the Welsh language is placed in stark perspective. Similarly, at the end of *Separado!* Rhys notes that the settlement of Patagonia by Welsh communities was supported and encouraged by the Argentine government as a means to claim territory in a border dispute with Chile. In both narratives of re-enactment of Welsh emigration, Gruff Rhys finds that utopian dreams of a 'Nova Cambria' are re-inscribed into nation-building, territorial expansion and the establishment of borders.

Separado!, directed by Dylan Goch, features Gruff Rhys on a small-scale 'tour' of Patagonia to promote his solo album *Candylion* (2007) and, ostensibly, to track down his distant cousin René Griffiths. Griffiths had a period of minor celebrity in Wales in the 1970s, when he would appear in BBC Wales programming to perform Argentinian Gaucho songs in Cymraeg, sometimes using lyrics that told stories from Welsh mythology. Griffiths would arrive in the studio on horseback, wearing a red poncho, performing a curiously hybrid cultural identity, in a nod to the typically mestizo hybridity of the gaucho. Lucy Taylor suggests that such hybridity was not the norm in Y Wladfa: 'Rather than hybridity, then, the indigenous and the Welsh lived parallel yet intersecting lives in which the Welsh were just one more group in a constellation of communities, retaining their own laws, customs and beliefs' ('Taylor 2019, p. 1076). Rhys calls Griffiths a 'Romantic Welsh Gaucho' in *Separado!*, and his presence on Welsh TV screens seems less an emanation of *hiraeth* than a kind of exoticised balladeering using traditional song. Griffiths' performances have a multiple activation, it seems to me, for the Welsh audience: at once alien and unusual, a character from the West (and Western), but also a character that re-inhabits the past, from traditional Welsh song and mythologies. Dark-haired and handsome, young and virile (the horse), Griffiths is a singing cowboy with a peculiarly Cymraeg inflection.

In a sense, in *Separado!* Griffiths is a McGuffin—he is only found in the last minutes of the film, in Cardiff, where Rhys now lives. A quest without a true object—'I know where I'm going, but I don't know where that is', Rhys says towards the beginning of the film—the narrative defaults to a series of encounters on the road, which echoes the Westward journeys of the Welsh settlers towards the Andes, and ends close to Esquel, a town among the mountains. There, the film concentrates on the ecological problems caused by gold mining in the area in interviews with local activists and historians. Throughout the film, there is a strong political sensibility and Goch and Rhys are mindful not to romanticise the Welsh settlements in the area—indeed, at one point Rhys implicates himself in what he calls a 'gang bang' of recent journalistic stories about Y Wladfa that portray it as a romantic historical curio. Goch and Rhys insist upon the historical context of colonialism at work even in the present day, so towns such as Trelew or Gaiman are not presented as a 'free Utopian Wales' of the settlers' dreams, but instead part of a historical process of colonisation, territorial expropriation, resource extraction and political repression. Trelew in particular was the site of an atrocity in 1972 when 16 political prisoners were murdered by the Argentinian Navy.

The fabric of the film is itself hybrid, deliberately rough and uneven. The deep grain of Super 8 film—we see Rhys with a camera towards the end of *Separado!*—is intercut with high-definition digital footage, and there are regular montage sequences in which the screen is broken into gridded frames which pass from right to left across the screen, mimicking the movement of the truck that Rhys drives across Patagonia. These sequences are largely set to Rhys' music, especially the track 'Gyrru Gyrru Gyrru' from *Candylion*, meaning 'I'm driving, driving, driving...' At one point he performs this with acoustic guitar to a small audience in the town of Trelew, a much more straightforward rendition than in the montage, which speeds up to form psychedelic patterns on the screen. The audiences he performs to are alternatively entertained and bemused by his use of electronic gadgets and noise-makers that create a strange, bleepy, rhythmic, extemporised track. At points, Rhys dons a red Power Rangers helmet through which he sings or hums; this is an absurd pop-cultural 'science fictional' device that is used in earlier parts of the film to 'transport' Rhys from Wales to Brazil, for performances in Sao Paolo, and thence to Buenos Aires and Patagonia. There is a curious, self-cancelling moment when Rhys and Lisa Jên Brown, a singer who comes from Rhys' hometown of Bethesda in North Wales, perform in 'Buenos Aires'; 'this performance never happened', says Rhys on the voice-over afterwards. The footage is apparently from a gig in Treorchy in Wales, but later in the film is again presented as part of the South American 'tour'. The actual 'real' status of the gig is put into question, under erasure, so to speak: did it happen or not? It is a point where the *verité* imperatives of the documentary road movie are put in brackets, the whole journey approaching something of a tall tale or dream: a South American Interior.

Both films suggest a mapping of a journey into 'unknown space' (Patagonia or the North American mainland) which compromises this sense of the colonialist experience of displacement and *hiraeth*. Although *Separado!* does not really do much with regard to giving voice to the experience of the Telhueche people, *American Interior* corrects this in Rhys' meetings with indigenous people whose own languages are on the brink of extinction. In *Separado!* Rhys suggests that the struggle for survival of the colonists in Y Wladfa 'mirrors the struggle for survival of the Welsh language in Wales', but the concern for the lost languages of others comes much more to the fore in *American Interior*. It is important to note, I think, that Gruff Rhys is one of the foremost pop musicians who works in Cymraeg, either solo or with the band Super Furry Animals. Most of his albums mix songs in English with songs in Cymraeg, but the Super Furry Animals' album *Mwng* (2000) was entirely with lyrics in the Welsh language, an important release by a major international group and a relatively explicit statement of opposition both to Anglophone domination and the imperatives of a global marketplace.

Throughout the film, Gruff Rhys is presented as a relaxed and affable presence. He is often portrayed with female companions and interlocutors, from his aunt in Bala who gives him a starting point in family history, to the older women of the Trelew local radio station, to Lisa Jên and his female cousin who accompanies him on the trip to the Andes, and who often drives the truck. If not quite masculine deferral, there is a self-effacement in terms of presentation here which softens the idea of the masculine quest and agency; at times, it is as though the truck is driving him, rather than vice versa. In relation to traditionally dominant Welsh masculinities, oriented around the stoicism and strength required of long hours of hard labour in the mines or heavy industry, or the generational conflicts suggested by Weissmann in her article on *Y Gwyll/Hinterland*, *Separado!* in particular revises masculinity through song, through music. Although Rhys explicitly places Cymraeg at the centre of the story of Welsh migration, music itself becomes a kind of transnational communication. Playing with the eccentric electronic musician Tony Da Gattora in Sao Paolo, who speaks neither English nor Welsh, while Rhys does not speak any Portuguese, they are able to interact together through shared musical gesture and intention. At one point in the film, questioned by an interviewer about this lack of linguistic understanding, Rhys says: 'in my experience, musicians don't talk that much anyway. Or even can't talk'. Rhys is known for his own lugubrious, halting speaking style, especially in English—in some ways, it is the slightly halting, thoughtful manner of the first-language Cymraeg speaker communicating in their second language. This undemonstrative style is purposeful, however, as well as humorous. The gaps and pauses in Rhys' speech force the listener to slow down, to think; it is a glitch in the intense flow of communication which estranges, makes us think about the language we are using: here, in this essay, English. Fluency in and of itself comes with a dynamic of power.

The importance of Rhys' music here goes beyond banalities about it being an 'international language'. As we have seen with the figure of René Griffiths, it offers the potential for hybridisation, of forms of expression which challenge the longings for home characterised by *hiraeth*. At the end of *Separado!* it is important that Griffiths is not located in Patagonia, nor has he made a 'reverse' migration to settle in Wales: he is part of both, the film claims, moving between Northern and Southern hemisphere summers, a figure of movement and re-location rather than dislocation.

84   B. BAKER

Smiling as he sits outside Cardiff Castle in the sun, playing and singing in the film's final shot, the 'Romantic Welsh Gaucho' becomes a plural figure, forever escaping, forever 'running away'.

Transmitting Welshness

Here is where music itself can help re-think masculinities as it migrates across borders, travels as mp3s, through digital networks, or forms a performative space where new kinds of communication and being can be imagined. Gruff Rhys' retracing of the path of Welsh settlement of Patagonia re-scripts a colonial narrative through music, through the multiple inheritances of Wales, England, North and South America that can be found in the film. Donning his Power Rangers mask and transporting 'into a parallel universe' (as the tag line of the film has it), *Separado!* remakes Welsh masculinity as much as it celebrates hybridity and intercultural exchange. Although it gestures towards *hiraeth* in its final movement towards home, the final encounter with René Griffiths works as an absurd coda, a kind of cancellation of the whole idea of the 'quest' to find the 'Romantic Welsh Gaucho'. In one sense he, like the performance in Buenos Aires, never existed. What does exist is the transmission across borders, one facilitated by both physical and digital networks that are central to the film. The film itself inhabits what Paul D. Miller calls 'a multiplex consciousness' of musical migration (Miller 2004, p. 61).

Jace Clayton, in his book *Uproot* (2016), traces the lines of transmission of digital technologies, from the use of Autotune in Berber pop music in Morocco to the dissemination of mp3s across global networks:

> When I first heard Jamaican voices sampled in mid-nineties jungle records I interpreted it as a form of respect. It was a kind of homecoming when I found ecstatic splinters of rap or reggae records that I knew and loved embedded in these alien-yet-familiar 12-inches from London. This was Paul Gilroy's notion of the Black Atlantic in action. The British academic approached history like a DJ, focusing on the edge-connecting 'routes' of transatlantic black culture instead of stable motherland 'roots'. The intensely physical dance music put these ideas into motion, full blast. (Clayton 2016, p. 183)

There remains, then, a tension between 'rooted and re-routed' cultural practices, that Clayton makes central to his title: 'Uproot' not only refers to the global circulation and displacements of pop music, but also the positive communities that can grow from these transmissions. The interplay of 'roots' and 'routes' is central to *Separado!* and *American Interior*. The ironic emphasis of the exclamation point in the title of *Separado!* turns separation and isolation into a cross-genre, cross-border shaggy dog story, where nothing is really separated at all. Our Patagonian cousin is our neighbour.

In the end, it is important that René Griffiths was first encountered by Gruff Rhys on television. A Cymraeg-speaking Gaucho singer, brought from Patagonia to the studios of HTV or BBC Wales for minority Welsh programming, himself embodies a fugitive, multiplex subjectivity. A figure of the age of global broadcast television, Griffiths is a figure not of looking back to traditional song in Cymraeg, but of cultural hybridity and newness. Rhys' use of a Power Rangers helmet to 'transport' himself from Wales to Brazil to Patagonia and back seems like a jokey science-fictional gimmick but again reinforces the sense that it is the *tele*-visual that transmits across borders. Hybridised with red poncho and a selection of electronic gadgets, keyboards and noise-makers, the helmet becomes a kind of icon in the film, a sign of the motility and transmissibility of popular culture across borders. *Separado!* in particular reorients 'hiraeth' towards what *A New Companion to the Literature of Wales* suggested was a 'yearning for an ideal spiritual state or emotional experience in the future, usually beyond time and space' (Stephens 1998, p. 317), in its direct communication of contemporary Welsh musical production to Patagonian communities, and re-articulates Welsh masculinity in utopian fashion. No longer determined by the generational conflict or succession of fathers and sons, nor the colonially compromised dreams of a *Nova Cambria*, Rhys is free to perform a hybrid, cyborg, feminised, multiplex subjectivity as his fugitive cousin always escapes, just out of reach, around the bend of the road.

Works Cited

Bauböck, Rainer. 2010. Cold Constellations and Hot Identities: Political Theory Questions about Transnationalism and Diaspora. In *Diaspora and Transnationalism: Concepts, Theories and Methods*, ed. Rainer Bauböck and Thomas Faist, 295–322. Amsterdam: Amsterdam University Press.

BBC/S4C. 2013–2016. *Y Gwyll/ Hinterland*.

Chatwin, Bruce. 1977/1998. *In Patagonia*. London: Vintage.

Clayton, Jace. 2016. *Uproot: Travels in 21st-Century Music and Digital Culture*. New York: Farrar, Strauss and Giroux.

Crossley-Baxter, Lily. 2021. The Untranslatable Word that Connects Wales. *BBC Travel.* https://www.bbc.com/travel/article/20210214-the-welsh-word-you-cant-translate. Accessed 15 May 2024.

Davies, John. 2007. *A History of Wales* (Revised ed.). London: Penguin.

Faist, Thomas. 2010. Diaspora and Transnationalism: What Kind of Dance Partners? In *Diaspora and Transnationalism: Concepts, Theories and Methods*, ed. Rainer Bauböck and Thomas Faist, 9–34. Amsterdam: Amsterdam University Press.

American Interior. 2014. Dir. by Goch, Dylan and Gruff Rhys. Ie Ie Productions.

Gustavsson, Madeleine, and Mark Riley. 2020. (R)evolving Masculinities in Times of Change amongst Small-Scale Fishers in North Wales. *Gender, Place & Culture* 27 (2): 196–217.

Kimmel, Michael. 1996. *Masculinity in America*. New York: Free Press.

Miller, Paul D. 2004. *Rhythm Science*. Amsterdam/New York: Mediawork.

Rhys, Gruff. 2014. *American Interior*. London: Hamish Hamilton.

Separado!. 2010. Dir. by Dylan Goch and Gruff Rhys. Ie Ie Productions.

Solnit, Rebecca. 2019. When the Hero is the Problem; On Robert Mueller, Greta Thunberg, and Finding Strength in Numbers. *LitHub.* https://lithub.com/rebecca-solnit-when-the-hero-is-the-problem. Accessed 15 May 2024.

Stephens, Meic. 1998. Hiraeth. In *The New Companion to the Literature of Wales*. Cardiff: University of Wales Press.

Taylor, Lucy. 2018. Global Perspectives on Welsh Patagonia: The Complexities of Being Both Colonizer and Colonized. *Journal of Global History* 13: 446–468.

———. 2019. The Welsh Way of Colonisation in Patagonia: The International Politics of Moral Superiority. *The Journal of Imperial and Commonwealth History* 47 (6): 1073–1099.

Ward, Michael R. M. 2015. *From Labouring to Learning: Working-Class Masculinities, Education and De-Industrialization*. London: Palgrave Macmillan.

Webber, Richard. 2010. The Welsh Diaspora: Analysis of the Geography of Welsh Names, National Assembly of Wales. https://www.gov.wales/sites/default/files/statistics-and-research/2018-12/061102-welsh-diaspora-analysis-geography-welsh-names-en.pdf.

Weissmann, Elke. 2021. Imagining the Welsh Nation in a Post-patriarchal, Post-National World: *Y Gwyll/Hinterland* and the Re-construction of Trans/national Masculinity. *NORMA* 16 (2): 118–134.

Williams, Raymond. 1960/1964. *Border Country*. London: Penguin.

———. 1964/1988. *Second Generation*. London: The Hogarth Press.

———. 1979/1988. *The Fight for Manod*. London: The Hogarth Press.

CHAPTER 5

Liminal Bodies: Disability and the Making of a Masculinity in J. M. Coetzee's *Slow Man*

Svetlana Stefanova

After an accident, the protagonist of J. M. Coetzee's *Slow Man* (2005b), Paul Rayment, undergoes an operation and loses a leg. He recognises his male identity as highly embodied and, through interactions on the border between socially 'normal' and 'deviant', attempts to reconstruct his self-hood. Within the dichotomy norm/alterity, he sees himself as incomplete, formless, lacking the plenitude attributed to a masculine identity—in other words, a 'deviation from the male norm'. He associates his disability with a loss of masculinity, hence loss of identity. The three main perspectives from which the body is understood—an organism and its biological structure, a metaphor and a means of communication of the incorporeal interior with the external world—interact creatively in the text.

Slow Man is not the first novel where Coetzee represents a body in pain—mutilated, wounded or ill. In *Waiting for the Barbarians* (1980), the crippled body of the barbarian girl that the Magistrate tries to decipher operates as a textual surface impregnated with symbolism. In *Life & Times of Michael K* (1983), *Foe* (1986) or *Age of Iron* (1990), representations of

---

S. Stefanova (✉)
Universidad Internacional de La Rioja, Logroño, Spain
e-mail: svetlana.stefanova@unir.net

© The Author(s), under exclusive license to Springer Nature Switzerland AG 2024
A. Thakkar et al. (eds.), *Border Masculinities*,
https://doi.org/10.1007/978-3-031-68050-2_5

87

disability and illness inform Coetzee's concerns with themes such as abandonment and loneliness, love and care, but mainly dignity. His characters are interpreted in relation to the meaning they give to suffering and pain. Terminal illness places Elizabeth Curren (*Age of Iron*) and Michael K in liminal states, legitimating their experiences and self-reflections. In *Slow Man*, Coetzee addresses the implications of disability for identifying the external parameters of male identity against a set of social and cultural norms. After a cycling accident, the retired photographer Paul Rayment suffers serious injuries and his right leg is amputated. Once at home, he finds it difficult to adapt to the limitations of his fragile body and the need for home care. After several failed attempts to find a nurse, Rayment is introduced to Marijana Jokić, a Croatian immigrant who earns his trust and affection with hard work and patience. The visits of Marijana's son Drago remind him of his own childhood and his 'three doses of immigrant experience': moving from France to Australia as a child, returning to France on his own and finally settling in Australia (p. 192). The metafictional dimension of *Slow Man* is generated by the intrusion of the Australian writer Elizabeth Costello, who seems to have created, at least partly, Rayment's story. When reading *Slow Man*, we should also bear in mind four events preceding its appearance: Coetzee moves to Australia in 2002; in November 2002 he breaks his collar-bone in a cycling accident in Chicago (Kannemeyer 2012, p. 583); in 2003 *Elizabeth Costello* is published and Coetzee is awarded the Nobel Prize for Literature.

Considerable criticism of *Slow Man* has been devoted to the analysis of two themes: the nature of authorship (see Zoë Wicomb (2009) and Mike Marais (2011)), and 'Coetzee's personal and literary migration from South Africa to Australia in 2002 and the implications of this relocation for his fiction' (see Elleke Boehmer 2011, Melinda Harvey 2011 or Sue Kossew 2011, from which this quote is taken). Intertextuality, with its many references to 'doubleness', is brought to the fore by Kenneth Pellow (2009) and Matthijs Baarspul and Paul Franssen (2018). Works that engage with disability (see, for example, Alice Hall (2012)) are inseparable from another major issue in Coetzee scholarship, namely the ethics of care. The issue of masculinity, which I want to address in this essay, has received little critical attention. Daniel Matias, the author of the only monograph on the topic to date, considers that much of the criticism on masculinities in Coetzee's fiction is on 'how the privileged white male acts in a different political context in which his political and cultural power is now largely diminished' (Matias 2017, p. 11). However, we should not overlook the importance of scholarly interest in male sexuality in the sequence of memoirs *Boyhood* (1997), *Youth* (2002) and *Summertime* (2009). In this sense, Boehmer's essay 'Queer Bodies' needs special attention for her remarkable queer reading of the memoirs, which she extends to some aspects of the economy of desire in *Elizabeth Costello* and *Slow Man*. In her examination of moments 'where desire involves a continual interplay of self-exposure and self-concealment', Boehmer (2009) offers an analysis of the visual representations of male (and sometimes female) legs as signifiers of erotic beauty (p. 128).

Fundamental for the understanding of critical research on men are concepts such as 'hegemonic', 'subordinated', 'complicit' or 'marginalised' masculinities (Kessler et al. 1982; Connell 1982, 1983). As Raewyn Connell (1995) remarks, initially, studies of masculinities 'centred on the idea of a male sex role' (p. 21). The male sex role remains a pivotal concept, together with power and sex difference, norm and deviance, and the social pressure on men to position themselves in relation to culturally legitimated norms, which are still discussed within studies of masculinities. Although Connell's (2009) later work does investigate the male body as part of a 'reproductive arena' (p. 11), Elizabeth Grosz (1994) remains correct to point out that '[t]he role of the specific male body as the body productive of a certain kind of knowledge (objective, verifiable, causal, quantifiable) has never been theorized' (p. 4). Recent conceptualisations of masculinities include Wetherell and Edley's (1999) 'multiplicity of masculinities', Anderson's 'inclusive masculinities' (2008, 2009) or Bridges and Pascoe's (2014) 'hybrid masculinities'. An important contribution to masculinity studies worth noting here is Michael Schwalbe's (2014) theory of 'manhood acts'. Interestingly, he defines masculinity-constitutive practices or 'manhood acts' as 'interactional rituals that produce the cultural objects we call "men"' (p. 56). Although my reading of Coetzee's novel is not based on Schwalbe's theory, I regard Rayment's encounters with several female characters as 'interactional rituals'. These rituals do not constitute masculinity, as in Schwalbe's work, but rather change the protagonist's perception of his own masculinity in the process of healing.

Theories on the body and embodiment are essential for the understanding of the relation between corporeality, subjectivity and identity in both feminism and studies of masculinities. The traditional identification of women with the 'negative', or at least secondary, counterpart of the dichotomies of mind/body, self/other, whole/blemished, has led to the interpretation of the female body as incomplete, formless and chaotic, somehow lacking the qualities related to its male counterpart. The female body, 'considered a monstrous error of nature', has often been articulated in terms of a defective, flawed, and impaired male body, and 'studied for her deviation from [the] male norm' (Schiebinger 1999, p. 24). Thus, the measure of perfection for both men and women appears to be a man, ideally young, white and healthy. Engagement with the relationship between corporeality and identity thus generates a logical dialogue between feminists and theorists concerned with disability. Feminist perspectives on 'difference'/'otherness' have greatly influenced theories that focus on disability, theories that examine 'society's attitudes and values concerning the body, what stigmatises it and what it considers 'normal' in physical appearance and competence' (Turner and Stagg 2006, p. 2).[1] Scholars interested in the intersection between masculinities and disability have pointed out that in Western culture 'the gender identity options' for disabled men are 'seemingly left as "failed", "spoiled" or in need of "reformulation"' (Robertson et al. 2020, p. 154) and that downplaying or rejecting hegemonic ideals are common coping strategies in experiences of impairment. While the wide variety of experiences featured in disability studies relate to a shared sense of stigma,[2] Rosi Braidotti (1999) explores 'deformed,' 'anomalous' or 'monstrous' bodies in discourse and positions 'the monstrous other [as] both liminal and structurally central to our perception of normal human subjectivity' (p. 292), an idea that intersects with the critical approach adopted in this essay.

The concept of 'liminality' offers a significant theoretical tool for the analysis of limits, borders and related phenomena. Extraordinary transformations often occur in temporal, spatial or mental liminal zones, and their analysis raises questions about the nature of boundaries and how they can be overcome. The anthropologist Victor Turner ([1969] 1976) discusses the concept of 'liminality', introduced by Arnold Van Gennep in his work *The Rites of Passage* (1909), explores the significance of rituals that mark transitional stages like birth, puberty or death, and describes their phases: (1) a separation, which 'comprises symbolic behaviour signifying the detachment of the individual or group either from an earlier fixed point in the social structure, from a set of cultural conditions […] or from both'; (2) a 'liminal' period, in which the ritual subject (the 'passenger') 'passes through a cultural realm that has few or none of the attributes of the past or coming state'; (3) a reaggregation, in which the passage is consummated (pp. 94–5). In his essay 'Betwixt and Between' ([1964] 1994), Turner describes the 'characteristics of transition' of the liminal (marginal) period and claims that initiation rites exemplify transition as they have 'well-marked and protracted marginal or liminal phases' (p. 5). I read Coetzee's *Slow Man* as an allegory of a ritual process of initiation into a new understanding of masculinities with Paul Rayment as a 'transition-being' or 'liminal *persona*', whose body is marked according to different social and cultural codifications, 'although they may be less readily observed or directly readable' (Grosz 1994, p. 141) than his physical disability. I suggest that, rather than creating a new category, Coetzee shows that the understanding of masculinities requires new codes able to avoid not only the dichotomy of male/female, but categorisation itself, a concern not dissimilar to that of Amit Thakkar in his chapter on Fiona Mozley's *Elmet* (2017) in this volume. I will go on to argue for the need to learn to read these codes and interpret the readings of others.

Separation: Scarring the Body

The narrative starts with the road accident, as a consequence of which Rayment undergoes an urgent operation and loses his leg. He awakes in hospital surrounded by deadly whiteness: 'white ceiling, white sheets, white light; also a grainy whiteness like old toothpaste in which his mind seems to be coated' (Coetzee 2005b, pp. 3–4).[3] He is forcefully separated from his earlier state, isolated from his community, and has to endure pain, as in the separation period that marks the beginning of the ritual passage. Liminality operates at various levels, hence the different interpretations of Coetzee's emphasis on whiteness, which can be associated with sterility, implying lack of manliness. Whiteness also relates to the symbolic expression of death in some cultures, thus constituting the third stage of the rite as an act of rebirth. The whiteness of the blank page, with its fearsome emptiness, signals an inward turn and challenges the protagonist to write himself into the world from scratch.

When doctors explain their decision to amputate his leg, they admit that old age aggravates his disability and that, at his age, the only possibility is an artificial limb. His first reaction is to refuse to accept his new state[4] and the idea of fitting a prosthesis: 'The picture that comes to [his] mind is of a wooden shaft with a barb at its head like a harpoon and rubber suckers on its three little feet' (p. 9).[5] Tim Mehigan's (2011) interpretation of these images alludes to the protagonist's transitional state. He discusses the meaning of the word *prosthesis* and claims that a prosthesis 'would provide Rayment, metaphysically and practically, with a thoroughly artificial transition to a new state of existence and, by implication, perhaps also of consciousness' (p. 195). I would argue further that Rayment's anxiety about the amputation of his leg causes a response similar to that caused by an act of violation. He feels vulnerable and displays the first symptoms of male fear often referred to as 'castration anxiety'. In this post-traumatic scenario, two interpretations of the Freudian concept converge: from the sociological point of view, the 'fear of regression' (Gilmore 1990, p. 29) and also the fear of 'losing control of one's body and forfeiting the ability to dominate others' (Preston 2017, p. 131). The very acknowledgement of such vulnerability leads to a symbolic shift from a mode of doing, i.e. self-reliance and independence, to a mode of being, inherently powerless and passive.[6] Perplexed by the sudden disturbance of his previous mode of life, Rayment appears to have lost connection with the surrounding world. Days and nights are spent in endless dozing as if he were still under the effects of anaesthesia. The metaphor of sleep in that initial moment implies disorientation and self-alienation, a period of passive expectation in the 'zone of humiliation,' unable to hide from the 'pitiless gaze of the young' (p. 13) which forces him to acknowledge the 'physical facticity' of his loss (Grayson 2021, p. 140). One of the characteristics of liminal personae is their structural invisibility, which is why they may be treated as corpses in their society; they 'may be buried or forced to lie motionless in the posture and direction of a customary burial' ([1969] 1976, p. 6).

The initial reaction of the protagonist to his accident is to correlate disability and loss of sexual desire. He is expected to 'experience gross desires' towards the young nurses at the hospital '*now that he is improving*', but he admits that 'he has no such desires' (p. 14, italics in original), which makes him feel emasculated for this clear deviation from the norm. Rayment is fully aware that male sexual potency is a primary social marker for manliness and that Western culture draws a link between heterosexuality and masculinity (Connell and Messerschmidt 2005, 851). Once he has located in disability his perceived loss of masculinity, he concludes that 'losing a leg is no more than a rehearsal for losing everything' (p. 15). The fear of formlessness becomes a fear of nonentity or loss of masculine identity. From that moment on and subject to the constant pressure of what is socially accepted as manly, the protagonist is involved in a series of experiences with different women, experiences that reflect his anxieties and his conscious search for a new understanding of his changed masculinity. Francis Cleaver (2002) describes this kind of '[s]elf-reflection and self-awareness [as] intended to lead to the construction of alternative concepts of masculinity', concepts that actively deny preconceived patterns (20). Rayment's encounters with women are themselves liminal processes, a succession of ritualistic trials that the protagonist has to undergo on his journey to self-knowledge.

The Ritual: Reading the Body

The first woman he meets is a nurse called Sheena, who takes care of him after his return back home. Sheena is portrayed somewhat crudely as 'fat, with a hard, lardy, confident fatness, and under all questioning unshakeably good-humoured' (p. 22). The first test comes when he tries to use the toilet. He fails and Sheena has to give him 'the potty'. She treats him as if he were a child, using patronising and demeaning language. Her attitude to disability shows that, in cultures where the idealisation of the body is powerful, 'much knowledge about how to live with limited and suffering bodies is not transmitted' (Wendell 1996, p. 109). These signs of vulnerability evidence the need to understand better how codes of masculinities are inscribed on the disabled body, especially since, as a consequence of his disability, Rayment's world dramatically shrinks 'to [his] flat and the block or two around' (p. 25). As in initiation rites, he is detached from his community so that he can empty his mind and heart from any influence from the 'exterior' and focus on the 'interior', on the self. The boundaries of his body mark the boundaries of his world. Domestic space, where the protagonist is trapped, has traditionally been assigned to women. Both women and disabled people are confined to a private space, as opposed to men, who are allowed unlimited freedom. In this sense, the domain of the 'model of man' seems to be the limitless open 'exterior'. Rayment understands that 'people lose limbs or the use of limbs every day', but for him, 'the cut seems to have marked off past from future with such uncommon cleanness that it gives new meaning to the word *new*' (p. 26, italics in the original). The pertinent question is: What is this new meaning and how does it relate to his masculinity and masculinities, more broadly?

The second nurse recommended by the social worker is a patient, respectful, efficient and cheerful Croatian immigrant, named Marijana Jokić. Unlike Sheena, Marijana is described as a 'positively handsome woman, well-built, sturdy, with nut-brown hair' (p. 30). The presence of, for him, an attractive woman only increases Rayment's painful feeling of having lost his manliness. It deepens his alienation from his body and emphasises the growing dissonance between body and soul: 'He still has a sense of being a soul with an undiminished soul-life; as for the rest of him, it is just a sack of blood and bones that he is forced to carry around' (p. 32). The 'doubling of self' into body sensations and soul-life reflects the extreme alienation as a result of the protagonist's encounter with his own 'otherness' (DeFalco 2010, p. 5). For Rayment, libidinal energy becomes the symbol of affirmative, visible energy. He is trying to 'remain a man, albeit a diminished man' and, while still under the effect of widely accepted concepts of male sexual conquests as an attribute of masculinity, a phrase from catechism class comes to his mind: '*There shall be no more man and woman, but ...* But what—what shall we be when we are beyond man and woman?' (p. 33, italics in original). The reference to catechism class resonates with Judith Still and Michael Worton's idea that rites of passage are often marked 'textually'. One of the examples they provide of 'entries into textuality' is the religious initiation in Christian communities where 'a child can be confirmed at any age as long as s/he can satisfactory answer all the questions of the relevant catechism' (Still and Worton 1993, p. 42).

For a man that cannot or does not want to fit into the stereotype, there is a mode of being that at first is 'impossible for the mortal mind to conceive' (p. 33) but that the protagonist will gradually discover in the course of his interaction with women as well as with men that represent hegemonic standards of masculinity. Yet, these relations are embodied and learning a different mode of masculinity requires him to bring the singularity of his disabled body into contact with the system of relations that constitute the idea of hegemonic masculinity. It is not that he does not feel a man anymore; he feels he is a man who is different from the model man, a 'man of some kind, the kind that fails to perform what man is brought into the world to perform: seek out his other half, cleave to her, and bless her with his seed' (p. 33). The mention of 'seed' points to a major example of the male roles operating in society: fatherhood. The protagonist is divorced and childless. Engaged in a process of self-affirmation, Rayment attempts to father Marijana's son by offering to pay for an expensive school the boy wishes to attend. The company of Marijana's children then reminds him of the fact that he has failed in yet another of the aspects of normative maleness. It becomes clear, then, that Rayment has failed to meet a number of requirements indicative for masculinity and that disability only accentuates his incomplete masculine identity, which is as incomplete as his own body after the amputation of his leg.

An old friend, Margaret, with whom Rayment had had a 'brief fling' years ago, comes to visit. The prevailing topic is inevitably sex and sexual relations and the protagonist again mirrors his anxieties in the reading by different women of his body. In this very brief encounter, Margaret comments broadly on his disability and masculinity, but her apparently well-intentioned and supportive words sound cynical. When she tries to diminish the importance of his injury and draws his attention to other aspects that can compensate, Margaret only emphasises his not belonging to hegemonic masculinity. She even asks him 'whether he would be able to perform the motions required of the active member of a sexual couple' (p. 37) and whether this is the end of his sexual life. Rayment thinks, 'Yet, what if it is indeed true? What if the snorting black steed of passion has given up the ghost? The twilight of his manhood' (p. 57). Understanding masculinity in this way as 'an essence or commodity, which can be measured, possessed or lost' (Cornwall and Lindisfarne 1994, p. 12) means that it is subject to changeable social mood and its 'market values', so to speak, can become obsolete.

While in the aforementioned 'humiliation zone', Rayment's embarrassment and shame, together with his visible vulnerability reveal his fragility, a condition traditionally attributed to women. If 'manhood is a relentless repudiation of the feminine' and 'the highest expectation of masculinity and the development of power are to destroy any vulnerability to shame' (Ayers 2011, p. 110), Rayment feels 'unmanly' under the scrutinising gaze of the women he meets. What is more, according to Margaret, 'amputees can be rather romantic' (p. 38), which means that he displays another (supposedly) female feature. We should not forget that, in rites, neophytes or initiates 'may be symbolically assigned characteristics of both sexes, irrespective of their biological sex. [...] They are symbolically either sexless or bisexual and may be regarded as a kind of human *prima materia*—as undifferentiated raw material' ([1969] 1976, p. 8, italics in original). Disability thus distances the protagonist from the dominant concept of masculinity in several ways. He is ascribed some 'female' features, such as corporeal identity projection, debility, dependence, externalisation of uncomfortable feelings and passions.

At the same time, he is treated by caretakers and medical staff as if he were a child, almost as if he were 'sexless'. As well as the nurses, Rayment also meets a psychotherapist, called Madeleine, who is in charge of reprogramming the 'old and now obsolete memory system' of his body and of helping him to accept his 'new body'. Madeleine treats old people as 'not very clever, somewhat morose, somewhat sluggish children in need of being bucked up' (p. 60). In this sense, disabled and elderly people seem to belong to a social category that is viewed and represented as ungendered. Gabriela Spector-Mersel (2006) argues that 'as a result of the ungendered image attributed to older persons, and the construction of older men as an invisible, paradoxical and unmasculine social category, Western hegemonic masculinity scripts are concluded at middle age' (p. 68). Whilst the final clause is contestable with certain hegemonic masculinities in politics or music, for example, it is true that women are also often treated in a patronising way and compared to children in need of men's protection, provision, and guidance. All these categories intersect in an aspect that can be determined as lacking one of the main features of hegemonic masculinity—self-sufficiency.[7]

Rayment's masculinity is also read against two clear examples of normative masculinity—Marijana's son, Drago, and her husband, Miroslav. Marijana's husband assembles cars and Drago has a motorcycle. Cars and motorcycles are symbolic of masculine power, often signifying masculine space, and as such, an extension of the male body. Mark Moss (2011) defines technology as 'a masculine enterprise' and argues that '[m]en who are not always exemplars of physical masculinity will often utilize masculine tropes in the technological realm' (p. xvii). Furthermore, Drago's intention to join a Defence Force Academy alludes to certain traits, such as physical force, bravery and discipline, which are expected from a warrior. The boy is young, athletic and vigorous as opposed to the protagonist, who is old, handicapped and apathetic. While Rayment's space shrinks after his accident, confining him physically to his home and psychologically to his own disabled body, Drago's masculinity is forged in the vastness of the country where he has grown up—Australia, where 'a climate of manliness prevails', favouring 'virtues such as self-reliance, action, and competitiveness' (p. 74). For Rayment, affectionate interactions are restricted and incomplete, reduced to the space surrounding his body and experienced as deeply private. The social extensions of Drago's body seem dynamic and unlimited in space as his image is boldly exposed to the public gaze.

The relation between body image and identity transforms the body into a site of speculations and feelings. Claire Colebrook (2011), departing from Lacanian thought, describes the body as a 'bounded organism, centered on a looking face whose gaze can be returned by the mirror, that not only represses the chaotically dispersed and relational manner of our existence; it also operates as a figure of reading' (p. 9). The body image is produced on the line between inside and outside, body and space, individual and culture, inertia and action, self and others. The narrative focuses not so much on Rayment's physical pain and the process of healing as on the immense transformation of his identity as a result of his perception of his new body image. He reads his body from the outside, through the eyes of others. His sessions with the physiotherapist only remind him of his dependence and make him shudder at the thought of an artificial limb. According to Grosz (1994), 'body-image disturbances may affect […] the ways in which the subject perceives and experiences his or her own body, sensations, or movements' or 'the ways in which the subject is able to position his or her body relative to the bodies of the others' (p. 70). In a world made by and for the able-bodied, disabled people are marked out for their disability. Their bodies are seen as physically unattractive and, as a consequence, not associated with sexual desire (Crawford 2014, p. 222). Instead of that, they are assigned to a kind of 'charity zone' managed by institutions and good-willed individuals, thus keeping them not outside, but on the margins of society. In rites of passage, according to one study, '"marginal" designates the unimportant, when not the unacceptable or even deleterious' (Aguirre et al. 2000, p. 2). But, unlike 'marginality', liminality 'suggests the existence of the second territory on the other side. A *limen* is a threshold between two spaces' (Aguirre et al. 2000, p. 6). Marginality implies discrimination, exclusion and inferiority with relation to a dominant centre, while liminality implies a transition, a crossover from one state to another. It requires an open, inclusive system with multiple possibilities. Rayment admits that he does not want to look natural, he prefers to feel natural, i.e. what torments him is the correspondence between body image and social acceptance. His reflection on the Venus of Milo as an ideal of feminine beauty mirrors his own fear of the public gaze: 'Why can the fragmentary image of a woman be admired but not the image of a fragmentary woman, no matter how neatly sewn up the stumps' (p. 59).

It is significant that Rayment, who relies heavily on the reading of his body image by others, is interested in photography and possesses a great collection of old pictures. A photograph occupies in a way the liminal zone between past and present, real and imaginary, objective and subjective reflection of a lived moment. Rather than mirroring the subject, '[i]t is part of, an extension of that subject; and a potent means of acquiring it, of gaining control over it' (Sontag 2005, p. 121). Questions concerning the veracity of photographs induce us to consider the photographer as a mediator between materiality and fantasy, who, like the novelist, 'makes reality atomic, manageable, and opaque' (Sontag 2005, p. 17). Rayment tells Marijana that 'he saved old pictures out of fidelity to their subjects, [...]. But that is not the whole truth. He saves them too out of fidelity to the photographs themselves, the photographic prints, most of them last survivors, unique' (p. 65). He remembers his 'first real job' as a darkroom technician and 'the little shiver of ecstasy' he feels, 'as though he were present at the day of creation', when 'the ghostly image emerged beneath the surface of the liquid' (p. 65). This attitude to photographs as a true record of reality marks the difference between Rayment's and Drago's responses to their self-image. While Rayment begins to lose interest in photography when colour and technology take over and images become easily manipulated, Drago has little respect for 'authenticity'. He takes some photographs from Rayment's collection and 'plays with the images' on his computer, assembling 'new' bodies with fragments taken from Rayment's collection and his family album. Drago's symbolic action shows that a young man, who in many ways fits into the model of dominant masculinity, not only is at ease with his body image, but he also takes advantage of the artifice of the image to create new forms, just as Rayment would, when the latter was a darkroom technician, before losing interest in photography, the difference being that Rayment seems unable to imagine a new body image the way Drago might be able to.

In a metafictional turn where such reimagining becomes possible, a well-known writer, Elizabeth Costello, the eponymous protagonist of Coetzee's earlier novel, appears in the narrative to play a decisive role in the culmination and the outcome of the ritual process. Her goal is not 'to support his ethical projects, nor to direct him toward true feeling in search for a deeper fulfilment of being', but 'to provide an outlet for the clamour of doubting voices in Rayment's head' (Mehigan 2011, p. 199). Nick Hodgin and Amit Thakkar's (2017) argument for the use of 'the scar motif', instead of terms such as 'working through', 'resolution' and 'closure', to avoid 'underplaying the permanence of the damage done by trauma' that the term 'healing' suggests, is particularly helpful to make sense of Costello's role in Rayment's painful adaptation to permanent disability (pp. 12–13). In this line of reasoning, rather than a process of healing, which implies closure, Costello takes part in a process that Hodgin and Thakkar would call 'scar formation' (p. 13). She appears unexpectedly and inexplicably in the story, invades Rayment's personal space and pushes him to compose his own identity, coming to terms with his scarred masculinity. Attwell (2011) argues that, after the entry of Costello, 'the novel becomes a struggle [between Costello and Rayment] for the control over the story of [Rayment's passion for Marijana] and its moral entangle ments' (p. 16).

Having witnessed Rayment's 'old-fashioned love' for Marijana, his passion, his dream of 'fathering' her children, Costello maintains that this relationship has reached a dead end and proposes an alternative. She offers to arrange a sexual encounter between the protagonist and a blind woman, called Marianna. Marianna's identity is an enigma and her life story, appearance and behaviour during their encounter allow for multiple interpretations. Although written differently, the two names, Marijana and Marianna, are pronounced in the same way. In the cases of both women, Rayment constitutes his own masculinity in terms of sexual interest or attraction, one which Marijana rejects but which Marianna is willing to satisfy. However, after Rayment's sexual encounter with the latter, he wants an assurance that she is 'truly' who Costello claims she is, 'that he has not been duped' (p. 115). He suspects that Marianna is either imagined and 'written' into his life story by Costello or Costello 'is writing two stories at once, stories about characters who suffer a loss (sight in one case, ambulation in the other) which they must learn to live with' (p. 118). Public gaze is invisible for Marianna, who has lost her sight as a result of a tumour and an operation, but like Rayment, she can sense people's repulsion. A close look at the relation between disability, sexuality and identity shows that, put together, disability and sex 'provoke contradictory responses ranging from denial, confusion, disapproval and disgust to fascination, obsession, surveillance and desire' (Goodley and Lawthom 2011, p. 90). Rayment and Marianna, 'two lesser beings, handicapped, diminished' (p. 113) embody these tensions between desire and disgust. During their 'experimental encounter', Rayment's main concern is his masculinity and the status of his body, reflected in his capacity for control and self-control: 'A man without sight is a lesser man, as a man with one leg is a lesser man, not a new man. This poor woman she has sent him is a lesser woman too, less than must have been before' (p. 113). Both of them push the limits of their senses, imagination and dignity, enduring what seems the impossible trial of having a pleasurable sexual experience without seriously damaging their self-esteem.

In initiation rites, the ritual subject faces unanswerable riddles, which here could be the symbolic meaning of Marianna's blindness, her life before disability, her unexpected desire to meet him, and Costello's suggestion that they might have met before. We should remember that 'the most characteristic midliminal symbolism is that of paradox, or being *both* this *and* that' (Turner 1992, p. 49, italics in the original). Following this line of thought, I will argue that Marianna is a disabled double of Marijana, a lesser Marijana, and at the same time a mirror reflection of Rayment's own perception of his diminished masculinity. A short story and an opera version of Coetzee's novel here might help solve the enigma of Marijana/Marianna. In the short story 'The Blow', published in June 2005a as an edited version *Slow Man*, the characters of Elizabeth Costello and Marianna are omitted. In the opera *Slow Man* (2012), with libretto written by Coetzee and music composed by Nicholas Lens, the characters are reduced to Rayment, Costello and Marijana, who, interestingly, is blind. Another interesting detail that Attwell (2015) found in the drafts of the novel is that 'Coetzee had written a thoroughly consummated relationship between Rayment and Marijana' (p. 220) but later apparently changed his mind, introducing Marianna, instead. One of the understandings of liminality that validates the interpretation of Rayment's encounters with the female characters as rites of passage is its reading as 'a fructile chaos, a fertile nothingness, a storehouse of possibilities, not by any means a random assemblage but a striving after new forms and structure, a gestation process, a fetation of modes appropriate to and anticipating postliminal existence' (Turner 1985, p. 295).

Before the encounter with Marianna, 'a woman of darkness', Costello insists on pasting flour and water on Rayment's eyes, so that darkness can free them from shame, which is mediated by vision.[8] In the dark, the protagonist is given the chance to confront his fears and doubts and live his masculinity without the social pressure created by daylight. As a symbol of chaos and the fear of the unknown, darkness blurs the boundaries of the body and attempts to neutralise the inscription of hegemonic masculinities on it, staging the 'fertile nothingness' and the 'store of possibilities' of the liminal phase. Thus, Rayment is not trying to *challenge* established role models or create a new concept of masculinity to adapt it to the nature of his disability, rather his concern about his 'diminished manliness' simply transforms the way he reads the scarred body. The reader might expect that after such an intense experience, seemingly created by Costello, involving fantasy, desire, affection and elements of passage rites like 'masks and monsters, symbolic inversions, parodies of profane reality' (Turner 1992, p. 55), the protagonist will emerge from his dark 'sacred enclosure' with a kind of transcendental revelation about life and death.

However, there is one last trial left—the disturbing and psychologically complex relationship with Costello. Rayment interprets his status as that of an 'initiate' in a 'rite of passage' and its meaning as a process of personal growth: '*We have crossed the threshold. Now we can proceed to higher and better things*' (p. 116, italics in original). For Craig Smith (2014), 'one of the lessons Rayment learns' is that 'to be human is to be a body capable of great suffering' (9). I would say that, in Coetzee's fiction, humanity is not so much about being capable of suffering, as about the meaning given to that suffering and its potential for personal transformation.

REAGGREGRATION: UNBINDING THE BODY

The role of Costello in the transformation of Rayment's conception of his masculinity as a result of his new disabled life condition is two-dimensional: as a woman and as a writer. The women Rayment meets and their reading of the corporal inscriptions of his 'diminished manliness' confront him with a multiplicity of masculine gender roles which he is forced to rethink, slowly transforming his perception of himself. Costello constantly reminds him of the limitations of his body and tries to convince him that, 'objectively speaking', old people like them do not need love, all they need is care. She recognises that 'care is not love' and makes a proposal for an 'ordinary' life: she will take care of him and in return he might take care of her. Even though he rejects this, I cannot agree with Jae Eun Yoo's (2013) claim that '[f]or Paul [Rayment], his ailing body is an excuse to push others away, and this self-containment leads to unfair judgments of others' and that he 'fails to take full responsibility for his own life and eludes any responsibility toward other people' (241). Although Rayment is aware of his limitations, he simply refuses to accept a 'diminished' type of masculinity reduced to care for an old disabled body.

In this context of refusal, Costello, the woman, reads Rayment's body as a self-evident site of his indisputable limitations due to disability and old age. By introducing him to Marianna, though, Costello, the writer, offers him the opportunity to explore a realm where all social norms are temporarily suspended, the limitations of the material body are overcome, the boundaries between past and present, real and imaginary are crossed, and the body is thought of as an emotional texture of initiations. She urges Rayment to 'live like a hero', to 'be a main character' of a story she is writing about him, a story she has full control of as an author. She seems to struggle for words when she tries to represent the complex web of liminal

102　S. STEFANOVA

processes that Rayment undergoes. It might be because, as Attwell (2008) argues, '[i]n order to encode desire, one needs the right code' (p. 234) or because, as Hayes (2010) puts it, 'neither the official institutions nor the literary practices of Australian modernity can find space to credit Paul's idea of himself with the authority he demands' (p. 258). Thus, the novel mirrors our anxiety about the limits and limitations of our body, our capacity to read the body, and the impossibility to narrate the acquired knowledge or self-knowledge using the existing terms and language codes.

Conclusion

Paul Rayment rejects what he believes are substitutions for desire, love, care and friendship, and claims authority over his life. He undergoes a painful process similar to the passage from boyhood to manhood, which in many ancient cultures is 'marked by initiations based on physical ordeals' (Still and Worton 1993, 39), and eventually refuses to be a 'hero'. The protagonist's new understanding of masculinity embraces the quest for authenticity and the decision to author his own life story. He recognises the signifying acts he is forced to perform in his gender-related ritual encounters, but refuses to strive for the status they grant. Following Sara Ahmed's (2004) words that '[b]odies take the shape of the very contact they have with other objects or others' (p. 1), I would like to suggest that in *Slow Man* it is the notion of masculinities that takes the shape of its protagonist's response to his contact with others. Coetzee does not struggle to articulate a new disability-inclusive gender style that his protagonist might be comfortable with. Rather, he distances himself from any normative models based on inclusion/exclusion, societal insecurities and self-bordering, to reflect instead his concerns not so much with what masculinity *is*, or to what category Rayment pertains, as with *how* the protagonist's reading of his new reality changes his understanding of his own masculinity.

Notes

1. Scholars working within Disability Studies reveal the corporeal dimension of human experience and expose the ways in which society excludes those who do not match the 'norm'.
2. Most critics understand the concept of stigma as defined by Erving Goffman (1986) for whom stigma is 'possessing an attribute that makes [a person]

different from others' and 'of a less desirable kind,' 'a person who is quite thoroughly bad, dangerous, or weak. He is thus reduced in our minds from a whole and usual person to a tainted, discounted one' (p. 3).

3. Further references to this edition are given after quotations in the text.
4. Lynne Segal (1995) describes 'denial, over-reaction and guilt' as 'the defensive responses to the desperation men feel when their male identity has not been adequately affirmed' (p. 131).
5. Melinda Harvey (2011) quotes these lines in relation to her idea of a 'surrealist world'. For her, *Slow Man* is 'a type of self-testing on Coetzee's part, post-Nobel Prize [whether he] can write a novel that has a protagonist who can't move, who won't act, who's getting old, who knows practically no one and who's boring as hell' (p. 24).
6. Sara Ahmed (2004) argues, 'To be passive is to be enacted upon, as a negation that is already felt as suffering. The fear of passivity is tied to the fear of emotionality, in which weakness is defined in terms of a tendency to be shaped by others' (p. 2).
7. Although physical self-sufficiency is an important aspect of hegemonic masculinity, its lack, due to old age or disability, does not exclude the possibility of other categories of male dominance, as shown by the recent incorporation of the category of 'trasnational business masculinity' (Connell and Wood 2005, pp. 347–364).
8. Timothy Bewes (2011) quotes Simone de Beauvoir's description of the shame of a young girl in adolescence in her seminal work *The Second Sex* (1949) and provides his own definition of shame as 'result[ing] from an experience of incommensurability, between the I as experienced by the self and the self as it appears to and is reflected in the eyes of the other' (p. 24).

WORKS CITED

Aguirre, Manuel, Roberta Quance, and Phillip Sutton. 2000. *Margins and Thresholds. An Enquiry into the Concept of Liminality in Text Studies.* Madrid: Gateway Press.

Ahmed, Sara. 2004. *The Cultural Politics of Emotion.* New York and London: Routledge.

Anderson, Eric. 2008. Inclusive Masculinity in a Fraternal Setting. *Men and Masculinities* 10 (5): 604–620.

———. 2009. *Inclusive Masculinity: The Changing Nature of Masculinities.* New York: Routledge.

Attwell, David. 2008. Coetzee's Estrangements. *Novel: A Forum on Fiction* 41 (2–3): 229–243.

———. 2011. Coetzee's Postcolonial Diaspora. *Twentieth-Century Literature* 57 (1): 9–19.

104   S. STEFANOVA

———. 2015. *J.M. Coetzee and the Life of Writing: Face-to-Face with Time*. Oxford: Oxford University Press.

Ayers, Mary Y. 2011. *Masculine Shame: From Succubus to the Eternal Feminine*. London and New York: Routledge.

Baarspul, Matthijs, and Paul Franssen. 2018. Settling for 'Something Less': J. M. Coetzee's *Slow Man* and the Shakespearean Bed-Trick Motif. *English Studies* 99 (5): 554–565.

Bewes, Timothy. 2011. *The Event of Postcolonial Shame*. Princeton and Oxford: Princeton University Press.

Boehmer, Elleke. 2009. Queer Bodies. In *J. M. Coetzee in Context and Theory*, ed. Elleke Boehmer, Katy Iddiols, and Robert Eaglestone, 123–134. New York: Continuum.

———. 2011. J.M. Coetzee's Australian Realism. In *Strong Opinions: J.M. Coetzee and the Authority of Contemporary Fiction*, ed. Chris Danta, Sue Kossew, and Julian Murphet, 3–18. New York: Continuum.

Braidotti, Rosi. 1999. Signs of Wonder and Traces of Doubt: On Teratology and Embodied Difference. In *Feminist Theory and the Body: A Reader*, ed. Janet Price and Margrit Shildrick, 290–301. New York: Routledge.

Bridges, Tristan, and Cheri Jo Pascoe. 2014. Hybrid Masculinities: New Directions in the Sociology of Men and Masculinities. *Sociology Compass* 8 (3): 246–258.

Cleaver, Francis. 2002. Men and Masculinities: New Directions in Gender and Development. In *Masculinities Matter! Men, Gender and Development*, ed. Francis Cleaver, 1–27. London: Zed Books.

Coetzee, J.M. 2005a. The Blow. *New Yorker*, June 27.

———. 2005b. *Slow Man*. London: Vintage Books.

Colebrook, Claire. 2011. Time and Autopoiesis: The Organism Has No Future. In *Deleuze and the Body*, ed. Laura Guillaume and Joe Hughes, 9–28. Edinburgh: Edinburgh University Press.

Connell, Raewyn W. 1982. Class, Patriarchy, and Sartre's Theory of Practice. *Theory and Society* 11: 305–320.

———. 1983. *Which Way Is Up? Essays on Sex, Class and Culture*. Sydney, Australia: Allen and Unwin.

———. 1995. *Masculinities*. Berkley and Los Angeles, CA: University of California Press.

———. 2009. *Gender: In World Perspective*. Cambridge: Polity.

Connell, Raewyn W., and James W. Messerschmidt. 2005. Hegemonic Masculinity: Rethinking the Concept. *Gender and Society* 19 (6): 829–859.

Connell, Raewyn W., and Julian Wood. 2005. Globalization and Business Masculinities. *Men and Masculinities* 7 (4): 347–364.

Cornwall, Andrea, and Nancy Lindisfarne. 1994. Dislocating Masculinity: Gender, Power and Anthropology. In *Dislocating Masculinity: Comparative*

Ethnographies, ed. Andrea Cornwall and Nancy Lindisfarne, 11–47. London and New York: Routledge.

Crawford, Cassandra S. 2014. Body Image, Prostheses, Phantom Limbs. *Body & Society* 21 (2): 221–244.

DeFalco, Amelia. 2010. *Uncanny Subjects: Aging in Contemporary Narrative.* Columbus: The Ohio State University Press.

Gilmore, David D. 1990. *Manhood in the Making: Cultural Concepts of Masculinity.* New Haven and London: Yale University Press.

Goffman, Erving. 1986. *Stigma. Notes on the Management of Spoiled Identity.* First published in 1963 by Simon and Schuster, New York, London and Toronto: Touchstone.

Goodley, Daniel, and Rebecca Lawthom. 2011. Disability, Deleuze and Sex. In *Deleuze and Sex*, ed. Frida Beckman, 89–105. Edinburgh: Edinburgh University Press.

Grayson, Erik. 2021. 'Even at This Late Juncture': Amputation, Old Age, and Paul Rayment's Prosthetic Family in J.M. Coetzee's *Slow Man*. In *Amputation in Literature and Film Artificial Limbs, Prosthetic Relations, and the Semiotics of 'Loss'*, ed. Erik Grayson and Maren Scheurer, 137–154. Cham: Palgrave Macmillan.

Grosz, Elizabeth. 1994. *Volatile Bodies: Toward a Corporeal Feminism.* Bloomington and Indianapolis: Indiana University Press.

Hall, Alice. 2012. *Disability and Modern Fiction: Faulkner, Morrison, Coetzee and the Nobel Prize for Literature.* London: Palgrave Macmillan.

Harvey, Melinda. 2011. 'In Australia You Start Zero': The Escape from Place in J.M. Coetzee's Late Novels. In *Strong Opinions: J.M. Coetzee and the Authority of Contemporary Fiction*, ed. Chris Danta, Sue Kossew, and Julian Murphet, 19–34. New York: Continuum.

Hayes, Patrick. 2010. *J. M. Coetzee and the Novel: Writing and Politics after Beckett.* Oxford: Oxford University Press.

Hodgin, Nick, and Amit Thakkar. 2017. Introduction: Trauma Studies, Film and the Scar Motif. In *Scars and Wounds: Film and Legacies of Trauma*, ed. Nick Hodgin and Amit Thakkar, 1–30. London: Palgrave Macmillan.

Kannemeyer, J.C. 2012. *J. M. Coetzee: A Life in Writing.* Trans. by Michiel Heyns. Melbourne and London: Scribe.

Kessler, Sandra, Dean Ashenden, Raewyn Connell, and Garry Dowsett. 1982. *Ockers and Disco-maniacs: Sex, Gender, and Secondary Schooling.* Sydney, Australia: Inner City Education Center.

Kossew, Sue. 2011. Literary Migration: Shifting Borders in Coetzee's Australian Novels. In *Strong Opinions: J.M. Coetzee and the Authority of Contemporary Fiction*, ed. Chris Danta, Sue Kossew, and Julian Murphet, 113–124. New York: Continuum.

106 S. STEFANOVA

Lens, Nicholas. 2012. *Slow Man*. Opera, libretto by J. M. Coetzee. Dir. by Maja Kleczewska. Perform. by Lani Poulson, Mark S. Doss, and Claron McFadden. Poznań, Poland, July 5.

Marais, Mike. 2011. The Trope of Following in J.M. Coetzee's *Slow Man*. In *Strong Opinions: J.M. Coetzee and the Authority of Contemporary Fiction*, ed. Chris Danta, Sue Kossew, and Julian Murphet, 99–112. New York: Continuum.

Matias, Daniel. 2017. 'Wooden Man'? *Masculinities in the Works of J.M. Coetzee (Boyhood, Youth and Summertime)*. New York: Peter Lang.

Mehigan, Tim. 2011. Slow Man. In *A Companion to the Works of J.M. Coetzee*, ed. Tim Mehigan, 192–207. Rochester, New York: Camden House.

Moss, Mark. 2011. *The Media and the Models of Masculinity*. Lanham, UK: Lexington Books.

Pellow, C. Kenneth. 2009. Intertextuality and Other Analogues in J. M. Coetzee's *Slow Man*. *Contemporary Literature* 50 (3): 528–552.

Preston, Jeffrey. 2017. *The Fantasy of Disability: Images of Loss in Popular Culture*. London and New York: Routledge.

Robertson, Steve, Lee Monaghan, and Kris Southby. 2020. Disability, Embodiment and Masculinities: A Complex Matrix. In *Routledge International Handbook of Masculinity Studies*, ed. Lucas Gottzén, Ulf Mellström, and Tamara Shefer, 154–164. London and New York: Routledge.

Schiebinger, Londa. 1999. Theories of Gender and Race. In *Feminist Theory and the Body: A Reader*, ed. Janet Price and Margrit Shildrick, 21–31. New York: Routledge.

Schwalbe, Michael. 2014. *Manhood Acts: Gender and the Practices of Domination*. Boulder and London: Paradigm Publishers.

Segal, Lynne. 1995. *Slow Motion: Changing Masculinities, Changing Men*. New Brunswick, NJ: Rutgers University Press.

Smith, Craig. 2014. On Not Yet Being Christian: J.M. Coetzee's *Slow Man* and the Ethics of Being (Un)Interesting. *Postcolonial Text* 9 (1): 1–18.

Sontag, Susan. 2005. *On Photography*. New York: RosettaBooks.

Spector-Mersel, Gabriela. 2006. Never-aging Stories: Western Hegemonic Masculinity Scripts. *Journal of Gender Studies* 15 (1): 67–82.

Still, Judith, and Michael Worton. 1993. Introduction. In *Textuality and Sexuality: Reading Theories and Practices*, ed. Judith Still and Michael Worton Manchester, 1–68. New York: Manchester University Press.

Turner, Victor. [1964] 1994. Betwixt and Between: The Liminal Period in *Rites de Passage*. In *Betwixt & Between: Patterns of Masculine and Feminine Initiation*, ed. Louise Carus Mahdi, Steven Foster, and Meredith Little, 3–22. La Salle, IL: Open Court.

———. [1969] 1976. *The Ritual Process: Structure and Anti-Structure* (6th ed.). Chicago: Aldine Publishing Company.

———. 1985. *On the Edge of the Bush: Anthropology as Experience*. Tucson, AZ: The University of Arizona Press.

———. 1992. *Blazing the Trail: Way Marks in the Exploration of Symbols*. Tucson and London: The University of Arizona Press.

Turner, David M., and Kevin Stagg. 2006. Introduction. In *Social Histories of Disability and Deformity*, ed. David M. Turner and Kevin Stagg, 1–16. London and New York: Routledge.

Wendell, Susan. 1996. *The Rejected Body: Feminist Philosophical Reflections on Disability*. New York and London: Routledge.

Wetherell, Margaret, and Nigel Edley. 1999. Negotiating Hegemonic Masculinity: Imaginary Positions and Psycho-Discursive Practices. *Feminism & Psychology* 9 (3): 335–356.

Wicomb, Zoë. 2009. *Slow Man* and the Real: A Lesson in Reading and Writing. *Journal of Literary Studies* 25 (4): 7–24.

Yoo, Jae Eun. 2013. Broken Tongues in Dialogue: Translation and the Body in *Slow Man*. *Texas Studies in Literature and Language* 55 (2): 234–251.

CHAPTER 6

Paul Auster's *The New York Trilogy*: Writing/Fatherhood/Borderlands

Chris Harris

Paul Auster's *The New York Trilogy* (1987) sits provocatively in any discussion of literature, borders, and masculinities. All three texts, *City of Glass* (1985), *Ghosts* (1986), and *The Locked Room* (1986) are concerned with a network of issues relating to writing and fatherhood in at least two contexts: father-figure influences in a patrilineal construction of the American literary tradition, and father-son relations in contemporary culture. They are also concerned with the conceptual borderlands between a range of binary oppositions including, amongst others, identity and otherness, reality and imagination, sanity and madness, connection and isolation, as well as success and failure in both literary and paternal spheres. The various artistic configurations that traverse thresholds and bind this trilogy of texts together, in what Auster has also described in a BBC World Service discussion as a 'triptych' (2012, 17:00), are at once multiple, rhizomatic, and strategically articulated. Auster states that the term triptych is better than trilogy to describe his work, but he opted not to use this term as a title because of the way it sounds: 'The New York Triptych'. The term is

C. Harris (✉)
School of Global Affairs, Lancaster University, Lancaster, UK
e-mail: c.harris7@lancaster.ac.uk

© The Author(s), under exclusive license to Springer Nature Switzerland AG 2024
A. Thakkar et al. (eds.), *Border Masculinities*,
https://doi.org/10.1007/978-3-031-68050-2_6

109

110   C. HARRIS

used, however, from the start and throughout in this reading to show how the various artistic configurations that connect the three texts, often in the form of repeated images and *leitmotifs*, can be imagined as crossing the boundaries of the three triptych panels. Such crossings are present, I would argue, however those panels are imagined or interpreted. *The New York Trilogy* is certainly polysemic by design, but as we will see it can be read as a complex and creative account of what it means to be an American writer, on the one hand, and what it means to be a contemporary father, on the other, with myriad overlaps, or border-crossings, within and between these two literary and autobiographical meditations.

Even at a superficial level, the evidence for this reading is apparent. Firstly, *City of Glass* relates the destructive relationship between Peter Stillman and his son Peter Stillman Jr through the eyes of a writer-cum-detective called Daniel Quinn. In this narrative of toxic fatherhood, Auster incorporates allusions to texts written by his global literary 'fathers' that include Marco Polo's *Travels* (1299, and 1579 in English), Miguel de Cervantes' *Don Quixote* (1605 for Part I and 1615 for Part II), and Edgar Allan Poe's *William Wilson* (1842). Secondly, *Ghosts* deals metaphorically with the idea of writers influencing writers—the construction of an overtly masculinised American literary tradition of fathers and sons—through an emblematic relationship between a writer-detective called Blue and a writer-detective called Black. Blue has previously been influenced by Brown and continues his work: 'Brown broke him in, Brown taught him the ropes, and when Brown grew old, Blue took over' (Auster 1987, p. 137). Extending these patrilineal influences into literary history and tradition, the narrative of *Ghosts* establishes relationships with key intertexts including Henry David Thoreau's *Walden* (1854), Nathaniel Hawthorne's *Twice-Told Tales* (1837 and 1842), and Walt Whitman's *Leaves of Grass* (1855). Finally, in *The Locked Room* the unnamed narrator is positioned as a father-figure to the child Ben whose biological father, Fanshawe, is missing and mistakenly presumed dead. From the margins of this narrative of surrogate fatherhood, Fanshawe exercises a continually spectral presence which is at once literary, epistolary (he writes letters to the narrator), and emotionally disturbing for the recipient. Living with the secret of his friend's separate life, the narrator earns a living by publishing Fanshawe's work as if it were his own, and at the same time he is living with Fanshawe's wife. Of course, the name Fanshawe is a direct reference to Nathaniel Hawthorne's *Fanshawe: A Tale* (1828). In sum, then, *The*

New York Trilogy is constructed on a visible framework of literary and social patriarchy.

That Auster should establish writing, fatherhood, and conceptual borderlands as prominent themes of his postmodern literary experiments in *The New York Trilogy* marks a thought-provoking continuity with *The Invention of Solitude* (1982). As he told Razia Iqbal in 2012 (7:30): 'that's the foundational work for me, [...] fiction I've written since has emerged out of a lot of the preoccupations that are articulated in that work'. The first part of *The Invention of Solitude*, *The Invisible Man* (written in 1979), is an autobiographical study focused on Samuel Auster, Paul Auster's father. At the start Auster recalls the moment when he heard of his father's passing and thereafter deploys that moment of sadness as a catalyst for a profound investigation of family life, family death, and the creative process. In this initial discourse on fatherhood, Auster provides testimony to the powerfully emotional impact his father had exercised in his lifetime through a meticulous study of the man, his character, and his characteristically distant ways of being. At the same time Auster establishes themes and ideas that would become enduring elements of his now recognisable literary aesthetic, including certain experiential borders beginning with the invisible line between life and death:

> One day there is life. A man, for example, in the best of health, not even old, with no history of illness. Everything is as it was, as it will always be. He goes from one day to the next, minding his own business, dreaming only of the life that lies before him. And then, suddenly, it happens there is death. A man lets out a little sigh, he slumps down in his chair, and it is death. (1982, p. 5)

In the second part of *The Invention of Solitude*, *The Book of Memory* (written in 1980–1981), Auster offers a different type of discourse on fatherhood which is narrated from the perspective of a father called 'A', presumably the writer himself. Significantly for his later writing, Auster chooses literary *dédoublement* as a method for examining his own experiences as a son and a father, and his own sense of having multiple identities:

> When the father dies, he writes, the son becomes his own father and his own son. He looks at his son and sees himself in the face of the boy. He imagines what the boy sees when he looks at him and he finds himself becoming his own father. Inexplicably he is moved by this. It is not just the sight of the

112   C. HARRIS

boy that moves him, nor even the thought of standing inside his father, but what he sees in the boy of his own vanished past. It is a nostalgia for his own life he feels, perhaps, a memory of his own boyhood as a son to his father. (1982, p. 85)

The Book of Memory explores simultaneously issues of fatherhood and questions of aesthetics, philosophy, narrative style, and form. Language, meaning, and chance are all present as topics for profound thought together with Freud's notion of the uncanny. And when Auster writes of 'chance', it appears to be exactly that sudden *frisson* of unease caused by a bizarre coincidence to which he is referring. In the 'First commentary on the nature of chance', for instance, Auster relates the story of 'M' who rents a room in Paris and discovers it was previously the 'chambre de bonne' (1982, p. 84) where his father hid during the Second World War. Noticeably, with reference to Quinn, *City of Glass* has as its second sentence: 'Much later, when he was able to think about the things that happened to him, he would conclude that nothing was real except chance' (Auster 1987, p. 3). In all these respects and more, then, *The Invention of Solitude* can be said to function as an important prelude to *The New York Trilogy*.

Such continuities of thought and writing in Auster's early publications have become talking points for literary and cultural critics. For Pascal Bruckner (1995, p. 27), for example, '*The Invention of Solitude* is both the *ars poetica* and the seminal work of Paul Auster. To understand him we must start here; all his books lead us back to this one'. In similar vein, John D. Barbour has convincingly argued that *The Invisible Man* and *The Book of Memory* both embrace issues of writing and fatherhood—in connection with solitude—as Auster searches for ways to illuminate the meanings of his life as a son to Samuel, as a father to Daniel, and as an aspiring novelist:

> Auster's memoir makes the experience of aloneness central to the relationship between fathers and sons. His portrait of his father shows the negative side of solitude in Samuel's self-absorption and failure to give his son love in ways that Paul could understand. Auster's portrayal of his role as father shows him trying to pass on to Daniel the positive meanings of solitude as linked to imagination, memory, and creativity. (2004, p. 31)[1]

Some of the main autobiographical continuities that build bridges between *The Invention of Solitude* and *The New York Trilogy* are certainly captured in this account, particularly with the links between isolation, fatherhood, and creativity. Barbour (2004, p. 31) further insists that at the time Auster was writing *The Invention of Solitude*, 'parenting' and 'imaginative writing' constituted his 'deepest commitments' and held a 'spiritual significance' for him. In this light, and especially when bereavement, divorce, as well as fatherhood, were all recent experiences in Auster's life, it is not surprising to find that various related issues would resurface in fictional form in *The New York Trilogy* only a relatively short time later. As we will see in what follows, Auster's desire to be a successful writer, and to be a good father, are not only two of the fundamental concerns which permeated his personal and writing life in the late 1970s and early 1980s, but also two of the major intellectual preoccupations that infuse all five texts collated in his 1982 autobiographical reflections and his 1987 'triptych'.

Thoughts Inspired by *City of Glass* (1985)

Auster has explained that the initial idea for *City of Glass* arose from an event in his own life that he later reconstructed in his writing as a meaningful coincidence. The famous opening line establishes this: 'It was a wrong number that started it, the telephone ringing three times in the dead of night, and the voice on the other end asking for someone he was not' (Auster 1987, p. 3). In a 2004 interview with James Naughtie for the BBC (02:15), Auster recounts how he had twice received a call asking for the Pinkerton Detective Agency and how he had twice simply ended the call because it was a wrong number. This had subsequently made him wonder what might have happened if he had pretended to be a detective instead. In the first text in the trilogy, the first panel of the triptych, Auster recreates this experience to begin telling the story of Daniel Quinn, a mediocre writer and widower living in a self-imposed isolation and anonymity in a New York apartment. Since the death of his wife and son five years earlier, a double trigger for Quinn's emotional struggle and social withdrawal, he has abandoned his hopes of being a celebrated literary talent and has chosen instead to earn a living by writing run-of-the-mill mystery novels under the pen name of William Wilson, with a detective protagonist called Max Work. He has not told anyone he is writing these novels. If asked, he pretends to be living from a trust fund left to him by his wife. Late one evening Quinn finds himself drawn into a search for a certain Peter Stillman who was imprisoned for nine years for incarcerating his son in a sealed room but who has served his sentence and is about to

114   C. HARRIS

be released. The permanently traumatised son, Peter Stillman Jr, fears for his life, as does his wife Virginia, his former speech therapist. To protect himself, Stillman Jr calls Quinn three times asking for Paul Auster of the Auster Detective Agency and on the third call, Quinn, pretending to be the fictional character Auster and assuming the detective mindset of Max Work, accepts a commission to track down the ex-con father. And in this way, the opening of *City of Glass* begins to unfold, starting with a fictionalised re-telling of a chance occurrence in Paul Auster's life and a problematisation of identity.

It is largely Auster's attention to the complexities of identity that situates *The New York Trilogy* as an exemplar of postmodernist style. In the words of Anne Berge (2005, p. 101), 'Paul Auster's *The New York Trilogy* […] has been read as a typical example of postmodern literature. One important feature is the theme of complex identity, and the novels can be read as an exploration of identity problems in the postmodern age'. In this context, *City of Glass* is both a story of tragically destructive fatherhood conveyed in and through the character of Peter Stillman and, as Quinn moves deeper and deeper into states of self-isolation, a story of an aspiring writer and would-be-detective's disappearance from the public eye and therefore failure to enter the annals of literary history or to solve the mystery. Both Stillman and Quinn follow pathways in life that lead to forms of isolation, madness, and imprisonment, real incarceration for one and metaphorical for the other. The two narrated lives are to some extent mirror images reflected in the glass environment around them that is New York. Moreover, these interrelated narratives tend to circle around one specific *leitmotif* that runs throughout the first novel, and throughout *The New York Trilogy*: the quest for omniscient understanding, the quest for the author-detective's all-knowing vision. Madeleine Sorapure (1995, p. 85) succinctly notes the writerly basis of this failure:

> *City of Glass* […] insistently frustrates the efforts of its author-characters to achieve an author's perspective on the events in which they are engaged. The novel frustrates, as well, the reader's or critic's attempt to locate the real Paul Auster behind the scenes.

This quest is repeatedly portrayed in *City of Glass* as endless, unfulfilled, a way into disconnection, loss of perspective, and eventual insanity. In this regard, Stillman is portrayed not only as an abusive father but also as an insane father who had locked his son in a windowless room for nine years to see if the isolated son would develop in such solitude the language of God, the prelapsarian language that united all peoples before the Fall of Man and before Fall of Language with the construction and destruction of the Tower of Babel. Stillman even ponders the reversibility of this mythical global history and the possibility of a return to an Edenic lifestyle with an innocent humanity untainted by the knowledge of evil.

Similarly, it is no coincidence that Daniel Quinn is identified with Don Quixote and introduced as a reader of Marco Polo or that Marco Polo is represented as a seeker of truth who is determined that when found, such truth, even Truth, should be set down in writing. As this modern-day Don Quixote and modern-day Marco Polo descends into madness, he follows Stillman through the streets of New York imagining that the steps spell out letters until the letters spell out words: The Tower of Babel. This, however, is postmodern metafiction, not psychological realism, and Daniel Quinn's fading reflections as forms of intertextuality reveal as much: 'He thought through the question of why Don Quixote had not simply wanted to write books like the ones he loved – instead of living out their adventures. He wondered why he had the same initials as Don Quixote' (Auster 1987, p. 130). Gradually Quinn abandons his life as a reclusive writer, becomes a vagrant, and finally returns to the empty Stillman apartment, undresses, writes less and less each day in a red notebook, and eventually vanishes altogether. Ultimately, in *City of Glass* Auster delivers two tales that intersect and interact with one another through quests for literary omniscience and fatherly success. He creates two male characters, both fathers, both writers, and tells two quixotic tales of disturbing failure in fatherhood. These tales are situated in the conceptual borderlands between reality and imagination, responsibility and irresponsibility, and in terms of metafiction, fatherhood, and authorship.

If the futile search for omniscience and rational explanation is one important *leitmotif* in Auster's imaginary tales from New York, the reader's search for the significance of the red notebook as a literary artefact is another form of *leitmotif* that criss-crosses the three constituent texts of *The New York Trilogy*. In practice, there are multiple red notebooks mentioned. Quinn has one, and so does Peter Stillman. At the end of *The Locked Room*, a red notebook is also to the fore in the *dénouement*—if such a word can be allowed in a discussion of Auster's postmodern narratives. Fanshawe offers a red notebook to the unnamed narrator who refuses it and destroys it. In the inevitable search by readers for meaning(s), there are some clues available though there are no definitive answers. Clues exist outside of the text. Auster has published a collection of autobiographical fragments under the title 'The Red Notebook' (1997a), and in an interview with the BBC in 2012 he admits to a penchant for spiral-bound notebooks with small squares on the paper. He explains that he buys them wherever he goes and uses them to compose fiction. He further comments on the significance of the notebooks for himself:

> I've always written by hand […] Notebooks have become for me a kind of emblem of the inner life, the inner life as expressed in language. And the notebook has become somehow a house for words for me. It's the dwelling in which, finally, I spend most of my time. What is the ultimate significance of this, you ask the meaning. I have absolutely no idea. (Auster in conversation with Gilbert 2012, 21:30)

What readers are to make of the red notebook as a literary device in *The New York Trilogy* is potentially illuminated by this statement. For each character who has a red notebook it could be understood, without doubt, as an 'emblem of the [character's] inner life, the inner life as expressed in language'. In Fanshawe's case, for example, he tells the narrator that it contains 'an explanation for what I did. At least an attempt' (Auster 1987, p. 311).

Clues also exist in the texts but bring apparent complications. The narrator of *The Locked Room* comments on Fanshawe's red notebook: 'Each sentence erased the sentence before it. Each paragraph made the next paragraph impossible […] as though in the end the only thing he wanted was to fail – even to the point of failing himself' (Auster 1987, p. 313). William Lavender (1993, p. 220) captures this deconstruction of self and text precisely for the first of the three novels: '*City of Glass*, then, is a deconstruction. Or a sabotage. It deconstructs the form of the novel, the canons of criticism, theory, and tradition, and it deconstructs itself, as it literally falls apart in its progression'. In this textualised act of deconstruction, the destiny of the failing writer in each narrative respectively is to disappear either into obscurity like Quinn, to another distant place like China with Blue, or into death as with Fanshawe.

Yet this bleak reading has a potentially opposite set of meanings too. For the narrator of *The Locked Room*, and potentially for the author Paul Auster, the disappearance of Quinn, Blue and Fanshawe might stand as a metaphor for the death of a self-absorbed personality and a self-defeating inner voice that has hindered any ability for each of them to thrive in life and society and to become a celebrated author (Quinn/Fanshawe) or a 'good' father (Blue/Fanshawe). In *The Locked Room*, the narrator moves beyond this realm of introspection, isolation, and failure when he destroys Fanshawe's red notebook on a train station platform. That same notebook could be understood as an emblem for an inner life that is a preparatory terrain for acts of creation, a borderland of consciousness that lies somewhere between self and other, between autobiography and fiction, and that can either become a psychological prison or a springboard to fulfilment. And if paternal fulfilment and success as a writer are the destinations, then the journey must begin, it would seem, with the death of the literary (fore)father. As Fanshawe nears the end of life, the narrator's last words are these: 'I came to the last page just as the train was pulling out' (Auster 1987, p. 314). The journey to authenticity and recognition can now begin, it just has not begun yet. There is a final hesitation and uncertainty, a final postmodern full stop.

If the red notebook facilitates thinking around the idea of borders, borderlands, and border-crossings, it is important to emphasise that borders are always present in *City of Glass* insofar as the main referents are literary and are concerned with form, especially with genre and conventions. *City of Glass* is an experimental text that swiftly establishes generic borders and just as briskly moves across them. Capancioni, Costantini, and Mattoscio (2023, p. 6) have argued that:

> the fruition of a cultural object—in the form of reading, watching, listening, etc.—can be interpreted as an act of border-crossing, because it entails crossing the medial borders of a text, as well as the epistemological border of interpretation.

Auster as character in his own fiction, Quinn, and other characters, are all constructed in ways that align with and illustrate this argument. As mentioned, the protagonist Daniel Quinn, a character who reads and writes mystery novels, has initials that are identical to those of Don Quixote for intertextual reasons. The narrator tells us that: 'what interested him [Quinn] about the stories he wrote was not their relation to the world but their relation to other stories' (Auster 1987, p. 7). In this vein, *The New York Trilogy* finds its principal meanings not in any realist endeavour to portray New York and its people, though there are certainly realist elements incorporated such as the architectural and engineering histories of the Brooklyn Bridge, but rather in the overt links with other works of

118 C. HARRIS

fiction. There are at least two levels to this systematic metafictional strategy: on one level there are deliberate connections and thematic overlaps such as Daniel Quinn's initials or the echoes of Edgar Allen Poe's *William Wilson* and the uncanny nature of *doppelgängers*; on another level *The New York Trilogy* is a text that cannibalises and carnivalises detective fiction both humorously and intellectually. Throughout the three texts, Auster plays with this principle: 'In the good mystery there is nothing wasted, no sentence, no word that is not significant' (Auster 1987, p. 8). Knowing that his readers will look for patterns, Auster enables the detective and the reader to be aligned, but their efforts cannot ever succeed. Quinn is a failing and ultimately failed detective and the reader can only fail too in any effort to find the logic that holds all the textual fragments together, for there is no such logic provided. Like certain examples of the French *nouveau roman*, Alain Robbe-Grillet's *La jalousie* (1957) for instance, clues lead to other clues but never to solutions, words lead to other words, and actions often lead to opposite actions with the ebb and flow of creation and cancellation, portraiture, and erasure, of meanings and characters, even events. *The New York Trilogy* offers three versions of a mystery novel and in each one the mysteries go unsolved. As Nealon (1996, p. 107) writes for *City of Glass*: 'The end of *City of Glass*, insofar as it is not an end, does not satisfy like a meal, as the consumable ends of many detective novels do. Instead, it brings the question of end ever closer, tries to ask that question in earnest'. So, for *City of Glass*, so for *The New York Trilogy*.

Further Thoughts Inspired by *Ghosts* (1986)

Auster has explained the genesis of *The New York Trilogy* to World Book Club listeners for the BBC. He did not set out to produce such a work. Instead, he was returning to old writing he had never published. Initially, at the age of about 23, he had opted to leave aside around one thousand manuscript pages with a sense of failure and defeat: 'I'm not capable of writing fiction. I can't write novels, I give it up' (Auster in conversation with Gilbert 2012, 14:45). Years later, in the 1980s, he decided to overcome this psychological hurdle and write a first novel by revisiting unfinished manuscripts. *City of Glass* emerged first out of this re-working of incomplete works of prose fiction, as did *Ghosts* afterwards from revisiting a series of unfinished plays. In *Ghosts*, the two detective-writers, Blue and Black, watch each other as each one writes in a small room on the opposite side of Orange Street, New York, the place where in 1855 Walt Whitman handset the first edition of *Leaves of Grass* (Auster 1987, p. 139). This principal 'staging' was originally conceived by Auster as a one-act play. In the conversation with Harriet Gilbert (16.01), Auster next explains that once there were two texts he knew there would need to be a third and *The Locked Room* began to take shape in his thoughts: 'There can't be just two, there has to be a third. This is a series of books that are all interconnected in some way even though they are separate'. In a sense then, *The Locked Room* was Auster's first novel to be composed and written over a single continuous period.

The title of the second novel, *Ghosts*, refers to the lingering presence of the 'great men' of the past. When the two detective-writers Blue and Black talk about Plymouth Church and the appeal of Henry Ward Beecher's sermons for Henry David Thoreau, Black states: 'Many great men have gone there [...] Abraham Lincoln, Charles Dickens – they all walked down this street and went into the church'. The next lines are these: 'Ghosts. Yes, there are ghosts all around us' (Auster 1987, p. 176). In a discussion of Auster's relations with his writerly self and with the works of earlier writers, James Peacock underlines the importance of self-other relations for Auster more generally but also warns against reductionist approaches by contemporary critics: 'Solipsism versus intersubjectivity, as an ethical, psychological and literary-historical issue, is surely the key agon in Auster's work, though not one reducible to a simple binary' (2011, p. 363). If the 'fathers' of America's literary tradition continue to influence the present moment with the reverberations of their lives and their writing, Auster makes it clear that humbler biological fathers, for whom fame is not an experience, also exert determining influences over their male offspring. Blue recalls walking across the Brooklyn Bridge holding his father's hand: 'The old man was born the same year the bridge was finished, and there was always that link in Blue's mind, as though the bridge were somehow a monument to his father' (Auster 1987, p. 151).

At this point in the narration one thought slides into the next on this theme of father-son relations. Firstly, Blue remembers the story of John Roebling and his son Washington as the engineers who designed the bridge, with son Washington continuing his father's work after the latter's death. Then Blue recalls a story from a magazine he has been reading called *Stranger than Fiction* in which, many years after a father's death, his son finds his father's body frozen in ice whilst out skiing in the French Alps. The father's body was frozen at a moment in his life when he was younger than the son who is now looking at his corpse 'like someone on

120 C. HARRIS

the other side of a thick window' (Auster 1987, p. 153). For the son, the experience produces the 'distinct and terrifying impression that he was looking at himself' (Auster 1987, p. 153). And here, there is a third sense of the ghostly in *The New York Trilogy*. In addition to literary fathers and biological fathers, there is also the double, at times even the *doppelgänger*. The narrator tells us in *Ghosts*: 'In spying out at Black across the street, it is as though Blue were looking into a mirror, and instead of merely watching another, he finds that he is also watching himself' (Auster 1987, p. 146). As Arce Álvarez has argued (2014, p. 47), the double in Auster's hands is not simply an echo of Edgar Allen Poe in *William Wilson* but much more: it is 'a metaphor of the creative act of writing'.

The creative act of writing, in turn, is represented in *Ghosts* as an activity that takes place in a psychological borderland (also in an enclosed physical space) where a writer's different selves continually meet, interact, and separate. The writer is therefore making daily decisions between committing to their creative or imaginative self and their other, more social, selves. This type of existential choice coupled with an exploration of a writer's subjectivity is given a place of high importance in Auster's fiction as he has explained relatively recently in interview with Laura Sims. When asked why he had created four parallel lives in his 2017 novel *4-3-2-1* for the protagonist Ferguson, he replied:

> I've often been exploring in my work the forces of what I would call contingency. Something happens, but it doesn't necessarily have to happen. So much of life is taking different forks in the road of life, you go left, you go right, sometimes these decisions seem arbitrary, but then they wind up determining a lot of what happens to you afterwards. And I've always been speculating, I think of human beings too, what if I had done this back then, instead of that? (14:07)

This world of forking paths and possible alternative lives is a hallmark of Auster's fiction and almost certainly connected to his readings of Borges. In a 2017 review of *4-3-2-1* in *The Guardian*, Paul Laity writes:

> In the novel's final pages, a crucial sentence refers to the 'endlessly forking paths a person must confront as he walks through life'. This is a nod to Jorge Luis Borges – a writer often cited in discussions of *The New York Trilogy* – and his story 'The Garden of Forking Paths', at the centre of which is, appropriately enough, a novel where all possible outcomes of an event take place simultaneously.

In *City of Glass*, Quinn sees two people getting off a train who could both be Peter Stillman from the old photograph he has, and in his guise as a detective he can only follow one of them. If he'd followed the other, the entire narrative would be different. In *Ghosts* Blue concentrates so much on his detective work, and writing, that the abandoned future Mrs Blue becomes 'the ex-future Mrs. Blue' (1987, p. 167). This story that Auster delivers consciously echoes Hawthorne's short story 'Wakefield' from *Twice-Told Tales* which is included in intertextual reference in a dialogue between Blue and Black. Later, when the 'ex-future Mrs. Blue' sees Blue by accident on East 26th Street, she is 'coming up the street with her two arms linked through the right arm of a man Blue has never seen before, and she is smiling radiantly' (1987, p. 166). She becomes furious with Blue and hits out at him. Blue's other possible life has dissolved: 'By the time he regains his composure and manages to return home, he realizes that he has thrown away his life' (1987, p. 167). Beyond this sense of other possible lives (a married life for Blue) that would have ensued from a choice not made (to contact her), Auster also includes doubles who are lookalikes (Blue resembles Walt Whitman) and others who are uncannily like another part of oneself: 'To enter Black, then, was the equivalent of entering himself, and once inside himself, he can no longer conceive of being anywhere else. But this is precisely where Black is, even though Blue does not know it' (1987, p. 192). In short, the narrative of *Ghosts* in its entirety presents New York as a literary borderland where writers of the past have a haunting presence and where writers of the present are also haunted by their own sense of having multiple identities and different possible futures, some more appealing than others.

FINAL THOUGHTS INSPIRED BY *THE LOCKED ROOM* (1986)

The most creatively accomplished of the three texts that appeared together in 1987 as *The New York Trilogy* is arguably *The Locked Room*. Of the three novellas in the trilogy, it is certainly *The Locked Room* that articulates the most sustained engagement with the processes of literary creation and literary transmission. Throughout this engagement, and throughout the trilogy, Auster toys specifically with the conventions of detective fiction and subverts them. Again and again, different characters *qua* amateur detectives, especially Quinn and Auster-in-the-text, seek answers but cannot find them. For instance, Sophie Fanshawe writes to the narrator for help in finding her missing husband. The narrator, in turn, reports:

122   C. HARRIS

'The police had found no trace of him, and the private detective she hired to look for him had come up empty-handed' (Auster 1987, p. 201). There appear to be existentialist maxims in operation. If a writer is not writing or if a character is not being written, or being read about, then he ceases to exist. Existence occurs in the practices of reading and writing.

While much has already been made in extant criticism of Auster's ability to thwart the reader's expectations of a detective novel, and to expose the limitations of detective fiction's enshrining of ratiocination in human life as the torch that sheds light on all, it is not ultimately the deconstruction of a popular genre that matters in relation to the thematisation of border masculinities in *The New York Trilogy*. Rather, it is a particular type of enquiry that repeats itself. As the first-person narrator of *The Locked Room* records: 'These three stories are finally the same story, but each one represents a different stage in my awareness of what it is about' (Auster 1987, p. 294). What this story, indeed these stories, reveal themselves to be about is the role that fathers and father-figures play in both the life of a writer as writer and the life of a writer as a father, citizen, and human being. As Dupre has already convincingly argued:

> Always in the background — and often in the foreground — are the literary fathers Auster has claimed for his own and the biological father who, in a perverse turn of events, may have inspired this complex and fascinating work with his silence. (Dupre 2007, p. 200)

To be unequivocally clear, however, there is no desire or attempt in this analysis to deliver a *reductio ab absurdum* with an argument for the presence of a single dominant theme or set of motifs and issues. It is one of the highest accomplishments of *The New York Trilogy* that, like Juan Rulfo's *Pedro Páramo* in the Latin American sphere (a text in significant ways about an archetypal Mexican father and cacique, as discussed in the chapter by Amit Thakkar in this very volume), a seemingly bottomless reservoir of interpretative possibilities continually inspires new readings and contextualisations. *The New York Trilogy*, like *Pedro Páramo*, has a critical reception so vast it has already become virtually unnavigable. The current emphasis on writing, fatherhood, and borderlands is therefore the pursuit of just one of the myriad interpretative possibilities; but one that adds a deliberately gendered perspective to our understanding of the texts in question. Stephen Bernstein's analysis of Auster's dismissal of traditional forms of closure for narrative fiction in *The Locked Room* is a pertinent reminder that literary critical enquiry can take us only so far in the search for meanings when postmodernity is the dominant aesthetic:

> Though Auster, of course, continues to write, *The New York Trilogy* itself collapses into its own sublime namelessness, vanishing into the same 'dead of night' during which Quinn's telephone rings at the beginning of *City of Glass* (p. 7). Thus, detective fiction's predictable linearity becomes a darkened moebius strip of deferral, with sublime darkness subsuming all. (1995, p. 105)

Bernstein, in a shorter version, says: '*The Locked Room* is finally Auster's powerful refusal to accede to the traditional category of closure, a refusal that makes repeated appeals to the sublime in order to frame its unimaginable task' (1995, p. 88).

The New York Trilogy reaches an end as the narrator of *The Locked Room* tears pages from the red notebook left for him by a dying Fanshawe and disposes of them one by one until none are left. The key passage, slightly preceding the final image of a departing train, is perhaps this one:

> If I say nothing about what I found there, it is because I understood very little. All the words were familiar to me, and yet they seemed to have been put together strangely, as though their final purpose was to cancel each other out. I can think of no other way to express it. Each sentence erased the sentence before it, each paragraph made the next paragraph possible. It is odd, then, that the feeling that survives from this notebook is one of great lucidity. It is as if Fanshawe knew his final work had to subvert every expectation I had for it. (Auster 1987, p. 313)

This ending is satisfying from a writerly perspective: writing about writing, metafiction. *The New York Trilogy* has consistently subverted its readers' expectations too, but not without another purpose being fulfilled more positively. That other purpose, for Auster, has been to identify and overcome an ongoing struggle in coming to terms with the lasting presence in a writer's life as writer and in a writer's life as a fellow human being of a biological father and a host of literary father-figures—before and beyond death. Such a coming to terms with the influential presence of a father and of father-figures is a feature of patriarchal societies and cultures, and so however idiosyncratically it may be experienced in a multitude of different

124 C. HARRIS

contexts, it is in and through a series of powerful experiential resonances that we hear the very heartbeat of this landmark trilogy.

In relation to concerns with literature and masculinities, what stands out about Auster's playful use of conventions drawn from the detective novel in *The New York Trilogy* is that all three texts are structured by a quest, an age-old literary trope which is the raison d'être for the intellectual and intertextual engagement with Cervantes and *Don Quixote*, as we have already established. They raise questions without striving to offer answers. As Auster told James Naughtie in 2004 (11:08):

> The traditional detective or mystery story answers questions and I feel what I do is I ask them, and I don't really give any answers. So, at times these stories might resemble detective stories but in the end they're not. I'm using the genre in the way, say, that Cervantes used chivalric romance for other purposes, or the way, say, Beckett used *Vaudeville* to do *Waiting for Godot*. It's a means to another end altogether.

Just as a detective is in search of answers, so too are Auster's characters. Yet the questions that matter in *The New York Trilogy* are not the superficial ones of the standard detective novel plot such as what the important clues are or who committed the crime. The truly meaningful questions in the three texts are of a different order: as a son will I ever be more than a living extension of the life lived by my father? As a father could I bequeath more positive and less negative influences than my father left for me? As a writer will I ever be free of the influence of yesteryear's literary giants in the sense of having my own style and approach? In the end, *The New York Trilogy* can be read as a complex reflection on a writer's coming of age, on his rise to a position of recognition and success and what this entails in relation to influences from fathers and father figures. The fact that Auster's own career was launched by this text is a supreme irony.

In this reading, the ending of *The Locked Room* acquires a position of high significance. The unnamed narrator walks away from Fanshawe (who is literally inside a locked room) and, as he walks to the train tracks to catch his train home, the narrator tears pages from The Red Notebook and destroys them: 'One by one, I tore the pages from the notebook, crumpled them in my hand, and dropped them into a trash bin on the platform. I came to the last page just as the train was pulling out' (Auster 1987, p. 314). This refusal to accept Fanshawe's request for a new publication from the red notebook, this 'killing' of Fanshawe represents the death of the writer-apprentice and the birth of the accomplished-writer, one who has assimilated influences but is no longer overpowered by them. The narrator is now free, free of Fanshawe and so of the American literary tradition as an enclosed imaginative space, and free also of other fatherly influences. He now identifies himself as a father to Ben: 'He's my son' (Auster 1987, p. 311). As he returns home, he is no longer an aspiring writer and would-be father; rather, he is a published writer and a hands-on father amongst other writers and fathers, living and dead.

Once more, one final time, it is possible for cultural critics to connect Auster's fiction and autobiography just as we did at the outset with references to *The Invention of Solitude*. Intriguingly, when asked in a 2004 interview (Naughtie, 7:20) about his motivations for putting a version of himself (or at least his name) into the novel, part of his response is about the seriousness of the challenges in his life at the time of writing, and about a perceived moment of forking paths: 'Just before I started this book I met my wife Siri Hustvedt who, I think, resurrected me from the dead. And I think that if I hadn't met her, I might have wound up something like Quinn, maybe not exactly like him, but emotionally like him'. This very contrast is clear in *The New York Trilogy*. Quinn inhabits, without escape, liminal psychological spaces that are, in the terminology of Anzaldúa, borderlands. Each borderland space is 'a vague and undetermined place created by the emotional residue of an unnatural boundary. It is in a constant state of transition' (1987, p. 3). In the end, however, Auster distances himself from the Daniel Quinn character he has created. The borderlands between the unnamed author of *The Locked Room* and Quinn, the troubled author of detective fiction, and so between celebrated writer/published author, and between troubled father of a deceased child/devoted father to a young boy, are left behind. In other words, the world of endless forking paths and alternative possible lives that is a hallmark of *Ghosts*, of *The New York Trilogy*, and of later works such as *4-3-2-1* (1997b) is itself contradicted in *The Locked Room* by the unnamed narrator's firm embrace of literary success and paternal responsibilities. *The New York Trilogy*, ultimately, and if read as an account of writing, fatherhood, and borderlands, does therefore reach a final closure of sorts (though certainly not a closed and happy resolution to all narrative conflicts). By so doing, Auster's first major novelistic contribution to American life and letters stands in defiance not only of literary genres and traditions, but also, ironically, of its own underpinnings: the inescapable *aporia* of postmodern writing and theory. The unnamed narrator of *The Locked*

126   C. HARRIS

Room departs the borderlands and enters his life as a successful writer and contented father. This reading, I would argue, is not contradicted by the unnamed narrator's final location on the platform of a train station, precisely because of the destruction of the red notebook. He is simply waiting to commit himself fully to his new life.

BRIEF REFLECTIONS AT THE END

Given this interpretation, in the final panel of the triptych, were anyone ever inclined to paint these panels now that there is a comic book edition—a graphic novel published in 1994 and re-issued in 2004—there might need to be an image of Paul Auster holding a copy of *The New York Trilogy*, the fictional writing that launched his career:

> Before the publication of *The New York Trilogy*, Paul Auster was known primarily for having edited the Random House anthology of twentieth-century French poetry and for having written several insightful literary essays. In the short time since the publication of the *Trilogy (1985–1986)* he has become one of America's most praised contemporary novelists. He has frequently been compared to authors ranging from Nathaniel Hawthorne to Alain Robbe-Grillet. (Barone 1995, p. 1)

Like the unnamed narrator of *The Locked Room*, Auster would no longer feel inferior to the writers of the American literary tradition whom he recognised as his cultural forefathers. Nor would he retreat into physical and psychological writerly isolation at the cost of all other possibilities in his life. Nor would he feel that he was destined to become a faltering, absent father, like Samuel Auster. Looking back at his father's death in *Winter Journal*, though, he still writes of a lasting regret:

> Thirty-two years ago today, and you have gone on regretting that too-abrupt departure ever since, for your father did not live long enough to see that his blundering, impractical son did not end up in the poorhouse, as he always feared you would, but several more years would have been necessary for him to understand this, and it saddens you when your sixty-six-year-old father died in his girlfriend's arms, you were still struggling on all fronts, still eating the dirt of failure. (2012, pp. 30–31)

With the publication of and critical acclaim for *The New York Trilogy*, Auster would cross the border from immaturity to maturity, leave borderlands in his fiction, and live his life with his new wife Siri Hustvedt and, from 1987, with their daughter Sophie. As we imagine him admiring an imaginary triptych, and examining its details, on Auster's face we perceive a gentle, but distinct, smile. Both in person and in artistic representation. Sadly, in May 2024 as this volume was going to press, Paul Auster's death was announced in the press. His passing marked his entrance into the pantheon of American writers where he will remain now with other literary giants, the writers he so admired.

NOTE

1. The death of Daniel Auster from a drug overdose in 2022, nine days after the death of his 10-month-old daughter Ruby, was widely reported in the media. These events are deliberately left unconsidered.

WORKS CITED

Anzaldúa, Gloria. 1987. *Borderlands/La Frontera: The New Mestiza*. San Francisco: Aunt Lute Books.

Arce Álvarez, María Laura. 2014. The Case of a Two-Fold Repetition: Edgar Allen Poe's Intertextual Influence on Paul Auster's *Ghosts. Journal of English Studies* 12: 35–48.

Auster, Paul. 1982. *The Invention of Solitude*. London: Faber and Faber.

———. 1987. *The New York Trilogy*. London: Faber and Faber.

———. 1997a. *The Art of Hunger: Essays, Prefaces, Interviews, and the Red Notebook*. New York: Penguin.

———. 1997b. *4-3-2-1*. London: Faber and Faber.

———. 2012. *Winter Journal*. London: Faber and Faber.

Barbour, John D. 2004. Solitude, Writing and Fathers in Paul Auster's *The Invention of Solitude. A/B: Auto/Biography Studies* 19 (1–2): 19–32.

Barone, Dennis, ed. 1995. *Beyond the Red Notebook: Essays on Paul Auster*. Pennsylvania: Pennsylvania Press.

Berge, Anne Marit K. 2005. The Narrated Self and Characterization: Paul Auster's Literary Personae. *Nordic Journal of English Studies* 4 (1): 101–120.

Bernstein, Stephen. 1995. Auster's Sublime Closure: *The Locked Room*. In *Beyond the Red Notebook: Essays on Paul Auster*, ed. Dennis Barone, 88–106. Pennsylvania: Pennsylvania University Press.

Bruckner, Pascal. 1995. Paul Auster, The Heir Intestate. In *Beyond the Red Notebook: Essays on Paul Auster*, ed. Dennis Barone, 27–33. Pennsylvania: Pennsylvania University Press.

128   C. HARRIS

Capancioni, Claudia, Mariaconcetta Costantini, and Mara Mattoscio, eds. 2023. *Rethinking Identities Across Boundaries: Genders/Genres/Genera.* Cham, Switzerland: Palgrave Macmillan.

Dupre, Joan Alcus. 2007. *Fighting Fathers/Saving Sons: The Struggle for Life and Art in Paul Auster's* New York Trilogy. PhD diss., City University of New York.

Gilbert, Harriet. 2012. Paul Auster: *The New York Trilogy.* Presented by Harriet Gilbert. BBC Sounds, *World Book Club,* November 4. Podcast, MP3 audio, 53:00. https://www.bbc.co.uk/programmes/p0104h52.

Iqbal, Razia. 2012. Winter Journal. Presented by Razia Iqbal. BBC Sounds, *Talking Books,* October 29. Podcast, MP3 audio, 25:00. https://www.bbc.co.uk/sounds/play/p0104lkj.

Laity, Paul. 2017. Interview: Paul Auster. *The Guardian,* January 20. https://www.theguardian.com/books/2017/jan/20/paul-auster-4321-interview.

Lavender, William. 1993. The Novel of Critical Engagement: Paul Auster's City of Glass. *Contemporary Literature* 34 (2): 219–239.

Naughtie, James. 2004. Paul Auster: *The New York Trilogy.* Presented by James Naughtie. BBC Sounds, *Bookclub,* September 5. Podcast, MP3 audio, 28:00. https://www.bbc.co.uk/sounds/play/p00fc3vt.

Nealon, Jeffrey T. 1996. Work of the Detective, Work of the Writer: Paul Auster's *City of Glass. Modern Fiction Studies* 42 (1): 91–110.

Peacock, James. 2011. The Father in the Ice: Paul Auster, Character, and Literary Ancestry. *Critique* 52: 362–376.

Sorapure, Madeleine. 1995. The Detective and the Author: *City of Glass.* In *Beyond the Red Notebook: Essays on Paul Auster,* ed. Dennis Barone, 71–87. Pennsylvania: Pennsylvania University Press.

CHAPTER 7

Gendered Borders/Bordered Genders in Maryse Condé's *Les Derniers Rois mages*

Laura McGinnis

Nowhere, arguably, is the question of borders and border crossings more intrinsic to identity than in the scattered archipelago of diverse geographical, national, political, linguistic and cultural entities known as the Caribbean. The populations of these islands are the product of complex border crossings through the widespread enslavement and transportation of African peoples across the Atlantic to islands conquered by imperial powers. This displacement was followed by the transgression of racial, cultural and social boundaries through the process of 'creolisation', the literal and metaphorical intermingling of these enslaved people with each other and with their white French, British, Dutch and Hispanic colonisers. This chapter takes as its context two francophone Caribbean islands, Martinique and Guadeloupe, which have a particular political status in the region: French colonies since 1635, both elected to become *départements* (administrative divisions) in 1946, with the same political status as those in mainland France. These islands thus share the historical border crossings of

L. McGinnis (✉)
Queen's University Belfast, Belfast, UK
e-mail: lmcginnis01@qub.ac.uk

© The Author(s), under exclusive license to Springer Nature Switzerland AG 2024
A. Thakkar et al. (eds.), *Border Masculinities*,
https://doi.org/10.1007/978-3-031-68050-2_7

129

130   L. MCGINNIS

their anglophone and hispanophone Caribbean neighbours but are marked by the specificity of their continuing relationship with France.

The multiple border crossings at the heart of this region have created a melting pot of cultures, languages and identities in complex *Relation* with each other. A concept expounded by Martiniquan theorist Édouard Glissant, *Relation* celebrates the complexity produced by the non-hierarchical and multifarious contact between cultures and privileges connectedness, favouring an all-encompassing vision of identity such that borders and boundaries become irrelevant. Drawing on the foundational *Mille plateaux* by Gilles Deleuze and Félix Guattari (1980), Glissant valorises the 'rhizome', which he describes as 'a multiple root, stretched out into networks', as a model for globalising identities that are open and relational (Glissant 1990, p. 23). He rejects investment in fixed identity and rootedness (the 'racine unique'—a single, unified root or origin), which he claims were key drivers of colonialism and slavery. Glissant argues that *Relation* is thus epitomised by 'the archipelagic reality in the Caribbean' as 'a space of encounter, of collusion, and of passage on the way to the continent of America' (Glissant 1990, p. 46). Significantly, Glissant considers the slave ship to be the crucible of *Relation* in the islands, simultaneously a site of death and unimaginable suffering and the generative space ('une matrice, le gouffre-matrice'—'a womb, the womb-abyss') which forged a new Creole people and culture.[1] As such, the Caribbean, as a complex network of multiple and diverse geographical, national, linguistic, cultural, political and social entities in non-hierarchical relation with each other, epitomises the multiplicity, diversity and exchange of *Relation* and the productive chaos of rhizomatic mobility.[2]

These historical border crossings have a wide-reaching impact, not only in the political sphere of these islands but also in the everyday behaviours and relationships of French Caribbean populations, as well as in the artistic and cultural output of the islands. Like other forms of identity, gender identity has been indelibly marked by the historical trauma of slavery, which continues to have profound repercussions for relations between the sexes. The study of men and masculinities in the French Caribbean remains relatively marginal, located as it is at the uneasy intersection of black masculinity theory,[3] anglophone Caribbean gender theory[4] and French masculinities theory.[5] In this context, gender is often considered to be synonymous with femininity, and the application of feminist theory and women's studies has, therefore, resulted in a number of works on the hitherto 'voiceless' women of the region.[6] Existing references to masculinities in the region are largely determined by the thesis of emasculation and compensatory hyper-virility prevalent in black masculinity theory.[7] This is a behavioural paradigm associated with enslaved black males and their descendants, whose identity has been shaped by the institution of slavery and its continuing legacy.[8] The enslaved Black male is dispossessed of his familial relationships by the White master, who symbolically occupies the roles of both father and partner on the plantation. The enslaved male attempts to compensate for this emasculation by performing exaggerated hyper-virility, most notably through promiscuity and sexual violence against his female partners. Although this behavioural pattern is key to the analysis of Antillean masculinity, this one-dimensional focus serves to reinforce gender binaries and, therefore, fails to account for the more nuanced masculine identities portrayed in some French Caribbean literature.[9]

Maryse Condé is the best known and most critically acclaimed Antillean woman writer. Her life and work were marked by a range of literal and metaphorical border crossings. Born in Guadeloupe, she lived in France, Africa, the United States and the Antilles. Many of her novels reflect this errancy[10] (an important element in Glissant's conception of *Relation*),[11] which Condé advocated as a source of creativity and inspiration for artists and writers,[12] and several of her protagonists, such as Francis Sancher in *Traversée de la mangrove*, tell stories of exile, migration and life as a foreigner on the margins of society.[13] Condé was a celebrated author, critic and intellectual, having held posts at prominent universities, including Harvard, Berkeley and Columbia, before her retirement in 2004. Her literary work has won many prestigious prizes, including the Prix de l'Académie Française, and she was named Chevalier de la Légion d'Honneur in 2004. Condé adopts a womanist perspective in her work, foregrounding women's lived realities and 'the perception of men through the prism of women's experience' (Fonkoué 2010, p. 78).[14] While gender has been a focus of some analyses of Condé's fiction,[15] these studies have been concerned primarily with femininity, and discussions of men and masculinities have remained marginal. Moreover, much existing criticism of Condé's work focuses on her early and generally better-known novels, such as *Heremakhonon* (1976), *Moi, Tituba, sorcière noire de Salem* (1986) and *Traversée de la mangrove* (1989).

Les Derniers Rois mages (1992),[16] one of Condé's less studied works, is a novel shaped by borders and border crossings, which are shown to have a determining effect on gender identity. Set mainly in the Americas,

132   L. MCGINNIS

oscillating between the Caribbean and South Carolina, yet suffused with continuing connections to Africa, the text deals with issues of cultural difference, exile, ancestry, marginality and the unquestioning glorification of Blackness. It tells the story of a royal African family, beginning with King Béhanzin, and explores the fates of his many descendants. The novel focuses on Spéro Jules-Juliette, an heir to this dynasty, whose grandfather, Djéré, was born of the king's liaison with a local girl during his exile in Martinique. Spéro is a painter who marries Debbie, an African American historian, and moves to the United States with her. Disillusioned by his personal and professional failures, alienated by his sense of disconnection in a foreign land and emasculated in his relationship with his wife and daughter, Spéro retreats into classic paradigms of hyper-virility, seeking solace in promiscuity and alcohol, and thereby replicating the dysfunctional behaviours of his father, Justin, and his grandfather, Djéré. In contrast, Debbie, a militant Black feminist, is the driving force in their relationship, appropriating Spéro's illustrious ancestry by translating the memoirs of his grandfather and taking sole responsibility for their daughter, Anita. Just as Spéro lives in geographical exile from his country of birth, his life is marked by his metaphorical (self-)exile in his relationships with his wife and daughter. His relationship with his American wife facilitates a dialogue between the bordered spaces of masculinity and femininity and the United States and the French Caribbean. The novel explores the intersection of geographical, political, spatial, sexual, racial and cultural borders.

Although less popular in studies of Condé's work than earlier novels, such as *Traversée de la Mangrove* (1989), *Les Derniers Rois mages* (1992) has received some critical attention, particularly in the years following its publication. To date, critics such as Ann Smock (1995) and Bonnie Thomas (2004) have explored themes such as race and identity. Smock examines the racial and cultural divide between Debbie and Spéro, while Thomas deals briefly with Condé's novel alongside texts by Simone Schwarz-Bart and Patrick Chamoiseau and focuses primarily on maternity. A key theme in much existing criticism has been geographical space, place and belonging: Mireille Rosello (1995) has written on the opposition of island and continent and insular versus outward-facing, 'relational' identity in Condé's novel, while Mildred Mortimer (1993) uses the themes of space and place to examine concepts of rootedness and belonging. Until now, however, there has been no analysis of masculinities, or of the gendered implications of border crossings (both literal and metaphorical), in the novel. This chapter will analyse the ways in which physical borders influence the constructed borders of gender, race and culture. It will pay particular attention to the ways in which Condé dismantles fixed categorisations and stereotypes such as hyper-virility, often through the irreverent style of her work. As Nesbitt notes, her writing is 'critical to [its] core. Her novels dismantle the pieties of everyday life to expose … the fragile narcissism of subjects who erect facades of ideology and self-importance' (Nesbitt 2013, p. 118). This destabilisation is often effected through narrative techniques such as humour, irony and satire. As Britton has argued, 'Condé irony or mockery is closely linked to the fictional text's ability to engage with the real and hence to speak the "truth"' (Britton 2004, p. 42). Through this irony and humour, Condé disrupts stereotypes and challenges binary categorisations and borders, physical and imagined, real and constructed.

Crossing Borders of Space, Place and Time

The novel centres on the transgression of multiple geographical borders at various points in time. Following the rambling inner monologue of Spéro Jules-Juliette during a rainy Sunday afternoon (10 December 1989), the work moves back and forth through time and space, charting the travels and the exile (both forced and self-imposed) of the protagonist and his ancestors, from prehistoric Africa to the present-day Antilles and United States. Indeed, the founding Ancestor's story is fundamentally one of migration and exile. Born in Africa as King of Dahomey (modern-day Benin), he was subsequently banished from his kingdom by French imperialists and, in 1894, was exiled to Martinique, where his son, Djéré, was born. When Djéré was five, his father took his wives and other children to live out his exile in Algeria, leaving Djéré and his mother, Hosannah, in Martinique. Similarly, the Ancestor's great-grandson, Spéro, settles far from his country of birth, Guadeloupe. Having married the African American Debbie, he moves to her birthplace, Charleston, in the south of the United States. Although his migration is voluntary, Spéro experiences his expatriation as a form of exile.

The transgression of geographical and spatial boundaries has important implications for the construction of gender identities. As Mortimer argues, Condé uses space as a metaphor for identity in the novel, such that 'spatial determinants of geography and landscape and spatial structures such as houses and rooms … become metaphors for the protagonist's search for self and its realisation' (1993, p. 758). Djéré experiences his abandonment by his father in precisely these spatial terms: banished from the paternal world, he goes to live in his grandmother's house, a matrifocal space,[17] characterised by the 'exclusion of the father, [and the] prolonged and over-invested relationship between the mother and son' (Gyssels 1996, p. 212). This symbolises Djéré's consignment to maternal space, which, arguably, has damaging repercussions for his construction of a masculine identity.[18] For Spéro, too, space is intimately connected with his masculinity. He experiences his exile in Debbie's birthplace, Crocker Island, as an emasculation, revealed in the recurring dream of his naked body being trapped and overrun by crabs:

> [T]hey crawled back up the length of his thighs, circling the large hill of his sex before entangling their legs in his pubic hair and quickly climbing the gourd of his stomach ... As they reached his throat, Spéro awoke ... For two years, he had been having the same dream, three or four times a week. (Condé 1992, p. 13)

The sense of anxiety and entrapment Spéro experiences in this dream reveals his profound unhappiness in Charleston, while the specific threat to his sex highlights the emasculating effects of his exile. His experience of rootlessness connects him to the Ancestor, as 'he no longer belonged anywhere. He, like the Ancestor, lived in exile' (Condé 1992, p. 170).

Conversely, Spéro's nostalgia for Guadeloupe is evoked throughout the novel by references to the sea, which both connects him to and distances him from his birthplace. The story ends with a description of the 'great soft, shifting, dark blanket' of water below him (Condé 1992, pp. 303–4). This invocation of the sea, a conventionally feminine entity, further underlines the emasculation of Spéro's exile. The homophone of 'sea' and 'mother' in French (*mer/mère*) links Spéro's longing both to his mother and his unrequited love for her and to his metaphorical 'motherland' of Guadeloupe. Spéro's longing to transgress physical and imagined borders to return to the mother/womb and the homeland is reflected in a mythical scenario at the end of the novel, in which the spirit of the deceased Ancestor returns from Kutome (heaven), enters the womb of a woman in labour and is reborn in the body of a child (Condé 1992, p. 294). In this magical realist scene, the Ancestor crosses the borders of life and death, body and spirit, the physical and the ephemeral, and masculinity and femininity. Through this re-birth and regeneration, the novel becomes circular, beginning and ending with the Ancestor at the heart of this noble African dynasty and ultimately crossing the boundaries of beginning and end. Likewise, Spéro repeatedly expresses his desire to 'start everything over again' (Condé 1992, p. 230), and the novel ends with him awaiting Debbie's return to ask her if they can start over by having another child. This cyclical sense of regeneration defies any neat solutions or conclusions, and the ending is left open to interpretation.

Gendered Borders: Africa, The Antilles and The Dynasty of the 'Rois Mages'

At the centre of the novel lies the story of Spéro's royal African ancestry, passed through the men of his paternal bloodline. As Rosello observes, the concepts of ancestry and origins are highly problematic in the Caribbean context, where 'a geographical politics of identity is indispensable … [R]eturns [to origins] are both indispensable and undesirable' (Rosello 1995, p. 568). Indeed, Rosello questions whether Aimé Césaire's seminal work of *Négritude*, the *Cahier d'un retour au pays natal* (1956), has legitimised this quest for origins, creating 'some kind of Césairean complex of the return to the native land' (Rosello 1995, p. 568). In light of this 'complex', the novel could be seen to chart a Negritudinal quest for origins in the geographically and psychologically distant continent of Africa. Crucially, both in the *Négritude* movement and in Condé's novel, this quest is 'exclusively masculine' (Haigh 2000, p. 115): just as *Négritude* fetishises masculine genealogy and the masculine originator, Spéro fixates on his paternal lineage, despite the uncertainty of this bloodline and his geographical and psychological distance from his unknown Ancestor. However, this supposedly illustrious heritage is undermined throughout the novel. The paratext warns that '[t]his is a work of pure fiction. The king in question had no descendants in Guadeloupe or Martinique' (Condé 1992). In this way and combined with the many inconsistencies and contradictions revealed throughout the novel, the entire saga is exposed as being fictional, its claims to legitimacy destabilised from the outset. The supposed origins of the dynasty also refute its masculine nature and situate it on the boundary between truth and fiction, history and mythology, as the founder of the dynasty, Tengisu, was apparently conceived during the union between a young woman and a panther (Condé 1992, p. 91). The search for paternal origins is further destabilised by the revelation that it is Djéré's mother, Hosannah, who instituted the ritual of commemorating 10 December following the death of her son's father. In addition, Spéro's ancestral quest is appropriated by Debbie and later by their daughter, Anita, the only one to complete the 'return to the native land' and thus fulfil the quest by travelling to Benin. In this way, Spéro's lineage is feminised, as it is passed to his only daughter since he has no male heir.

Condé explores the gendered impact of this ancestry, which affects male and female characters in various ways. Spéro's father and grandfather, Justin and Djéré, fetishise their glorious heritage; however, this fixation leads to their stagnation, and they become 'two layabouts, two alcoholics … [who are] sometimes violent' (Condé 1992, p. 56). Through Djéré and Justin, Condé thus presents 'the paralyzing results of excessive preoccupation with the past' (Nyatetu-Waigwa 1995, p. 559). Their depiction as 'Rois mages' in the French title (a Biblical reference to the Wise Men who follow the Star of Bethlehem to visit Jesus after his birth) is therefore ironic,[19] deriving from a nickname given, in jest, to Djéré and later to Justin, undercutting the elevated self-perception of this male line and 'work[ing] to turn an attitude, which is considered arrogant and unproductive, to derision' (Moudileno and Higginson 1995, p. 628). These men, who value the myth of their glorious African origins over their contemporary Antillean reality, become agents of a regressive and repressive nostalgia, incapable of living in the present. Paradoxically, the fixation on the hyper-masculine quest for origins leads to the paralysis and metaphorical impotence of these men.

Like his ancestors, Spéro fails to live up to this supposedly hyper-masculine dynasty. The humour and irony of his portrayal both highlight the gap between his arrogant self-perception and reality and emphasise his divergence from the stereotype of hyper-virility. His name, Spéro Jules-Juliette, sits uneasily with his character: while the evocation of hope in his forename contrasts sharply with his languishing and indifferent attitude to life, which ultimately results in his failure and despair, the 'Jules-Juliette' is absurdly repetitive, and the 'Juliette' feminises him from the outset, a striking contrast to the hyper-masculine lineage of which he boasts. Spéro is shaped by a dysfunctional maternal relationship, fuelled by his mother's lack of affection for him. His unfulfilled craving for maternal affection haunts him into adulthood: 'Marisia always remained Spéro's great love. No other woman ever had the same effect on him' (Condé 1992, p. 63).

Spéro's adult relationships with women constitute a compensatory attempt to gain the love of his distant mother.

Spéro's alienation is exacerbated by his professional failure. Despite his talent in watercolours, Debbie persuades him to use pigments in his paintings. In so doing, he fails to produce any work deemed worthy of exhibition or purchase in Charleston. Debbie's driving role in his (ill-fated) career serves to emasculate him, and he fails to overcome both her influence and his own sense of inadequacy. As Moudileno and Higginson argue, Spéro's failure as an artist is not due to his lack of talent; rather, it is a result of his own weakness of character, coupled with Debbie's domineering influence, as 'he has let himself be trapped in the notion of a political engagement through art, thus repressing his own creative impulse' (1995, pp. 631–2). Unemployed and penniless, Spéro finds himself 'in the same position as Justin or Djéré, forced to rely on handouts from Debbie' (Condé 1992, p. 223). Spéro's failures link him to his father and grandfather, placing him in a metaphorically impotent lineage. Through humour, irony and skilful characterisation, Condé thus expertly debunks the fixation on a single, hyper-masculine African origin. She undermines the gendered borders of the Negritudinal quest and, indeed, of this dynasty, instead advocating a multifaceted, relational approach to geographical and political borders.

Bordered Genders: Debbie and Spéro

Conventional gender categorisations are also symbolically problematised, destabilised and even reversed in the novel through the characterisation of the protagonist, his wife and his ancestors. The marital relationship between Spéro and Debbie is marked in bordered and gendered terms. The distance in their geographical and cultural origins becomes a metaphor for their relationship; although Spéro moves to America, they soon drift apart, divided by new borders and obstacles. Having married Spéro for his illustrious ancestry, Debbie assumes this heritage, taking control of the story and translating Djéré's *cahiers* (notebooks) for publication.[20] In this way, she dispossesses Spéro of his own history. She infantilises and demeans him at home, leaving his monthly allowance in '[an] envelope with his name on it, set among those of the domestic staff', which 'humiliated Spéro to the core' (Condé 1992, p. 42). Spéro's greatest hope for mediation of the distance between them is his daughter, Anita. However, this hope quickly fades as Debbie 'conquers' their daughter for herself.

138 L. MCGINNIS

Debbie excludes her husband from his paternal role, banishing him to the periphery of the guest bedroom:

> Under the pretext that the baby was ill, Debbie had monopolised her completely. She put her to sleep in her bed, having relegated Spéro to one of the guest rooms … From the solitude of his sheets … he once again felt like a foreigner, an exile! (Condé 1992, p. 31)

The spatial dynamics of this passage highlight Debbie's symbolic, imperialistic conquest of space in their relationship, a highly charged action in the post-slavery context. The marital home becomes a bordered space ruled by Debbie, in which Spéro is emasculated, displaced and consigned to the fringes. This depiction of the domestic space evokes Glissant's presentation of the slave ship as a site which is paradoxically both maternal and unknown. Rather than producing a glorious and soul-affirming return to his (hyper-masculine) African origins, the domestic space metaphorically induces in Spéro a grotesque return to the suffering and devastation of the 'gouffre-matrice'—the 'womb-abyss'—of the slave ship. Moreover, Spéro's exclusion from his role as husband and father and the destabilisation of his masculine identity is reminiscent of the dispossession of enslaved Black men from the paternal role. His paternal inadequacy also reflects and perpetuates Justin's and Djéré's unviability as paternal role models. These stymied models of fatherhood constitute a dysfunctional yet important divergence from conventional forms of masculinity and represent an important type of border masculinities: those masculine subjectivities consigned to the edges of traditional categories. Indeed, Condé seems to remind us that paternal presence is no guarantee of involvement or engagement in children's lives.

In response to his feelings of emasculation and alienation and excluded from the newly feminised space of the marital home, Spéro retreats in despair to the exclusively masculine, homosocial space of the bar, where he seeks comfort in excessive drinking, while 'asking himself what purpose he had on this earth' (Condé 1992, p. 271). He also resorts to extramarital affairs, justifying his behaviour as compensation for his fragile self-esteem: 'all these conquests gave him back his self-confidence, in these times when he had such need of it' (Condé 1992, p. 272). Spéro represents the self-pitying male who holds his wife responsible for his dissatisfaction, seeing his infidelity as the logical consequence of his unhappiness. As Spear notes, 'Condé frequently ridicules her characters' soul-searching by ironic portraiture' (1993, p. 723). Through free indirect discourse, Spéro becomes a mouthpiece for men's perceptions of gender roles and identities, the inflated melodrama and hypocrisy of his self-victimising attitude provoking humour and encouraging the reader to laugh at his expense. Spéro's attempts to justify his behaviour are undermined by the humour of his self-pity:

> Debbie had started to lie with her back to him in bed and, his pride wounded, he refused to touch her hostile flesh [...] It was therefore inevitable that he would start to think about improving his appearance in the mirror of another woman. (Condé 1992, p. 228)

His hypocrisy is highlighted when, despite his own adulterous transgressions, he condemns Debbie for 'bringing shame on his name' and 'making him a laughing stock' (Condé 1992, p. 279), as 'a woman who takes a younger male lover brings disrespect upon herself!' (Condé 1992, p. 285). The absurdity of his excuses is intensified by his recourse to racial stereotypes of the hyper-sexed Black male to explain his behaviour, undermined by the narrator's ironic intrusion: '[d]idn't they know? African, American, or Antillean, the Black male is not cut out to be monogamous' (Condé 1992, p. 41). Condé derides both racist stereotypes of the Black male and his exculpatory recourse to such stereotypes. Moreover, despite his apparently marginalised position, Spéro undeniably benefits from what Raewyn Connell has termed the 'patriarchal dividend'—the 'advantage men in general gain from the overall subordination of women', whether or not they conform to patterns of hegemonic masculinity (1995, p. 79). Spéro drinks to excess, indulges in affairs and is largely excused for his behaviour; by contrast, when Debbie (allegedly) engages in such behaviours, Spéro condemns her for behaving inappropriately and is worried about the repercussions for his own reputation. In this way, Condé undermines the recurring portrayal of men as victims of slavery, revealing how they benefit from male privilege. She simultaneously refuses to vindicate her male characters' dysfunctional behaviours through recourse to exculpatory myths of emasculation and compensatory hyper-virility as responses to historical trauma, a tendency which only perpetuates such dysfunctional male behaviour.

Spéro's self-victimisation also reveals his own insecurities and his fragile sense of identity. For instance, he questions whether Debbie's alleged affair is a result of his inferior masculinity and sexual prowess: '[d]id he not satisfy her? […] What did she see in this Isaac? His youth? His beauty? […] His sex which never lowered its head nor gave up the fight? Because this was the only possible explanation!' (Condé 1992, p. 286). The ironic tone of the final exclamation derides the direct attribution of women's conjugal (dis)satisfaction to male sexual prowess. Isaac's superior looks and youthful virility contrast sharply with Spéro, an unfaithful, indifferent, indolent—and even impotent—husband. While the humour and irony of free indirect discourse convey Spéro's limitations, the passage also suggests his own sneaking realisation of these weaknesses, revealing his vulnerability. Furthermore, in the course of the novel, Spéro comes to understand and acknowledge his mistakes, such as his 'failure with Anita', for which '[h]e was responsible by omission, by irresponsibility' (Condé 1992, pp. 261–62). He begins to question his own narrative, coming to the sudden realisation that '[he] had been a terrible father' and '[a] bad husband—a very bad husband' (Condé 1992, p. 230). While Condé undermines, derides and condemns Spéro's behaviour, she also conveys his vulnerability, his self-awareness and reflexivity, and the complexity of the experiences which have caused him to act in this way: 'deep down, he was a little boy who was unsure of himself' (Condé 1992, p. 62).

Undermining *Négritude*? Troubling Racial and Cultural Borders

Condé's criticism is not reserved for her male characters; she also uses irony and humour to highlight the flaws, inconsistencies and hypocrisies in Debbie. As Leah Hewitt argues, through the 'shaky marriage' between Debbie and Spéro, 'Condé enacts a reciprocal critique in which neither spouse escapes the other's (and our) sharp scrutiny' (1997, p. 212). The distance between Debbie and Spéro is reinforced by the borders of their individual cultural, racial and gender identities.

Committed to the principles of Black Pride, Debbie is fixated on the glorification of ancestry and origins and celebrates a single African origin (the 'identité-racine' that Glissant rejects), investing in purity and linearity of origins and constructing artificial racial borders. Through Debbie's shortcomings, Condé makes a fundamental criticism of *Négritude* itself as a binary model of identity focused on the African origins of Black and mixed-race populations. Debbie's simultaneous attachment to the Black Pride movement and her misreading of her own and Spéro's family histories highlight the fundamental contradiction at the heart of *Négritude*—paradoxically, the racist universalism it claimed to redress—by considering all dark-skinned peoples to share a cultural heritage and thus eliding their individual identities. For instance, she refuses to accept the racial hybridity of her Barbadian father. She also becomes disillusioned with her family history following the revelation that her father became a civil rights activist not after meeting Martin Luther King Junior, as she believed, but as a result of a much less glorious encounter—namely, a violent beating he received in April 1960 after using the 'Whites Only' bathroom of Woolworths. Unable or unwilling to confront her own prejudices and constructed hierarchies, Debbie protects herself from what she cannot reconcile to her own narratives of history by 'put[ting] away her typewriter' (Condé 1992, p. 98) and choosing to focus instead on Spéro's ancestry.

In her celebration of blackness and the single African root, Debbie fails to grasp the cultural differences between herself and Spéro. For instance, she chooses to ignore the racial hybridity of Spéro's heritage (which is so fundamental to Caribbean identity)—particularly his mixed-race Antillean mother—and fixates on the African origins of his paternal family. Condé thus condemns this singular, transnational model of Blackness and its valorisation of African origins over the hybrid reality of American and Antillean populations. She highlights the limitations of this binary model of identity through Spéro's critical voice, warning of the dangers of becoming trapped, like Debbie, in 'the prison of race' (Condé 1992, p. 105). Condé thus demonstrates that women can be just as oppressive as agents of a regressive, reductive, nostalgic vision of identity as their male counterparts. Moreover, Debbie's role as militant Black feminist is undermined by her treatment of Spéro, whom she humiliates and relegates to the periphery of their home and of family life. As Mortimer argues:

> Debbie's punishment of Spéro, her use of humiliation and physical distancing, ironically subverts the politically correct behaviour to which she subscribes. In effect, she parodies the racist tactics she abhors; Debbie becomes responsible for "putting a Nigger in his place". (Mortimer 1993, p. 760)

Ultimately, the novel presents 'a scathing satire of the religion of racial heritage ... Debbie and Spéro's "roots" have made them exiles; they wander banished from love' (Smock 1995, p. 676). By undermining both characters, Condé highlights the reductive and regressive nature of the construction and glorification of borders and fixed identities. In addition, Condé demonstrates that Spéro's desire to forget the past is just as dangerous as Debbie's obsession with the single African root. Using his critique of Debbie's glorification of race as an excuse to opt out of all political purpose and all attachments to heritage, he commits himself to forgetting the past; however, 'his way of forgetting is thoughtlessly to repeat' (Smock 1995, p. 676). Ironically, despite the connotations of hope in his name, Spéro is just as unproductive in his approach to history as Debbie. In this way, neither Spéro's choice—to forget entirely—nor Debbie's choice—to construct an artificially coherent history—represents a viable way of coming to terms with the past. Rather, Condé seems to advocate a more relational, rhizomatic approach, suggesting the limitations of binary conceptions of identity. In the novel, the future lies in reconciling continents—Africa, the Antilles and the United States—and the two main protagonists, Spéro and Debbie. The novel ends with a potential new beginning, as Spéro seeks reconciliation with Debbie by having another child. Condé seems to suggest that making connections, rather than reinforcing borders and boundaries, offers a more hopeful future, both for her characters and for the world(s) in which they exist.

Conclusion: Beyond Borders, Beyond Binaries

As a writer, Condé refused to be restricted by binaries and narrow categorisations. As Spear argues, '[s]he has always advocated the writer's freedom to write beyond borders, for literature itself should not be limited to any geopolitical constrictions' (1993, p. 729). In this sense, her vision of identity is antithetical to the single-origin narrative of *Négritude*. *Les Derniers Rois mages* (1992) demonstrates the ways in which adherence to fixed geographical, spatial, cultural and psychological boundaries leads to stagnation and misunderstanding, epitomising Glissant's vision of identity as 'a system of relation [...] which contests [...] universalism' (Glissant 1990, p. 156).

This contestation of universalist categories is also key to Condé's portrayal of gender identities. She moves beyond conventional portrayals of masculinity and femininity and beyond one-dimensional characterisation. She uses irony and humour to highlight the flaws, contradictions and hypocrisies in both Spéro and Debbie. While refusing to absolve men of their dysfunctional and irresponsible behaviours, Condé nuances her male characters through an examination of the socio-historical repercussions of slavery and colonialism that have contributed to these constructions of masculinity in Antillean society. As Rosello claims, '[e]ach geographical place'—and, I would argue, each character—'is like an island, related to every other island by means of complex and ambivalent connections. None is really more important, or more original, or more authentic than any other' (Rosello 1995, p. 574). This non-hierarchical focus on multiplicity and diversity exemplifies Glissant's vision of *Relation*: various spaces, places, characters and identities in the novel all exist in complex relation with each other.

However, I would argue that the troubling of borders in Condé's work represents a more negative vision of identity than Glissant's *Relation*. Rather than exploring the productive potential of relationality, Condé focuses on breaking down unified, universalist ideas and identities. In narrative terms, the form of the novel—a rambling, non-linear and non-chronological series of reflections by Spéro—'allows separate fragments ... to appear at uneven intervals ... favour[ing] the interference of heterogeneous patterns superimposed on each other and the migration of themes and images among different contexts' (Smock 1995, p. 673). In addition, the use of free indirect discourse and the large number of peripheral characters undermines the convention of a single, dominant narrative voice. The multiple, non-hierarchised viewpoints have a de-centring effect and depart from the traditional (male) author(ity) figure and an omniscient narrator. Moreover, Condé offers no reassuring reconciliations or neat conclusions; rather, the ending is left open to interpretation. Thus, in contrast to the constructive and productive potential of relationality in Glissant's thought, border crossings in Condé's novel, whether related to traditional geographical, gender, cultural or racial categories, represent an opportunity to debunk unified and universalist myths such as *Négritude*. While she offers no guarantee for the future, the ending of the novel is 'nonetheless a crossing...' (Smock 1995, p. 674): an intersection in the paths of two individuals and the geographical, racial, political, cultural and gendered borders they represent.

NOTES

1. An interesting exploration of the maternal imagery inherent in Glissant's *Relation* can be found in Stanka Radović (2007).
2. This is also elaborated in his earlier text, *Le Discours antillais* (1981).

3. Black masculinity theory focuses primarily on the African American context, from which Martinique and Guadeloupe are distinct both in their French heritage and in their ongoing 'neocolonial' relationship with their colonising power, as well as in geographical scale.

4. The anglophone Caribbean context differs from the francophone one, perhaps most notably in the English-speaking islands' status as independent political identities.

5. French masculinities theory is itself limited by the consideration of gender studies as an 'Anglo-Saxon' preoccupation. Of the existing masculinities studies texts based on French literature and culture, many fail to consider masculinities beyond the metropolitan French context. See Lawrence Schehr (2009).

6. Such works include Haigh's *Mapping a Tradition: Francophone Women's Writing from Guadeloupe* (2000), Wendy Goolcharan-Kumeta's *My Mother, My Country: Reconstructing the Female Self in Guadeloupean Women's Writing* (2003), and Jennifer Jahn's 'Martinican Women's Novels: Oppression, Resistance, and Liberation' (2008), amongst others.

7. Most notably, Thomas's *Breadfruit or Chestnut? Gender Construction in the French Caribbean Novel* (2006), and Stéphanie Mulot's 'Redevenir un homme en contexte antillais post-esclavagiste et matrifocal' (2009) are both predicated on notions of hyper-virility.

8. Rooted in the North American context, this theory has been articulated perhaps most famously—and controversially—by Robert Staples in articles such as 'Masculinity and Race: The Dual Dilemma of Black Men' (1978). This theory has been subject to extensive criticism by black feminist critics such as bell hooks.

9. Thomas, the critic who has written most extensively on gender construction in the region, makes the case for gender 'fluidity' in her work (2004, 2006), drawing on the work of Judith Butler, but, through her reliance on binary terminology and recourse to stereotypes such as the 'weak male' and 'strong female', perhaps inevitably ends up re-inscribing gender binaries.

10. For instance, the themes of exile and marginality, in various forms, are central to novels such as *Une Saison à Rihata* (1981), *Ségou: Les murailles de terre* (1984), *Ségou: La terre en miettes* (1985), *Traversée de la mangrove* (1989), *La Migration des cœurs* (1995), *Desirada* (1997a), and *La Belle Créole* (2001).

11. Glissant argues that '[t]he wanderer [*l'errant*] is no longer a traveller, nor a discoverer, nor a conqueror' (1990, p. 33). Glissant considers errancy and rootlessness to be a key part of the Caribbean experience, with repercussions for modern society.

12. As Condé stated in an interview, 'it's this wandering that engenders creativity. In the final analysis, it is very bad to put down roots. You must be errant and multifaceted, inside and out. Nomadic' (Pfaff 1996, p. 28).
13. Condé's work is often read through this prism of exile and migration, as encapsulated by the title of an edited volume on Condé's work, *Maryse Condé: une nomade inconvenante* (Cottenet-Hage and Moudileno 2002).
14. All translations of secondary sources are my own.
15. Works foregrounding gender (and particularly femininity) in Condé's work include Shelton's 'Condé: The Politics of Gender and Identity' (1993); Thomas's *Breadfruit or Chestnut?* (2006), Lillian Manzor-Coats's 'Of Witches and Other Things: Maryse Condé's Challenges to Feminist Discourse' (1993), and Françoise Lionnet's *Autobiographical Voices: Race, Gender, Self-Portraiture* (1991), amongst others.
16. Condé (1992). An English translation of the novel is available, entitled *The Last of the African Kings* (1997b). Further references to the novel will be made with page numbers referring to the French edition. All translations of the text are my own.
17. A term often used in the Caribbean familial structure, matrifocality refers to a household in which the mother is head of the family as a result of paternal absence.
18. Mulot (2009) argues that the matrifocal nature of French Caribbean society often gives rise to compensatory displays of hyper-virility.
19. Although 'Rois mages' translates as 'Wise Men' or 'Magi', the title of the official English translation by Richard Philcox loses this Biblical reference (*The Last of the African Kings*). As well as a wise man or mage/magus, the term 'mage' also implies a wizard, magician or sorcerer—connotations which are lost in the English translation of 'African Kings'.
20. The term 'cahier' recalls, of course, Césaire's foundational *Cahier d'un retour au pays natal* (1956). Like Césaire's poem, Djéré's *cahiers* trace the origins of the dynasty back to Africa.

Works Cited

Britton, Celia. 2004. Breaking the Rules: Irrelevance/Irreverence in Maryse Condé's *Traversée de la mangrove*. French Cultural Studies 15 (1): 35–47.
Césaire, Aimé. 1956. *Cahier d'un retour au pays natal*. Paris: Présence africaine.
Condé, Maryse. 1976. *Heremakhonon*. Paris: 10/18.
———. 1981. *Une Saison à Rihata*. Paris: Laffont.
———. 1984. *Ségou: Les Murailles de terre*. Paris: Laffont.
———. 1985. *Ségou: La Terre en miettes*. Paris: Laffont.
———. 1986. *Moi, Tituba, sorcière noire de Salem*. Paris: Mercure.
———. 1989. *Traversée de la mangrove*. Paris: Mercure.

146   L. MCGINNIS

———. 1992. *Les Derniers Rois mages.* Paris: Mercure de France.

———. 1995. *La Migration des cœurs.* Paris: Laffont.

———. 1997a. *Desirada.* Paris: Laffont.

———. 1997b. *The Last of the African Kings.* Trans. Richard Philcox. London and Lincoln: University of Nebraska Press.

———. 2001. *La Belle Créole.* Paris: Mercure.

Connell, R.W. 1995. *Masculinities.* Cambridge: Polity Press.

Cottenet-Hage, Madeleine, and Lydie Moudileno, eds. 2002. *Maryse Condé: une nomade inconvenante.* Guadeloupe: Ibis Rouge.

Deleuze, Gilles, and Félix Guattari. 1980. *Mille plateaux: Capitalisme et schizophrénie II.* Paris: Minuit.

Fonkoué, Ramon A. 2010. Voix de femmes et figures du mâl(e) en littérature francophone: Nicole Brossard et Maryse Condé. *Nouvelles études francophones* 25 (1): 75–89.

Glissant, Édouard. 1981. *Le Discours antillais.* Paris: Seuil.

———. 1990. *Poétique de la Relation (Poétique III).* Paris: Gallimard.

Goolcharan-Kumeta, Wendy. 2003. *My Mother, My Country: Reconstructing the Female Self in Guadeloupean Women's Writing.* Oxford: Peter Lang.

Gyssels, Kathleen. 1996. *Filles de solitude: Essai sur l'identité antillaise dans les (auto-) biographies fictives de Simon et André Schwarz-Bart.* Paris: Harmattan.

Haigh, Sam. 2000. *Mapping a Tradition: Francophone Women's Writing from Guadeloupe.* London: MHRA.

Hewitt, Leah. 1997. Afterword: The Critical F(r)ictions of Maryse Condé. In *The Last of the African Kings*, trans. Richard Philcox. Lincoln and London: University of Nebraska Press.

Jahn, Jennifer. 2008. *Martinican Women's Novels: Oppression, Resistance, and Liberation.* Unpublished doctoral thesis. University of Cambridge.

Lionnet, Françoise. 1991. *Autobiographical Voices: Race, Gender, Self-Portraiture.* New York: Cornell University Press.

Manzor-Coats, Lillian. 1993. Of Witches and Other Things: Maryse Condé's Challenges to Feminist Discourse. *World Literature Today* 67 (4): 737–744.

Mortimer, Mildred. 1993. A Sense of Place and Space in Maryse Condé's *Les Derniers rois mages. World Literature Today* 67 (4): 757–762.

Moudileno, Lydie, and Francis Higginson. 1995. Portrait of the Artist as Dreamer: Maryse Condé's *Traversée de la Mangrove* and *Les Derniers Rois mages. Callaloo* 18 (3): 626–640.

Mulot, Stéphanie. 2009. Redevenir un homme en contexte antillais post-esclavagiste et matrifocal. *Autrepart* 49: 117–136.

Nesbitt, Nick. 2013. *Caribbean Critique: Antillean Critical Theory from Toussaint to Glissant.* Liverpool: Liverpool University Press.

Nyatetu-Waigwa, Wangari Wa. 1995. From Liminality to a Home of Her Own? The Quest Motif in Maryse Condé's Fiction. *Callaloo* 18 (3): 551–564.

Pfaff, Françoise. 1996. *Conversations with Maryse Condé*. Lincoln: University of Nebraska Press.

Radović, Stanka. 2007. The Birthplace of Relation: Edouard Glissant's *Poétique de La Relation: For Ranko. Callaloo* 30 (2): 475–481.

Rosello, Mireille. 1995. Caribbean Insularisation of Identities in Maryse Condé's Work: From *En attendant le bonheur* to *Les Derniers Rois mages. Callaloo* 18 (3): 565–578.

Schehr, Lawrence R. 2009. *French Post-Modern Masculinities: From Neuromatrices to Seropositivity*. Liverpool: Liverpool University Press.

Shelton, Marie-Denise. 1993. Condé: The Politics of Gender and Identity. *World Literature Today* 67 (4): 717–722.

Smock, Ann. 1995. Maryse Condé's *Les Derniers Rois mages. Callaloo* 18 (3): 668–680.

Spear, Thomas C. 1993. Individual Quests and Collective Memory. *World Literature Today* 67 (4): 723–730.

Staples, Robert. 1978. Masculinity and Race: The Dual Dilemma of Black Men. *Journal of Social Issues* 34 (1): 169–183.

Thomas, Bonnie. 2004. Identity at the Crossroads: An Exploration of French Caribbean Gender Identity. *Caribbean Studies* 32 (2): 45–62.

———. 2006. *Breadfruit or Chestnut? Gender Construction in the French Caribbean Novel*. Oxford: Lexington Books.

CHAPTER 8

A Very English Caciquismo?: Land, Badlands and Habitus in Fiona Mozley's *Elmet*

Amit Thakkar

This chapter will consider a violent, rural, Spanish American model of behaviour, caciquismo, meaning rule by (almost always) male local bosses, called caciques.[1] The figure of the cacique is of indigenous origin, but, as I have noted previously (Thakkar 2012, pp. 125–159), the practice emerged from a largely community-centred endeavour before the Spanish conquest to become a more individualistic enterprise based on land ownership. The post-independence Spanish American cacique has evolved and survived various attempts to curb his power. Multiple forms of caciquismo exist today in Spanish America, including neo-, national and urban caciquismo, all relying on physical violence or the threat of such violence. The type of caciquismo associated with Spain, meanwhile, is a kind of political clientelism rooted in an originally nineteenth-century practice of administrative, bureaucratic and electoral control by an individual in a given region.[2] Such political matters can and do also occupy the Spanish American cacique, though more relevant for my purposes is the fact that both Spanish and Spanish American forms of caciquismo involve

---

A. Thakkar (✉)
School of Global Affairs, Lancaster University, Lancaster, UK
e-mail: a.thakkar@lancaster.ac.uk

© The Author(s), under exclusive license to Springer Nature
Switzerland AG 2024
A. Thakkar et al. (eds.), *Border Masculinities*,
https://doi.org/10.1007/978-3-031-68050-2_8

149

150   A. THAKKAR

manipulating and/or ignoring surrounding public structures in order to maintain a local, private hierarchy.

To date, there has been little serious discussion of the potential for *non*-Hispanic variants of caciquismo.[3] Apart from some lexicographical interest in the term during the years of the Spanish Empire (see López Fadul 2000), it has not been widely discussed, understood or used in English-language discourse. Whilst this is no doubt due to the absence of caciquismo as a historical reality for most of the Anglophone world, such an absence does not preclude the widespread relevance of the term. I will examine the potential that caciquismo has to help us understand analogous masculinities in the work of the modern British novelist Fiona Mozley, specifically *Elmet* (2017), which was nominated for the Man Booker Prize in its year of publication. In attempts to categorise the novel, critics and readers variously discussed it as a kind of Yorkshire western, a Yorkshire noir, a Robin Hood tale and even a gothic fable with elements of gangster and horror fiction. In such border-dissolving works, 'readers are encouraged to be an artist, to think outside conventions and create alternatives', as Claudia Capancioni (2023) argues in reference to Ali Smith's *How to Be Both* (2014). In this case, I was encouraged by Mozley's novel to expand the borders of the concept, term and practice of caciquismo.

Whilst malevolent rural English landlords abound in older English literature, especially that of the nineteenth century (Tobin 1993), and although we even have an urban, post-war cacique in the industrialist Mr Brown in John Braine's *Room at the Top* (1957), also set in West Yorkshire, the term 'cacique' has never been applied to any of these characters and, if it ever had, it would almost certainly have been considered inappropriately exotic, even insulting. Caciquismo is considered a somewhat 'backward' form of local rule in Spanish America (as is its variant in Spain), an obstacle to progress, and certainly, therefore, never a phenomenon pertaining to areas considered 'developed'. It would be a stretch to claim that this has changed, that there might be a recent trend in cacique-like characters in modern English literature set in England, but there is a comparable female model of such behaviour (a cacica) in *Hot Stew* (2021), Mozley's acclaimed second novel, set in Soho, London, and another recent novel of interest is Scott Preston's *The Borrowed Hills* (2024), from the same publisher as that of Mozley's novels, in which a powerful local farmer William Herne exhibits many caciquismo-related traits in the wake of the 2001 foot-and-mouth epidemic in Cumbria. What is certain is there is no space in the current chapter to deal with the 'cacica' figure in *Hot Stew*, nor Herne in Preston's novel. The initial inspiration for this chapter, moreover, is the violent, manipulative behaviour of the protagonist of the novel *Pedro Páramo* (1955), the eponymous cacique of the masterpiece written by the Mexican author Juan Rulfo, and the extent to which Pedro serves as a model for the study of caciquismo in fiction elsewhere. Despite being set in early twentieth-century Mexico, Pedro's exploitative behaviour will serve as a point of comparison to that of a similarly dominant character in *Elmet*.

The analysis of caciques in fiction (Nason 1973; Thakkar 2012) tends to tie their behaviour with specific socio-historical contexts in which actual caciques exist, such as those of rural Spanish America over the centuries. Without such an obvious context for the existence of caciquismo in England, one might be tempted to avoid comparison. However, the link to historical reality is not the point. Just as Raewyn Connell's taxonomy of masculinities (1995) departed from its original inspiration in Australian masculinities to become a model for analysis throughout the world, so too concepts and models arising in Spanish America, such as caciquismo, can be applied to the non-Hispanophone world. What is revealed by an analysis of Mozley's novels which departs from the problematisation of land-related, class and particularly gendered borders is that a fictional form of cacique-like local domination in a rural area, called a cacicazgo in Spanish, underlines the border-crossing relevance of caciquismo as a phenomenon based not so much on historical reality as on insidious, socially damaging values that transcend nations and encompass patriarchal, bordering practices even in putatively progressive countries such as the United Kingdom. I argue that responses related to habitus rather than political action via institutions—which are steeped in the illusion of 'consent'—can be a model for contesting caciquismo, wherever the practice exists. The first half of the chapter deals with the conceptual apparatus for this argument, starting with a discussion of the relationship between caciquismo and hegemonic masculinities, moving on to a discussion of the role of habitus. Whilst I reference the novel throughout, the second half is a closer reading of *Elmet* in light of that apparatus.

Caciquismo and Fluid Hegemonic Masculinities

The pairing of caciquismo with British forms of masculine domination in the twenty-first century may seem bold, but it is in keeping with the volume's focus on the application of conceptual approaches across geographical and temporal borders. The longest chapter of my monograph on Rulfo (Thakkar 2012) involves the analysis of the aforementioned cacique Pedro Páramo, placing his activity in the context of generally Spanish American forms of local boss behaviour, rather than those considered solely Mexican. Whilst other detailed overviews of more modern caciquismo exist (Middlebrook 2009), I have found the cacique attributes outlined by the early twentieth-century Ecuadorean thinker Alfredo Espinosa Tamayo (1910), which I shall reprise further in this chapter, most useful and specific for my purposes. Pedro's territorial control, which I summarise later, is a springboard for my analysis of Mozley's David Price, for whom 'territory' is a key aspect of the claim to local power in *Elmet*, as the following brief summary of the novel will clarify.

Arriving into a patch of wild land ostensibly owned by Price, in West Yorkshire near the East Coast Main Line, is the towering figure of John Smythe, 'a foot taller than the tallest … Daddy was gargantuan' (pp. 190–1). Smythe is a bare-knuckle fighter, referred to as Daddy throughout by his son Danny Oliver, the novel's narrator, who is fifteen years old by the end of the novel, and who accompanies Smythe to the copse with his elder sister Cathy Oliver. Both children have the name of their mother, who had inherited land, a farm, though it is not confirmed that this inherited land is the wild patch where Smythe's family now builds their home. The mother has anyway disappeared from the lives of the family before their arrival, the children having previously been left in the care of their now deceased grandmother, Granny Morley, when they lived further north, by the sea. Price holds 'the largest acreage of any of the local farmers' (p. 76) and rules his territory just like a cacique, with an iron fist, or at least the fists of those who work for him. His henchmen extract rent from those occupying the many houses he owns in the villages nearby, and the former council houses he bought and profited from after Margaret Thatcher's right-to-buy scheme in the 1980s left many buyers unable to pay off their mortgages. They also force labour from those who are in debt to him and ensure they work just 'for a tenner at end of day' (p. 152). Resistance to these practices is mounted first by Smythe himself, and then in concert with a local, comfortably retired former mining union boss,

8 A VERY ENGLISH CACIQUISMO?: LAND, BADLANDS AND HABITUS... 153

Ewart Royce, and his wife, Martha, together with whom effective action is taken in the form of a rent strike, initially forcing local farmers to improve wages, only for them to renege on their promises after consulting with Price. This concerted action by workers is as close to one based on 'consent' as the characters oppressed by Price ever manage: they form a seemingly tight unit of solidarity around a bonfire prepared by Smythe in a scene more suggestive of clandestine activity in the coffee plantations of Guatemala than of official union behaviour.[4]

Price, who seems to have known the mother of the family, refuses to hand over the land around the copse to Smythe—who used to work and fight for Price himself—unless Smythe wins a fight that Price calls, against a similarly gigantic man brought over from Ukraine. Interestingly, Preston's *The Borrowed Hills* also features a pivotal bare-knuckle fight scene between the protagonist Steve and his nemesis George, echoing the fact that the hierarchy within any cacicazgo ultimately draws on raw physical strength. The fight is, ultimately, a way to allow John to claim the wild land as his own on a basis that Price can easily ignore if he wishes. There are several prior hints that this promise would not be respected, but after winning the fight, the odds are even further stacked against Smythe: it turns out that Cathy has murdered one of Price's two sons, the younger Charlie, in the depths of the woods during that very fight, defending herself from a presumably sexually motivated attack. The climactic penultimate chapter in the house Smythe built in the copse sees him being tortured to death by Price before a gang that the latter has gathered, among whom some had previously worked against Price. This is the least of Price's problems, as he is outwitted by Cathy herself, who burns the house down, along with Price, his men and her own dying father; all after killing a man Price had ordered to take her to a bedroom and 'make the most of her' (p. 289), just as she had fended off and killed Charlie earlier. Instead of believing Cathy's confession to his son's murder earlier during this ordeal, then, Price orders her to be raped even when he could just kill her there and then. Due to this error, she is able to overcome the rapist, returning with the equipment to create the final conflagration. The undoing of Price is, therefore, that he never believed Cathy could have killed his son Charlie, even when she admitted it to him, because—as his remaining, elder son Tom says—she's 'a little girl' (p. 289). The remainder of the plot concerns Danny's escape from this inferno and his travels across the country in search of his lost sister, all recounted in italicised chapters which interweave with the main narrative from the start, eschewing linearity just as Rulfo's fragmented novel does.

The behaviour of Price, and that of his nemesis, Smythe, presents us with typological challenges related to masculinities. Connell's categories of hegemonic, complicit, subordinate and marginalised masculinities (1995) are now common and current fare within masculinities studies, but Christine Beasley advocates additional terms such as 'sub-hegemonic masculinity' because the category of 'hegemonic' slips too easily between different versions of domination. She argues that there is rarely a single hegemon, and that, in fact, '[h]egemonic masculinity, even at the local level, may be seen as hierarchical and plural' (2008, p. 98). Connell's understanding of 'gender regimes' as localised, already fluid entities, remains useful alongside Beasley's understanding of plural, hierarchical hegemonic masculinities. According to Connell, a gender regime 'may reproduce, but may in specific ways, depart from, the wider gender order (i.e. the whole societal pattern of gender relations)' and will broadly include local factors related to the gendered division of labour, relations of power, emotions and culture (Connell 2006, p. 839).

Price and Smythe are both 'sub-hegemonic', in the nuancing provided by Beasley, but Price does not legitimise his masculinity—as a model of behaviour—so much as merely *enforce* certain modes of acquiescent behaviour within the regime of his local community through sheer economic wherewithal. Smythe is a rival sub-hegemonic masculinity, a second hegemon, not because he holds any levers of economic power like Price, but because he is a culturally charismatic figure due to his fighting prowess and his principled behaviour, which attracts praise, loyalty and following. At any one moment, though, the logic of patriarchal society demands that—on a local level, at least—only one of the two top men is 'top man'. Thus, Beasley is right that at the local level, there can be more than one hegemon (Price and Smythe, in this case) and Connell is right that there can be a fluctuating hierarchy (Price is the hegemon to begin with, then Smythe, then neither when both are killed) because, as Connell states, the position of hegemon is 'always contestable' (1995, p. 77).

Hegemony and Territory

Etymologically, hegemony denotes 'leadership', from the Greek hegemon, meaning 'leader', but in its Marxist apprehension, it is also a group of individuals with interconnected and interdependent economic and political interests, for whom consent to 'lead' is manufactured in society via the domination of institutions, the generation of certain discourses and the control of production. Referring specifically to 1930s England, Antonio Gramsci states that 'landowners and the industrialists have permanent interests which bind them together' (1936, p. 156). These groups are now joined arguably by the most powerful hegemonic interests in the economic sphere, which are financial and property-owning, as indeed we see in *Hot Stew*. As a way of binding these 'complicit embodied identities', it is easy to see how 'the mobilisation of consent' might be a 'great advantage' (p. 93), as Beasley argues. However, in the twenty-first century, such influential interests collude too brazenly in the creation of forms of institutional control designed to garner only an illusory 'consent'. This illusory consent manifests not just through ostensibly 'democratic' institutions, for example, the first-past-the-post system of general elections in the United Kingdom, but also in localised practices such as 'consultations' prior to major economic manoeuvres like land acquisition or the 'restructuring' of organisations, or even apparently reached agreements between workers and employers, as we see described above within the local gender regime in *Elmet*. Such illusory consent will always out itself as illusory since its mechanisms are there to maintain the status quo, both in economic and in socio-cultural terms, by gaining rubber stamps rather than genuine approvals. These 'complicit embodied entities', whether at a state, institutional or local level, actually pay scant regard to institutional forms of consent, instead depending for their survival on almost automatic modes of routine behaviours and assumptions, on habitus.

For a sub-hegemonic masculinity like Price, the need for this habitus of everyday acquiescence is predicated on a precarious claim to 'his' land. While 'land' has the modern sense of definite boundaries, e.g. political, geographic and economic (property), it also has a wider connotation beyond such certitude. In its most rudimentary and original conception, land is merely the opposite of sea and, in this latter sense, it does not belong to anything but the planet itself. Indeed, in most romance languages, at least, land is 'tierra', which can mean both 'land' and 'earth/ Earth'. The word itself is therefore conceived of as both private and public, in the most fundamental sense of being planetary rather than belonging to any one individual. According to Gayatri Spivak's notion of planetarity, after all, we only 'inhabit [Earth] on loan' (2015, p. 291), a notion echoed in the title of Preston's *The Borrowed Hills*, of course. This sense of the word 'land' as 'planetary' does not exist in English but, in

Elmet, private human ownership seems temporary, subject to an irrepressible natural *territorial* force in the rural setting of the novel: 'the ghosts of the ancient forest could be marked when the wind blew. The soil was alive with ruptured stories that cascaded and rotted then found form once more and pushed up through the undergrowth and back into our lives' (p. 6). The repetition of the word 'and' reinforces the planet's unrelenting permanence. The language here provides a language for the Earth, which almost speaks to us through the literary techniques deployed by Mozley: it 'lives and breathes' (p. 202), as Smythe will say.

The underlying impression of such words is that, though humans can pretend to own land, the planet in fact owns humans. This impression extends to the force of water. In the town by the North Sea where the family lived before, the salty air displays a punitive, almost parental claim to the brother and sister, as it '*whipped* our faces so that they were near red raw and the salt *combed* our hair and *dug* under our fingernails' (p. 35, my emphasis). Mozley's references to the forces of the planet also hint at the precariousness of the 'consent' upon which human claims to territory are based since such claims are set against natural forces that are beyond human control, and those natural forces are far more durable, more likely to 'win'. Thus, land ownership is imbricated within human societal structures of economic, political and therefore social power precisely to reinforce an already tenuous claim to literally planetary territory, a claim that is not 'approved' by nature, making it therefore all the more contingent on illusions of social and political 'consent'. But this chapter relates to whether it is really consent upon which land ownership and acquisition are based or the customs, the habitus, of a given population on which such claims are *given up* to powerful interests and whether that habitus can be challenged by an alternative one. Our passivity is critiqued and a more positive response is invoked subtly in *Elmet*, a novel which demonstrates that such an alternative does indeed exist, even if it requires self-sacrificing courage to enact it.

Consent, Borders and Habitus

Resistance to private, hegemonic land acquisition can and does occur consciously, of course, rather than through any unconscious habitus as such, arising most prominently in areas of the world where neoliberal economic projects force the displacement of subaltern groups. In their study of such acquisition and resistance in India, Kenneth Bo Nielsen and Alf Gunvald Nilsen (2017) state that it is only through the mechanisms of hegemonic control, in their case those of law, that subaltern groups can and do practise resistance. Thus, 'institutions, discourses, and technologies of rule that attach to the state also become sites of contention where subaltern resistance can be articulated and pursued' (p. 205). Nielsen and Nilsen question the extent to which such resistance can be successful, though, since the same modalities by which they are suppressed are those by which they must resist. Those modalities represent a phoney apparatus of 'legitimate' resistance, making that resistance redundant and the idea of consent illusory. As we see in *Elmet*, Price merely ignores public institutions, created by and founded on 'consent', in his dealings. In fact, being off 'any kind of official radar' (p. 190) suits both Price and his victims. His tenants operate under a system akin to colonial debt peonage since they cannot pay their rents to him, instead paying him practically in kind with informal work: 'That way he did not have to organise wages and they were his to run like dogs' (p. 76). State-related matters like tax, working conditions and inflation-linked wage increases are irrelevant to Price. For Jon Beasley-Murray (2010), the problem with apprehensions of power relations based on hegemony, including the field of subaltern studies, is that they assume that domination still works by consent when, in fact, that notion is meaningless where the state or any hegemon, including a local cacique we could say, is present and actively dominant through habitus. In fact, capital and power work through biopolitics, that is to say, through the multitude in the form of our bodies (in a way similar to Foucault´s biopolitics) and through our (almost anaesthetised) everyday activities, habits, attitudes and interactions: habitus.

The problems that Nielsen and Nilsen describe in India are not restricted to that country, of course. In both developed and developing countries, very little has changed in terms of the options for resistance, especially when it comes to lawful, hegemonically sponsored land acquisition. Since the path to resistance via hegemony's own mechanisms of control is limited and often non-existent in all practical terms, what are the alternatives? If appeals to outdated laws, such as India's colonial Land Acquisition Act of 1894 or the Mexican Subsoil Laws of the 1917 Constitution, cannot be trusted to produce social justice and, indeed, were not designed sincerely enough to do so, what is the recourse? Both of Mozley's novels encourage us to see that recourse to justice can be engineered by changes in habitus that are tortuously conceived and maintained in the face of hegemonic attempts to restrain them. These resistant practices are not always successful but such changes in behaviours do at least constitute a long-term alternative to engagement with traditional institutions of power by creating new forms of habitus which defy the border-generative practices by which hegemony seeks to sustain itself. Smythe intuits as much when he reads an offer of a deal from Price whereby he would hand over the land to Danny and Cathy if Smythe returns to work for him full-time:

> It's idea a person can write summat on a bit of paper about a piece of land that lives and breathes, and changes and quakes and floods and dries, and that that person can use it as he will, or not at all, and that he can keep others off it, all because of a piece of paper. That's part means nowt to me. (p. 202)

Price's border-generative practices do not just entail the creation of literal borders; they also implicate the creation of class and gender hierarchies. More generally, in society, such practices include social, legal, bureaucratic and academic classifications, which are all dependent on creating borders. For Pierre Bourdieu, the act of classification misleadingly creates 'distances which are kept or signalled' (1984, p. 165) between groups of people, a process of differentiation which might be exemplified by the activities of collusive interests in land-owning practices, for whom the parcelling of land via borders is indispensable to their hegemony. But what if, unlike Smythe, and just through habitus, through their acquiescence to both land borders and hierarchies, ordinary people also collude in this classifying, bordering process? Habitus, after all, is a learned, almost automatic 'disposition that generates meaningful practices and meaning-giving perceptions' (p. 166).

Thus, the practices of bordering, of classifying, without wishing to conflate the two, have this in common: their ability to proliferate thought processes, which then become so difficult to escape that complicity with their underlying structuring systems becomes the norm. For Bourdieu, the 'disposition' in question is one built on capitalism and the tastes, perceptions, practices, etc. associated with it. *Elmet* constitutes a call for an alternative habitus and a change in the usual characteristics of Bourdieu's 'disposition': in our tastes, or at least in our ways of thinking about nature, for example, as mentioned earlier. One extended reading of the novel, the only one so far it seems, is based on the space of the 'mythic rural' where 'alternative collectivities' can be rekindled from older notions of the commons, of 'recommoning the land' rather than from a far-from-perfect 'social contract' (Johansen 2023, p. 649). The present analysis places this call for alternative land ownership in the context of masculinities, habitus and nature. We need *not* consider nature a force that is at odds with us, for

8 A VERY ENGLISH CACIQUISMO?: LAND, BADLANDS AND HABITUS... 159

that is the position of capitalist border-generators, including landowners, who are threatened by the universality of the planet, the possibility (reality, really) that it belongs to everybody and nobody. Nature can instead become a source for *post*-hegemonic relations in which land becomes not a site of private acquisition, of borders, but a less bounded source of inspiration for all and thus a source of affective resistance to the supposedly consensual, supposedly rational binary of powerful/subordinate in human power relations. The language of Mozley's novel itself, with its respect for nature's little nuances, as demonstrated in the lines I have so far quoted, is merely one aspect of that inspiration. The very lifestyles of the three characters in its central family form the bedrock of a call to resist borders and border-generative practices with alternative values based on a motley, and apparently contradictory, blend of brute strength, compassion, solidarity and land husbandry (as opposed to ownership).

Caciquismo, *Pedro Páramo* and *Elmet*

There are plenty of caciques in Spanish American writing, among the most memorable being don Alejo in the Chilean author José Donoso's *El lugar sin límites* (1966), *The Place without Limits*, a title that itself evokes borderlessness, Lázaro Pizarro in the Mexican writer Héctor Aguilar Camín's *Morir en el Golfo* (1985), *Dying in the Gulf*, again a title that alludes to the usefulness for such individuals of unmonitored—if not quite unbordered—spaces, and indeed the eponymous cacica Doña Bárbara in Rómulo Gallegos' novel (1929), whose 'barbarism' hints at the conceptually artificial division between civilisation and barbarism, a common theme in Spanish literature of the nineteenth and early twentieth centuries.[5] Meanwhile, Miguel Delibes' *Los santos inocentes* (1981), *The Holy Innocents*, presents a rural Spain in which the cruelties of patriarchal landlordism are also prevalent.

Rulfo's 1950s novel *Pedro Páramo* presents us with a cacique who is—not untypically for such a figure—able to entirely control the destiny of an entire town, most of which he seems to own, in the northwest of Mexico. Pedro's mistreatment of Comala's inhabitants takes many forms that correspond to circumstances and behaviour typical of a Spanish American cacique, according to the aforementioned Espinosa Tamayo, namely, their taking place in a remote rural setting, the exercise of arbitrary and violent power, unbridled self-interest in commercial operations, cruelty and indifference to human need, extralegality sustained by nepotism, hypocrisy,

160   A. THAKKAR

sexual abuse of women, unabashed manipulation of political processes (more a feature of Spanish caciquismo, as mentioned above) and, finally, unyielding resistance to political or social progress (Espinosa Tamayo 1979 [1918], pp. 276–280; Thakkar 2012, p. 131). Pedro's caciquismo, which outlasts even his death as the town's inhabitants are left in purgatory by his refusal to cooperate with the priest, is a snapshot of a centuries-long pattern of behaviour of largely male domination via land control (Thakkar 2012, pp. 152–159). I am less concerned here with the evolution of Spanish American caciquismo from its community-centred origins to a version marked more by 'surrogate tyranny on behalf of the state' (Thakkar, p. 154) than I am with the behavioural patterns of the twentieth-century cacique, as outlined by Espinosa Tamayo. It is precisely through these behaviours that a cacique, or cacica (see Ochoa and Guengerich 2021), represents and reinforces a more universal gender order, predicated on bordering and classifying processes not dissimilar to those enacted by the Spanish Empire—hence, the connotation of 'backwardness' that the term 'cacique' holds.

Whilst it is tempting to see the cacique as a 'hegemon' whose rule is based on consent, it is, in fact, habit rather than consent that makes their control over a community possible. To understand how and why this might be the case for Price in *Elmet*, and with due respect to Loic Wacquant's warnings about 'refracting Bourdieu through the prism of native sociological lenses' (1989, p. 30), it is useful to note Beasley-Murray's assertion that, in a Latin American setting and beyond, consent is less important than habit and affect:

> The fact that people no longer give up their consent in the ways in which they may once have done, and yet everything carries on much the same, shows that consent was never really at issue. Social order is secured through habit and affect: through folding the constituent power of the multitude back on itself to produce the illusion of transcendence and sovereignty. (2010, p. ix)

The resonance of this statement with Pedro's 'transcendence and sovereignty' is clear in the final stages of that novel since he is able to condemn the town to penury and starvation and to signal this condemnation merely by folding his arms in dismay at the death of the woman he loves. At this point, the town's dependence on habit, as opposed to consent, is laid bare, as it ceases to function. In stark contrast to the raging battles around the town for national control, to gain the consent to rule, due to the Mexican Revolution, and the ensuing Cristero War, there is no resistance, no attempt to challenge Pedro Páramo's power in Comala, a town which is subject, instead, to the whims of a cacique precisely because it maintains habits rather than expressly giving consent to that cacique. The novel's ending makes clear that, while Pedro himself dies, the system of caciquismo reigns supreme, given that all the characters and inhabitants of his town are condemned to the purgatory his actions and inaction, his alone, have made inevitable. Habitus here is sustained by violent practices such as the denial of education, the rape of women and the absence of legal support, but ultimately submission to power is maintained through an overarching habitus of submissive practices, supported by a Catholic belief in redemption through confession (denied by Pedro's effective banishment of the priest), rather than in explicit permission for the cacique to behave in the abusive way that he does.

The reader may be forgiven for thinking these matters do not pertain to the modern Western world, such is the pervasive rhetoric about development and underdevelopment. A caciquismo-informed reading of *Elmet* makes clear that the activities of Price are comparable to those of Pedro Páramo, even if the context of habitus in this novel is secular rather than Catholic and the location is entirely different. According to the Ted Hughes' quote from *Remains of Elmet* at the start of the novel,

> Elmet was the last independent Celtic kingdom in England and originally stretched over the vale of York ... But even into the seventeenth century this narrow cleft and its side-gunnels, under the glaciated moors, were still a 'badlands', a sanctuary for refugees from the law. (no page number)

Both Comala and Elmet have the quality of a 'badlands', a hotbed of extralegality, and the main source of the drama of both novels, at least initially in *Pedro Páramo*, is a struggle over land-related legacy. In *Elmet*, Smythe constitutes a threat that caciques like Price rarely take well to: a stranger (an 'offcomer' in Preston's *The Borrowed Hills*), or 'forastero' in Spanish. This is because the cacique, according to Espinosa Tamayo, is averse to 'any alien autochthonous element ... [which could] bring subversive ideas' (p. 276).

BORDERS AND BADLANDS IN *ELMET*

At the end of the novel, Cathy kills two rapists as well as starting a fire that erases the whole local gender regime. In order to unpack this climactic ending, I refer to Connell's understanding of gender relations on three levels, namely, power, production and cathexis. In terms of power, to take the first, we are more primed than Price for Cathy's murder of two men more powerful than her in different senses (Charlie due to wealth/class and the second man due to sheer physical power). In contrast to the reader, Price is completely unaware of how easily she can use a gun, how sure her aim is, how easily she can skin a hare or mallard, how physically strong she is. All of these abilities belong to the second aspect of Connell's schema, production, since hunting and preparing meat is how she helps John, her dad (Smythe), to maintain their alternative lifestyle in the copse, which also involves land husbandry and the ability to defend oneself. But Price is also unprepared for how passionately committed to her family she is, and this is the realm of cathexis, of emotion, critical to the aforementioned local gender regime, and explained by Connell as follows: 'the way in which attachment and antagonism among people and groups are organized along gender lines, including feelings of solidarity, prejudice and disdain, and sexual attraction and repulsion' (2006, p. 839). Price assumes traditional gender relations pertain in his patch of wild land, due to his wilful obliviousness to the convergence of cathectic and production relations in creating the physically powerful, almost literally explosive, character that Cathy is, with her strong attachment to family and her repulsion towards the predatory behaviour of Charlie and Tom. In a reading based on resentment (Price's, not Smythe's) and the 'mythic rural', Emily Johansen succinctly puts it thus: 'Cathy's violence, perhaps even more legibly than Daddy's, is framed by the novel as a rejection and fury in the face of gendered expectations of behaviour and bodies' (2023, p. 650).

Price's assumption of the primacy of the traditional gender order is based on these 'expectations', on habitus. This is made understandable to the reader as Mozley initially encourages the idea that a conventional gender order indeed does pertain. Earlier in the novel, this basic male-female hierarchy manifests in the way Cathy feels powerless to resist as she is attacked by male school bullies on a beach in their seaside town, an event which foreshadows later confrontations with the sons of Price. The hierarchies related to the particular gender regime of Smythe's family at that early point seem to underline such strictly clear ranks. Smythe is clearly in charge; even the family's dogs seem aware of this as they 'turned their faces up to their masters on every other step. The dogs looked at me [Danny] and Cathy. We looked at Daddy' (p. 54). But there are hints for the reader in the relationship between the siblings that the male-female hierarchy is not at all to be taken for granted. It helps that Cathy is the older sibling but it is also she who is more physically able, who can hunt, who displays strength and courage at difficult moments, who ultimately resists Price by strangling his son, killing another sex attacker and setting fire to the house at the end. It is generally Danny who cooks, likes the 'inside' rather than the outside, 'making house nice and that' (p. 67), and is happy to gain an education through Daddy's friend, Vivian. He exhibits non-conventional masculinity by wearing the latter's clothes in secret and ultimately performing sexual favours for Bill, a trucker, in return for shelter and warmth. Neither Cathy nor Danny turns out to conform to the established gender order, one that is based on gender borders, another type of classification, to recall Bourdieu, this time borders created on the quite simple terms that men will be men and women will be women. Despite this unconventionality with regard to gender, male privilege in this novel is certainly not 'invisible' (Kimmel 2003) since the raw facts of survival require brute strength associated literally with male fighting power, even though—by the end—Cathy contests that privilege with her own (literally) naked strength.

The family's habitus is an alternative one. The gendered division of labour is not stereotypical, and there is no need for a regular job, with a regular payslip, and integration into the surrounding patriarchal economic structures (the farms are all owned by men). The masculinities of Danny and his father correspondingly exhibit a certain defiance of convention, but they each represent strikingly different modes of being a man. It is clear from the outset that living in the copse is John's choice since we are told that he could have gone into construction but chose not to (p. 19). The desire to work with nature, rather than obliterate it, is a major feature of the alternative habitus and is most apparent in the way both Danny and Daddy treat animals. At school, before they move, Danny examines insects during the break or sea creatures at the beach afterwards, but he always returns them 'back to their homes and to their lives' (p. 31), just as Daddy hunts as humanely as he can (p. 114), and ensures the family's chickens are in a coop attached to the family home, rather than 'needlessly cold' (p. 164). Although John and Danny share this compassion, John calls his son a 'funny lad' (p. 67), a term Danny hears now and again, especially after the novel's key fight; one particular individual all but ascribes him the tag of femininity, which does not displease or disturb Danny for whom such classification is neither to be mocked nor accepted. As with many features of adult behaviour, for Danny, such bordering practices are just the way things are, and his response is a shrug: 'Well, it's fine by me' (pp. 229–230).

Thus, to return to Beasley's discussion on the plurality of hegemonic masculinities, it must also be the case that there are a plurality of *subordinate* masculinities, among which a sub-category of indifferent subordination might be heuristically of use. But Danny's indifference vis-a-vis attempts to classify and border him is unsurprising by this point in the novel since we have already seen such indifference in terms of *class* boundaries. After a telling-off for Cathy from the school headmistress, in which the latter places the blame for the beach incident on Cathy rather than on the attacking boys, who are from a 'nicer' part of their town, Daddy at least 'outwardly' agrees with the headmistress and offers an insincere apology since it 'was simply the way people saw things […] It was the way the world was. We just had to find methods of our own to work against it and to strengthen ourselves however we could' (p. 44). To some extent, then, rather than bonding on supposedly 'effeminate' behaviour like being kind to animals, it is actually a habitus marked by *apathy* towards bordering practices, both social and terrestrial, which means father and son, otherwise so unlike each other, get on so well.

Danny does not necessarily actively promote through his narrative or dialogue any alternative habitus. Mozley's writing reinforces it in more subtle ways. One is by deploying the past simple repeatedly in relation specifically to Danny's methodical actions, his acting out of his 'femininity' in activities like kitchen chores that might otherwise seem irrelevant. In a scene which typically conveys Danny's uncomplicated interest in not being particularly masculine throughout the novel, his domesticity is casually delivered in a succession of very simple verbs, a technique seen elsewhere in the novel but very evident here: 'I *busied* myself in the sink. I *washed* and *dried* the tall glasses that had been in the basin since the night before and *placed* them on the table next to a full jug of water' (p. 96, my italics). This is in the house of Vivian, of roughly the same age as Smythe, a 'feminised' place where Danny finds refuge and comfort with a quasi-mother figure with whom knowledge, talking and cooking are more important than hunting and defending oneself. In contrast, the actions and behaviours of the sons of Price correspond to a more traditional habitus in which the gender order, not just that of men over women, but of 'superior' men over 'lesser' men, is prevalent, where 'the proper order of things' (p. 116) means Tom, the elder son, is always 'the second only in the universe' (p. 116), in other words, second to his father.

At stake for the Prices is their own habitus marked by these traditional, bordered hierarchies where each layer of a hierarchy 'knows its place', so to speak, whether this place is one related to class or gender. In Bourdieu's terms, and not unlike those of Judith Butler (1990), this knowledge of one's limits is reinforced through repetition of expected norms within a given 'life-style': 'the countless pieces of information a person consciously or unconsciously imparts endlessly underline and confirm one another' (169). It is therefore significant that it is precisely in the realm of *non*-bordered spaces, the unclaimed lands—a wild within the wild—in which Cathy meets these boys. This is where the germ of a challenge to class and gender borders arises, culminating in her using her physical strength, a quality stereotypically not associated with a girl in this habitus, to overturn both a gender order and a class order in which men like Price do not expect to be challenged. They do not expect it due to the 'countless [self-reinforcing] pieces of information' Bourdieu refers to above: socially reinforcing information which classifies and determines misleading class and gender borders.

Whilst the threat to their values simmers on this class and gender plane, the challenge to Price from Smythe is primarily related to a very material factor, land, on the face of it: 'We lived here on his doorstep yet he had no access to our lives. We did not pay him rent, we did not work for him, we did not owe him anything. So he feared us' (p. 124). But John and his family evidently threaten Prices' values as well: the word 'price' is even suggestive of a common criticism of such people who 'know the price of everything but the value of nothing'. It is clear, in the discussion of this novel so far, that the values of Price correspond to those of a cacique like Pedro Páramo, but it would be inaccurate and unsophisticated to simply reverse the schema and declare Smythe a kind of antithesis to the cacique model. There are aspects of Smythe that actually conform to the cacique model: the remote rural setting that Espinosa Tamayo posits as crucial for cacique activity also applies to the activities of Smythe, whose alternative lifestyle must remain undetected by authorities to survive matters such as council tax, income tax, education and care services for the children, etc. There is, therefore, a degree of Espinosa Tamayo's category of 'extralegality' in everything Smythe does (and does not do), and although for

Espinosa Tamayo, the cacique attribute 'nepotism' refers to patrilineal inheritance of huge swathes of land, is it not the case that Smythe wants to deliver a similar inheritance, albeit on a far smaller scale, for his own children? For this same reason, his activities are governed by 'self-interest', another of Espinosa Tamayo's cacique attributes explored in my earlier work (2012). If Smythe shares with Price a propensity, then, for a remote setting in which to indulge in extralegal activities in the service of their respective offspring, which is really a kind of existence based on self-interest, what is there left of Espinosa Tamayo's cacique definition on which they might diverge?

Whilst the *where* and at least some of the *why* of Espinosa Tamayo's attributes of a cacique are shared by the two antagonists, it is the *how* through which they ultimately differ. John practises violence in his productive activity of fighting because it is a way to survive, not because it is a way to socially or economically subdue another person into a position of abject subordination or to confirm hegemony, which is the motive of Price and his sons, who 'smashed up bars for fun in the knowledge their father could pay for the damage [...] had ridden their quad bikes over their neighbours' crops' (pp. 76–77). Because of the absence of that desire on John's part to exercise power over others, there is no cruelty, hypocrisy or sexual abuse of women in his behaviour. In fact, he actively strays from any situation where his desire to avoid subjugating others might be tested, for example when advising Cathy not to confront the boys who attack her on the beach. He behaves with respect to the point of a fault in the way he deals with the mother of his children, whose absences distress them and who, it appears, had a relationship with Price before meeting John, with Danny perhaps hinted to be the result of that union ('Your daddy—if he is your Daddy [...]', p. 292), ironically underscoring Danny's repeated reference to Smythe as 'Daddy' throughout the novel. The flight of the mother from the land, with Smythe, is recounted by the contrastingly misogynous Price as one of almost daylight robbery, in which Smythe also makes off with 'a pile of cash, my wife's jewellery and a pair of 1960s Holland & Holland guns' (p. 292). Here, the objectification of the mother, in a list including guns, evokes a more entrenched sexual violence based on ownership of both women and land. As Johansen notes:

> Daniel's mother, rather than an autonomous agent of her own escape, is simply another item in the list of property with which Daddy absconds [...] the land on which Daddy builds their home is simply a later addition to the same list. (2023, p. 652)

Now, Smythe can hardly be considered a reconstructed masculinity in the mould of the classic 'new man', and he shares the self-interest and extralegality of Price, but he is clearly not an exemplar of cacique-like violence and cruelty either. He is, therefore, a masculinity unburdened by classification, unbordered, a subjectivity which defies categorisation, neither toxic nor saintly—paradoxically, a borderless identity.

Within the 'badlands' of *Elmet*, Smythe can be elusive to authorities who would seek to classify, to border him, and it is only in this wild outland that he can carry out a lifestyle that defies such bordering practices that cannot be classified as either patriarchal or modern. In the absence of such authorities, it is Price—as the initial sub-hegemonic power—who tries to contain Smythe, to make him conform to local, illegal practices of his own, including settlement of territory by violence and the administering of cruelty. But Smythe refuses to do any more of Price's dirty work for him when offered the chance. He instead helps and encourages those farm workers whom Price seeks to exploit, using the unmonitored spaces within this unbordered territory to mete out 'just' violence. He physically takes out a certain Mr Coxswain, who had failed to pay back Smythe's work-injured friend Pete (p. 25) and organises locals into a powerful form of civil disobedience, the rent strike. If the land he inhabited was subject to civic supervision and scrutiny, with all the bordering and classifying practices that civic authorities practise, he could not possibly help in the ways that he does or even raise his children in the border-indifferent way that allows them to be as gender-unclassifiable themselves as they are.

Conclusion: *Elmet* and Hope

Further research on the protean, border-crossing qualities of the Spanish American cacique would be of interest. The central villain, or cacique, in Mozley's second novel, *Hot Stew*, is in fact a cacica, a female version of this usually male figure. Agatha Howard is a ruthless London property tycoon who aims to mobilise all her connections in the public sector (the police), the private sector (various businesses) and the underground criminal world to evict women from a Soho brothel, where the women (and clients) are relatively happy, in order to knock it down and develop flats and restaurants. In her treatment of individuals affected by and related to this venture she displays many of the features I have noted in Price, especially the recourse to physical violence, extralegality, cruelty, indifference and, at one point, the apparent sexual exploitation of a male employee.

The Spanish American cacique clearly crosses both gender and geographical borders, just as the Argentinian 'gaucho' does, as Brian Baker demonstrates from a 'very Welsh' angle in another chapter in this volume. The fact that it does, as I have argued here, indicates that gender, ironically, is not the only issue. What needs addressing is the *manner* of the practice of power via land or property ownership. Smythe/Daddy, after all, also presumes to own land. He also has the emotional capacity and bodily strength to act physically violently where he feels it is necessary to do so, just as Price has the emotional tenacity and financial wherewithal to do so. John sticks to firm moral principles, though, and does not engage in unnecessary cruelty or physical violence. Even if he might not be Danny's real, physical 'Daddy', he is his moral daddy, exemplifying how land ownership combined with physical, financial and/or emotional strength need not result automatically in caciquismo. He demonstrates that consent need not be given up to hegemons and that an alternative habitus and alternative daily practices are far more threatening to caciquismo than not giving consent through institutions (there is no reference to parliamentary or local party politics in the novel).

Similarly, Danny and Cathy, whilst they challenge gender stereotypes, also help to create and sustain a lifestyle devoid of the stranglehold of modernity, in the form of either technology, digital or otherwise (no phones, no laptops; the passing trains are as close as they get), or exploitative power relationships, including any based on hegemonic power structures dependent on phoney consent. That they ultimately fail to maintain that lifestyle, even if Cathy appears to have taken down Price and his gang in the closing apocalyptic fire, does nothing to reduce the fact that that consent is never given to Price. More broadly, and with a degree of hope, *Elmet* sensitises the reader to the fact that the planet, with which humans only have a temporary and tenuous relationship, has also been arbitrarily organised, crisscrossed with fields, according to borders generated by capitalism, of which claims to territory are only one, and that any such hegemony based on habitus, on our habitual acquiescence to those borders—to repeat the words of Connell on hegemonic masculinities—is 'always contestable' (1995, p. 7).

Notes

1. I will not be italicising caciquismo, cacique or (the female version) cacica, since a minor intention of this piece is to promote understanding, currency and usage of these terms within Anglophone discourse.
2. See Joaquin Costa (1901), *Oligarquía y caciquismo como la forma actual de Gobierno en España: urgencia y modo de cambiarla* (Madrid). For an account of the evolution of the Spanish version of caciquismo, see Carmelo Romero Salvador, *Caciques y caciquismo en España* (1834–2020) (Los Libros de la Catarata 2021).
3. Robert Kern (1973) is one exception.
4. One might be reminded, for example, of the opening of Gregory Nava's film *El Norte* (1983), in which just such a clandestine meeting around a fire, by an old colonial ruin, is organised by oppressed workers in Guatemala.
5. Two excellent works which deal with fictional Spanish American caciques are by José Carlos González Boixo (1996) and Robert Kern (1973).

Works Cited

Aguilar Camín, Héctor. 1985. *Morir en el Golfo*. México D.F: Edicions Océano.

Beasley, Christine. 2008. Rethinking Hegemonic Masculinity in a Globalizing World. *Men and Masculinities 11* (1): 86–103.

Beasley-Murray, Jon. 2010. *Posthegemony. Political Theory and Latin America*. Minneapolis: University of Minnesota Press.

Bourdieu, Pierre. 2010 [1984]. *Distinction: A Social Critique of the Judgement of Taste* (1st ed.). Taylor & Francis Group.

Braine, John. 1957. *Room at the Top*. London: Eyre & Spottiswood.

Butler, Judith. 1990. *Gender Trouble: Feminism and the Subversion of Identity*. London: Routledge.

Capancioni, Claudia. 2023. 'This Particular Art [Is] All About Walls': Nomadic Poetics of Identity in Ali Smith's *How to Be Both*. In *Rethinking Identities Across Boundaries: Genders/Genres/Genera*, ed. Claudia Capancioni, Mariaconcetta Costantini, and Mara Mattoscio, 183–202. Cham, Switzerland: Palgrave Macmillan.

Connell, Raewyn. 1995. *Masculinities*. Los Angeles: University of California Press.

———. 2006. Glass Ceilings or Gendered Institutions? Mapping the Gender Regimes of Public Sector Worksites. *Public Administration Review 66* (6): 837–849.

Delibes, Miguel. 1981. *Los santos inocentes*. Valladolid: Editorial Planeta.

Donoso, José. 1966. *El lugar sin límites*. Mexico City: Joaquín Mortiz.

170   A. THAKKAR

Espinosa Tamayo, Alfredo. 1979 [1918]. *Psicología y sociología del pueblo ecuatoriano*. Quito: Banco Central del Ecuador, Corporación Editora Central.

Gallegos, Rómulo. 1929. *Doña Bárbara*. Barcelona: Editorial Araluce.

González Boixo, José Carlos. 1996. The Underlying Currents of Caciquismo in the Narratives of Juan Rulfo. In *Structures of Power, Essays on Twentieth-Century Spanish-American Fiction*, ed. Terry J. Peavler and Peter Standish, 107–125. New York: State University.

Gramsci, Antonio. 1971 [1936]. *Selections from the Prison Notebooks of Antonio Gramsci*. London: Lawrence & Wishart.

Johansen, Emily. 2023. Making Sense of the Rural White Working Class: The Contemporary Novel of Rural Retreat and the Politics of Resentment. *Textual Practice* 37 (4): 642–666.

Kern, Robert, ed. 1973. *The Caciques, Oligarchical Politics and the System of Caciquismo in the Luso-Hispanic World*. Albuquerque: University of New Mexico Press.

Kimmel, Michael. 2003. Foreword. In *Masculinities Matter! Men, Gender and Development*, ed. Frances Cleaver. London and New York: Zed.

López Fadul, Valeria. 2000. A Cacique By Any Other Name. https://www.folger.edu/blogs/collation/a-cacique-by-any-other-name Accessed April 2024.

Middlebrook, Kevin J. 2009. Caciquismo and Democracy: Mexico and Beyond. *Bulletin of Latin American Research* 28 (3): 411–427.

Mozley, Fiona. 2017. *Elmet*. London: John Murray.

———. 2021. *Hot Stew*. London: John Murray.

Nason, Marshall R. 1973. The Literary Evidence Part 1: The Term Caciquismo, Its Variants and Its Literary Scope'. In *The Caciques, Oligarchical Politics and the System of Caciquismo in the Luso-Hispanic World*, ed. Robert Kern, 27–42. Albuquerque: University of New Mexico Press.

Nielsen, Kenneth Bo, and Alf Gunvald Nilsen. 2017. Law Struggles and Hegemonic Processes in Neoliberal India: Gramscian Reflections on Land Acquisition Legislation. *Globalizations* 12 (2): 203–216.

Ochoa, Margarita R., and Sara V. Guengerich. 2021. *Cacicas. The Indigenous Women Leaders of Spanish America, 1492–1825*. Norman: Oklahoma University Press.

Preston, Scott. 2024. *The Borrowed Hills*. London: John Murray.

Rulfo, Juan. 1989 [1955]. *Pedro Páramo*. Madrid: Cátedra.

Smith, Ali. 2014. *How To Be Both*. New York: Anchor.

Spivak, Gayatri Chakravorty. 2015. *Planetarity (Box 4, Welt)*. *Paragraph*, 'Translation and the Untranslatable'. July 38 (2): 290–292.

Thakkar, Amit. 2012. *The Fiction of Juan Rulfo: Irony, Revolution and Postcolonialism*. Woodbridge: Tamesis.

Tobin, Beth Fowkes. 1993. *Superintending the Poor: Charitable Ladies and Paternal Landlords in British Fiction, 1770–1860*. New Haven: Yale University Press.

Wacquant, L.J.D. 1989. Towards a Reflexive Sociology: A Workshop with Pierre Bourdieu. *Sociological Theory* 7 (1): 26–63.

CHAPTER 9

Superheroes, Spectacles and Hoods: 'Dances of Identity' in Uncommon Spaces

Saul Pandelakis

In movies, as supposedly in real life, men do not make passes at women who wear glasses. So they do not, and in the unlikely event that they do, it is only to let their female counterparts dramatically remove their spectacles, untie their austere bun and reveal their good looks. A woman should not wear glasses, Hollywood tells us, for instance, in *The Big Sleep* (Hawks 1946) where Humphrey Bogart tells a charming bookseller, 'I was just wondering if you have to...', and then points at his own eyes as if the very word 'glasses' could not be uttered. The bookseller complies and removes her glasses, then proceeds to let her hair down. This transformation is sanctioned by Bogart's approval: she is transformed by those seemingly small changes into a new woman. A similar accomplishment can be observed in *Now, Voyager* (Rapper 1942), in which Bette Davis lets go of her old self and, consequently, of her glasses (Shingler 2008). As she admits feeling 'undressed' without her spectacles, her psychiatrist breaks them in half, adding, 'Good for you to feel that way'. To be more seductive, to become true women, girls have to let go of their glasses. Richard

S. Pandelakis (✉)
Université de Toulouse, Jean Jaurès, Toulouse, France
e-mail: saul.pandelakis@univ-tlse2.fr

© The Author(s), under exclusive license to Springer Nature Switzerland AG 2024
A. Thakkar et al. (eds.), *Border Masculinities*,
https://doi.org/10.1007/978-3-031-68050-2_9

171

Dyer speaks in such cases of a 'character development constructed through dress' (1998, p. 111). Just as the new 'outfit' puts the changed body on display, glasses and hair hint at a shift in personality on the face itself. It is thus not about a very concealing outfit here but a single, little accessory that has the power to change a character immensely. Mary Ann Doane depicts the role of glasses when associated with a female character:

> The woman who wears glasses constitutes one of the most intense visual cliches of the cinema. The image is a heavily marked condensation of motifs concerned with repressed sexuality, knowledge, visability (sic) and vision, intellectuality, and desire. The woman with glasses signifies simultaneously intellectuality and undesirability; but the moment she removes her glasses [...] she is transformed into spectacle, the very picture of desire. (Doane 1982, pp. 82–83)

In light of Doane's argument, the compulsive removal of glasses is one of the ways used by women to negotiate between identities perceived as incompatible. From the desexualised intellectual to the seductive lady, glasses work to bridge identities inasmuch as they separate them, this mere object operating as a line in the sand in the space of femininity. Hollywood films allow intelligent women to be seductive on the condition that they downplay their own talents, to perform their femininity according to the standards of seductiveness: Doris Day in *Teacher's Pet* (Seaton 1958) becomes a pinup, the bookseller lets go of her spinster attributes in *The Big Sleep*, as teenage Laney will later do in *She's All That* (Robert Iscove 1999). While it would certainly be relevant to focus on the glasses used by female characters, I would like to deploy the aforementioned proverbial assertion ('men don't make passes...') as a prompt to cast a wider net on this object, to investigate its role in the onscreen performativity of male bodies in entertainment films. Spectacles identify a very wide range of male and female characters, from nerds to serious scientists, from teachers to spinsters. Are glasses on screen bound to be dropped to signify newly found seductiveness? If so, what exact use do male characters make of glasses, and how does this usage connect to their masculinity and overall gender performance?

Masculinity and femininity are to be understood here as dynamic spaces of negotiations, across which characters can wander about in the course of a given fictional text. In this context, it seems at first that male and female characters use props similarly to navigate different and sometimes conflicting identities—notably the glasses. The scope of this essay obviously forbids me to list all the occurrences of glasses in American cinema, but two examples can quickly shed light on their instrumentality. In *The Big Sleep*, Bogart uses dark glasses to disguise himself as an 'egghead' before meeting and attracting, as his regular self without the glasses, the bespectacled bookseller mentioned earlier. Here, glasses stand out as more than an accessory. As significant as a full-body costume, they characterise the nerd, the harmless man who appears to be as intelligent as he is socially ineffective. Intellectualism, marked as passive, is a quality heroism needs to separate itself from, in this case in the form of two different settings, two different bookshops. The later case of *Executive Decision* (Baird 1996) is exemplary of this necessity for the wannabe hero to break from the realm of the mind. Faced with the necessity to take action and to become a true hero, Kurt Russell's character accidentally breaks his glasses, hereby 'mark[ing] his transition from a man who knows something about terrorism to one who does something about it' (Lichtenfeld 2007, p. 177).

The trope which sees a nerdy man become a hero (or conversely, a man taming his heroic identity by donning the nerd's attire) has never been more dramatically re-enacted than in the case of Superman. The character, both in comic books and on screen, uses the glasses as the powerful transforming device that articulates two opposite male identities, structured by a symbolically charged set of binaries (mind/body, passive/active, soft/hard, etc.). Taking Superman's seminal example as a cue for further inquiry into heroic male identities on screen, I wish to first scrutinise the use(s) of glasses in superhero narratives, from Richard Donner's 1978 feature to more recent productions in the subgenre. I aim to ground my argument by analysing earlier Hollywood productions in which glasses come to play a pivotal role. By positing the recurrence of the use of glasses as a semantic device, I will demonstrate that such use to shift from one identity to another is not only a requirement of the Superman canon but, more widely, a reworking of a primitive male *masquerade* in the context of superhero film. I will argue that Doane's coining of the term can intersect with Stanley Cavell's understanding of the 'dance of identity' (2005, p. 73), notably in the case of *Superman III* (Lester 1983).

Glasses can, of course, function as a mere sartorial element; however, they are also a material object, a product whose first function is to enable vision. While glasses provide fictional characters with the ability to engage in a transformative process, they are themselves two-sided, between visibility (including what they say of their owner) and functionality (what they

174   S. PANDELAKIS

do for them). I aim to shed light on this duality by first turning to Laura Mulvey's theory of 'the gaze' (1975). Her famous article has been widely discussed, and it is not my intention here to use Mulvey's framing of 'to-be-looked-at-ness' as a main theoretical tool. However, her approach will provide me with a foundation upon which to better understand the essential role of glasses in heroic and superheroic contexts. It will also prove a great resource as Mulvey considers the act of looking as a spatial process, where the spaces I described above as 'dynamic' incarnate and organise power relations. Giuliana Bruno's approach to cinema as an atlas (2002) will also provide me with useful theoretical tools to remap the performance of gender. Bodies can be said to inhabit spaces, but they are also spatial *components* of that space. Rethinking bodies in this fashion enables me to look at borders between identities, borders that are central in the making of 'gender architectonics' (Bruno 2002, p. 85). Finally, I aim to look at more recent productions (in both film and TV series) that indicate that the glasses masquerade, not yet obsolete, has been in part rewritten using new props—possibly bringing to bear an even more fluid and uncertain paradigm, especially in the context of TV with *Dexter* (2006–2013) and *Mr. Robot* (2015–).

From the clear-cut Superman model to more fluid performances, I will demonstrate that gender is produced on screen in spatial terms, according to a geography that engages familiar terrains, unknown outskirts and the policing of borders. This very text bears witness to a shift in my approach towards the hero's masquerade. While I started my work on the superhero masquerade hoping to uncover the fabric of heroism, my framework has somewhat shifted to investigate how these travels from one identity to another bespeak gender-transitioning acts—with a queer perspective that does not take 'masculinity' or 'feminity' as defined spaces or solid compounds, but rather as fluid, ever-changing sites of production (Halberstam 1998, p. 17; Butler 2014 [1993], p. x). As my examples will surely deploy a rather narrow array of white cis males, this choice should in no manner indicate that the performance of masculinity belongs to them, or that their performances do not affect female, non-white and/or trans bodies, to name a few. Considering gender in spatial terms allows me to blend the usual feminine/masculine terminology that often accompanies considerations based on gender. To back this original intuition, I draw again from Giuliana Bruno's understanding of the cinematic experience as a journey in space. Her observations make way for a spatialised understanding of gender performativity when she talks about the 'gender nomadism' (2002, p. 81) brought forth in specific places.

GLASSES AND LOOKED-AT-NESS

Laura Mulvey's article 'Visual Pleasure and Narrative Cinema' (1975) offers an insightful framework for the examination of glasses and the related experience of seeing. In her view, the gaze of the male protagonist is mirrored by the gaze of the male spectator and partakes of a male-centred perspective. Mulvey posits that the compulsion to look, interiorised by movies at large, follows a basic structure: 'cinematic codes create a gaze, a world, and an object, thereby producing an illusion cut to the measure of desire' (1975, p. 17). As men often issue the look, women are constantly made the *object* of this all-encompassing gaze. Male characters objectify women by gazing at them, thus making sure to control both the action and the space of the narrative. In this framework, looking means assigning a position to a female or feminised other, locating it in a space where they are deprived of agency. Mulvey goes on to show that female characters can inspire or motivate the action, yet they will rarely resolve the situation themselves. This firm grid has been widely discussed, notably by Richard Dyer, who, in his study of the male pinup, suggested that being subjected to the look did not necessarily equate with adopting a passive position (1982). It is also necessary to note that, in mainstream film, and mainly only from the eighties onward, several productions have worked around or against the set of expectations tied to female characters. Focusing on male characters, however, I would like to use Mulvey's article as a starting point inasmuch as the categories she outlines (looking/being looked at) are warped by the use of glasses. Mulvey hints that this gendered setup extends beyond domination solely over female characters when she states: 'The male protagonist is free to command the stage, a stage of spatial illusion in which he articulates the look and creates the action' (1975, p. 13).

In this case, looking seems to implicate the relationship between a character—who is, true, often male—and his surroundings. Mulvey's system has proven to be quite clear-cut, but a quick look at several bespectacled characters, male or female, proves that men can actually entertain a similarly complex relationship to the act of seeing, understood as a vector of power. *Bringing up Baby* (Hawks 1938) offers one of the first examples of a 'square' on screen. The glasses conceal Cary Grant's good looks, and an

176 S. PANDELAKIS

affected pronunciation contributes to further downplay the appeal ordinarily associated with his persona, even if it should be noted that the tendency to wear a disguise is also a part of Grant's persona on screen (Cohan 1992, p. 397). He seems at first to endure the same anti-glasses tyranny experienced by *The Big Sleep*'s bookseller and Bette Davis in *Now, Voyager*. As soon as the glasses are off, Katharine Hepburn sanctions his new appearance by observing: 'You're so good-looking without glasses'. Interestingly, though, the glasses do not help Grant's character, Dr. Huxley, to see the world around him more clearly; they are not a vector of power. The scene at the restaurant where Huxley seems bound to destroy everything he touches (including Hepburn's cocktail dress) is significant in that regard. The situation later builds up around the chase of Baby, the eponymous leopard, with a snowballing turn of events consistent with the conventions of the comedy genre. Glasses, and more broadly, the very act of seeing are then made pointless and contribute to the portrayal of a man losing his grip on his surroundings: he is dominated by space, and the space of his masculinity is consequently rewritten. Huxley even loses his spectacles during the chase and later states: 'The things I have been doing today I could do just as well with my eyes closed'. While women's glasses function first and foremost as a 'signifier [...] of unattractiveness' (Doane 1982, p. 82), men's glasses are usually connected, though not in Grant's case here, to the very act of seeing, perceiving, and furthermore, participating in a more or less successful understanding of the world. Audrey Hepburn comes herself to this sour realisation when she addresses Cary Grant in *Charade* (Donen 1963): stating that he does not really need his glasses, she tries them on and realises with embarrassment the extent of her mistake. Glasses therefore enter the film's discourse as a potentially damaging fashion accessory for Cary Grant's image but, very quickly, they are reestablished as a functional object—following Mulvey, as an object of potential control over space.

Over the years, comic books and movies alike have underlined the necessity for the superhero to take on a disguise that protects his identity and ensures the safety of his loved ones. What better way for Superman to go unacknowledged than to dress as his exact opposite? The bland Clark Kent has come to incarnate the other side of Superman, prompting comic book readers and filmgoers to wonder how Kent could get away with it and how Lois Lane (whose face, unencumbered by glasses, suggests she has perfectly good sight) did not realise her colleague and Superman were one person. Being looked at, Superman also acts as an onlooker: his almighty gaze enables him, for instance, to check the health status of Lois's lungs (in the 1978 version) and operates as a quick x-ray exam after an accident (*Superman Returns*, Singer 2006). Scott Bukatman interprets Superman's eyes as the core of his heroism, speaking of 'a magistral gaze upon a known and controlled urban landscape' (2003, p. 197). Kent's glasses and his perceived inability to see exist in tension with the superhero's super look. Supposedly meant to correct an imperfect gaze, the glasses come to play the role of a mask, as many commentators argue (Bukatman 2003; Brownie and Graydon 2015, p. 20). This transparent mask (Bukatman 2003, p. 213), alongside the grey suit, construct Kent as an embodiment of the average modern man. Bukatman thus synthesises the relationship between Superman and his alter ego: 'Superman and Clark subvert one another: the man who sees everything meets the man who is not seen' (2003, p. 214). Engle makes a similar point by stating that 'Clark Kent […] is the epitome of visible invisibility […] someone whose extraordinary normality makes him disappear in a crowd' (Engle 1987, p. 85). Both of Superman's identities are extreme: one is highly visible, thanks to his stunts and colourful costume; the other is almost impossible to locate. How those two radically different personalities cohabit has much to do with the glasses, a prop that stands at the border between them.

Heroic Geographies: The Blind Spot

As if glasses had a life of their own, they are constantly put on and off in the various Superman narratives. In 1978, the switching between the two personalities was a central comedic highlight: in a significant scene, the audience sees Superman visiting an enamoured Lois, then leaving right before Kent appears at the door. While Lois goes off-screen to get ready for dinner, Clark remains at the centre of the frame, enacting a short series of micro-gestures that give shape to an ever-returning temptation.[1] Removing his glasses, he straightens his back and boasts the iconic Superman grin—only to realise he cannot let Lois know the truth and has to allow Superman to *fade into* Clark Kent's image. I want to emphasise here how this process is ultimately visual. The transformation, as well as the passing from one identity to another, is processed through the cinematic image, ripped at its core to open a new, heroic space. While the transformation (necessarily incomplete since Superman is wearing Kent's costume) involves the whole body, it is mainly triggered by the glasses. Putting them on and then removing them constitutes a performance

(Brownie and Graydon 2015, p. 76) and, moreover, a choreography that epitomises a ciphered space between the two identities.

What I am more interested in, then, is neither Superman nor Clark Kent, but the transition from one persona to another, and how the glasses help with this shift. Mary Ann Doane's framing of the term 'masquerade',[2] stemming from Joan Riviere's original coining of the term (1929, pp. 306–308), can help us understand this crucial transformation. Doane defines feminine masquerade as a process of constructing one's own gender, which she coins as 'a hyperbolisation of the accoutrements of femininity' (1982, p. 82). It can be perceived as a display of excess, but it is one of the main ways gendered identities become assertively visible. Since femininity is deemed more flexible and appears more evidently constructed (notably through masquerade), women can easily shift their identities using various priming rituals (makeup, hairdos, etc.). Ann Chisholm, drawing from Lacan and Doane, suggests that every masculine attempt to assert itself through display is in itself feminising (2000, p. 141). Using dress to reveal his identity, the male superhero incidentally defuses the masculinity embodied by his superpowers. The costume and the abilities seem here to work in contradictory ways: building one's masculine power leads to deconstructing it.

Much has been done to define each facet of the Superman character and their respective cultural implications. To solve the character's doubleness, commentators often weigh in favour of one or the other of Superman's identities (Hoët 2007), alternately choosing one or the other as the 'true' identity. The masquerade, which acts as a gendered performance, seems to carry along with it an understanding of gender as an expression of an essential truth. My focus being on the trajectories that tie identities, the border(s) between them, rather than the identities themselves, I shall try to overcome such a binary outlook. The Superman movies continuously interrogate the essence of the link imperfectly unifying Superman and Clark Kent and provide different explanations each time. The space between the two personalities seems more telling than the personalities themselves: the more Kent and Superman are defined as opposites, the more their connection seems impossible and calls for mediation. The transformation from one identity to the next then resorts to emblematic shortcuts: phone booths and revolving doors function as magical dressing rooms; as for the ripping of the shirt, it suggests a clothes change—only to see this process hidden by way of editing. This is another question possibly hanging on the audience's minds: *how* does he put the costume on?

Generally, Hollywood productions do not seem keen on showing men dressing and have found many ways to circumvent this issue.[3] As feminine dressing and undressing rituals are frequently integrated into a film, its masculine equivalent leaves room for uncertainty and anxiety. Here we return to dressing as a signifier of gender difference. Therefore, the simple act of changing clothes is marked by erasure every time and produces a paradox: if we wish to see Superman—the man with a super, all-powerful look—our own vision as a spectator has to be blurred.

Between the prowess of Superman and Clark Kent's dull life, there is an operation that cannot be seen. We, the audience, do not know if this blank spot stands for a man pulling up tights or for a magical operation that would enable him to get dressed. Our not knowing is compensated for by our *seeing*, but imperfectly so: the image of Superman follows the image of Kent, and the magic used here is as much the hero's prerogative as a twist resulting from the possibilities of the cinematic apparatus. *Superman III* offers an interesting starting point to help us understand the function of this blind spot holding together the superhero's two identities. In the opening scene, Clark Kent gets caught in the city's chaos, which results in a collective burlesque dance, where every little accident snowballs into a major disaster. When this situation escalates, Kent can no longer discreetly help the Metropolis denizens and chooses to transform into Superman. Importantly, it is not a phone booth that gets used as a fitting room this time but a photo booth. As I have argued elsewhere (Pandelakis 2009), the use of this specific prop is strongly reminiscent of Fred Astaire's dance in *The Band Wagon* (1953), identified by Stanley Cavell as 'a dance of identity' (2005, p. 73). Just as Astaire jumps from one attraction to the other in the Penny Arcade, Kent effortlessly goes from one disaster to another. Fred Astaire does not linger in the photo booth, which is a mere accessory in his celebratory dance. Clark Kent could be said to be dancing as well, but the pictures that result from this performance fail to solve the identity issue. When Superman comes out of the booth, all dressed up and ready to operate, he is careful to take the incriminating pictures of his switch. He rips the photo strip (composed of four shots) in two, giving the Superman half to a young passer-by. The superhero thus protects his identity as Clark Kent, but the series of photos, as they are shown to us, reaffirm the existence of this blank area standing between the two identities. This *locus*, because of its materialisation through the photographic medium, seems to simultaneously stem from space and time negotiations. The absence of the *in-between* pictures speaks not so much of a forbidden space (for we cannot step into the phone booth with Superman) as of an erased chunk of time. In the case of Astaire dancing to reassert his identity, Cavell is prompted to ask: 'Just how and where has this man managed this metamorphosis or quasi-metempsychosis (not finding a new body but finding his body anew)?' (2005, p. 72). This question, partially answered by Astaire's performance, is applied to the figure of Superman only to remain unsolved—if not altogether unsolvable.

Most superheroes have to transform. Iron Man must put on armour while Hulk must rip his clothes to become his super-human self. Being superheroic means being able to achieve a transition, to move from A to B. One could argue that this transformation is merely a morphing, and the reason why we do not see Superman transform has been, until recently, the lack of technical ability to portray him doing so. If Superman does not dress up but organically evolves from one state to another, morphing should reveal the details of this change. Morphing is a staple of the early tales of body doubles. The 1931 version of *Dr. Jekyll and Mr. Hyde* (Rouben Mamoulian), evidently unable to display a harmonious transformation, proceeds by breaking this process into small time units, linking them by means of shots fading into one another. This approach implicates tedious make-up work to construct the appearance of the face in each time unit. Such complicated processes can be avoided, as in the *Incredible Hulk* TV series (1978–1982): the body of Bruce Banner being dramatically different from the Hulk's, the transition is veiled by radical choices in editing, such as a close-up on the squinting of an eye, which comes to signify an entire body swap. With CGI, morphing ceased to be a limit, and all sorts of transformations became available on screen (from *The Mask* (Russell 1994) to *The Matrix* (Wachowski and Wachowski 1999), or more recently *Wolverine* (Mangold 2013)). Superheroes, however, did not all benefit from this new possibility. The Hulk can now organically stem from the various bodies of Eric Bana, Edward Norton or Mark Ruffalo, but in many instances, Superman is still seen ripping his shirt open and resorting to phone booths (*Superman Returns*). When showing bodies turning into their other is made possible, some filmmakers choose not to, here indicating that the technical limitations never were the issue. Between the common man and the super-self, a distance subsists: the border between two male identities swells up and becomes a space of uncertainty, to be inhabited in the course of a dance. This dance, in geographic terms, gives expression to a form of *horror vacui* (Mattern 2021), as if constant movement could veil the empty foundations of male heroism.

While *Superman Returns* replays the old phone booth paradigm, the more recent rewriting of the character in *Man of Steel* (Snyder 2013) seems to indicate an interesting shift in the making of the superhero. The very title points out a more primitive outlook on the superhero. Instead of using actual names, the phrase 'man of steel' clouds the character's traditional duality: he is made of steel (superheroic) but is also just a man (the 'normal' side). Very early in the narrative, the matter of hiding behind a mask is made entirely pointless, since Lois Lane finds him after what seems a rather short investigation. Rather than using the names 'Superman' or 'Clark', which tie the character to his doubleness, the film emphasises the superhero's alien status and his Krypton origins by using the name 'Kal-El' beyond the scope of its opening scene. Kal-El is also first seen on screen as a bearded, bare-torso man surrounded by flames, an iconography very far from the usual Superman canon. Later, the character appears as a drifter going from town to town in northern America, a framing that ties him to the maladjusted veteran Rambo in *First Blood* (Kotcheff 1982). In this movie, contemporary to the first *Superman* franchise, there is no room for duality as Rambo is a rock-solid, inescapable identity. Far from using any type of masquerade to move from an obsolete version of himself to a renewed self, the soldier is faced with the inability to come back to normalcy. Displaced to American territory, the heroic repertoire of war combat appears hysterical and pathological. It is thus quite telling to see *Man of Steel* openly quoting *First Blood* and associating Superman with a set of values so far removed from the character's filmic tradition. This 'new' Superman still navigates the space of the self, this time tied with national identity as well as gender: marked by Rambo's visual heritage, he carries the burden of trauma after being displaced from his Krypton homeland.

This framing of Superman is not isolated and parallels other rewrites of superhero narratives. In the first *Spider-Man* series (2002–2007), Peter Parker's identity as a nerd is frequently stressed narratively (through canonical high school scenes) and visually (by showing him wearing thick, black glasses). These glasses appear sometimes broken (signifying Peter's vulnerability) but are most often shed. In *Spider-Man 2* (2004), the loss of his powers is first manifested by the return of myopia, stressed by a blurry POV shot and the comeback of the glasses. While the glasses are less central in Spider-Man's performance as such, they still signify the hero's impeded relationship with normalcy. When Peter regains his powers in the same story arc, the glasses fall on the ground—the camera panning on the devastated city of New York. This is no longer Peter's point of view that

182 S. PANDELAKIS

the glasses embody but ours; *we* are the normal people gazing through the glasses, while Spider-Man has recovered his true self and gone on to perform high feats. This use of the glasses is rather ambiguous, and in no case isolated. *Superman Returns* makes use of an identical shot framing young Clark's body behind his spectacles: if the object is not as such a point of entry in an elaborate masquerade, it continues to incarnate, on a symbolic level, the touchpoint between two bodies.[4]

HOODS AND CAPES: THE SPACE OF NORMALCY

All superheroes deal with normalcy, pictured either as the extra, time-consuming obligations of domestic life (*Spider-Man III* (Raimi 2007); *Kick-Ass 2* (Wadlow 2013)) or as an unattainable state of bliss where superheroic duties would cease to exist (*Superman II*, (Lester, 1981) *Avengers: Age of Ultron* (Whedon 2015)). Between the superhero and the normal man, there always remains a space, an in-between that presents the character to be whole. M. Night Shyamalan's *Unbreakable* (2000) chooses normalcy as a core issue but unexpectedly tears it from the traditional dualities that accompany its depiction. Here, Bruce Willis's character, David Dunn, accidentally discovers his powers after surviving a train wreck. This process of revelation is prompted by a mysterious gallery owner, and Dunn's own son soon urges him to further investigate his own exceptionality. While most superhero films stress their character's uniqueness by repeatedly displaying their abilities to transform, *Unbreakable* stretches the transformative ability to the length of a movie, with the climactic feat or self-discovery coming much later, in the closing sequences of the feature.

This awareness of his abilities slowly emerges because the powers are not exactly powers; they are small differences, a potential that makes Dunn slightly out of the ordinary. This gentle, incremental approach tends to erase the usual colourful depictions of the superheroic self. Dunn does not wear a unitard, nor does he climb walls or choose a dazzling pseudonym to brand his exploits—he is even very reluctant to perform exploits in the first place. Shyamalan seems to methodically peel all traces of a common superheroic visual culture off Willis's body, relying for the cinematography on a grey-blue palette that contributes to normalise the actor's heroic persona. This process prompts Brownie and Graydon to observe that the director 'indirectly position[s] its hero as a superhero without a costume' (2015, p. 52). While *Unbreakable* sheds many aspects of the comic book heritage, it is inaccurate that the costume is entirely displaced. The process of erasure engaged by Shyamalan operates as a blank space open for rewriting. This erasure can be understood, in a sense, as the opening-up of the in-between space—the small space that was so carefully located and contained in the case of the early Superman movies. Shyamalan is also aware of the pop aesthetics of superheroes, but these are circumscribed to the graphic space of comic books and to the flamboyant attire of Elijah Price. Dunn's costume, if it deserves such a name, is barely an object; it takes the most primitive form of a raincoat, which, when backlit, makes the ordinary man look like a caped and hooded figure. Shyamalan thus makes sure to construct this visibility through the cinematic apparatus rather than positing its reality in the narrative's world. The existence of the hero as an intensely mediated figured is made all the more visible when Dunn's son discovers a crude sketch of a mysterious hero on the morning paper's front page.

Unbreakable remains unique in its normalising yet non-comedic approach to the superhero. As a first standalone feature, disconnected from any source material, Shyamalan's film appears rather isolated in an ongoing era of superhero extravaganza, where less familiar characters see their adventures brought to the screen (Ant-Man, Green Arrow) and franchises are rebooted as soon as they come to a close (see the *Amazing Spider-Man* instalments, Webb 2012, 2014). I wish to argue here that while the glasses (and the associated double body paradigm) still loom over superhero productions, *Unbreakable* seems to have inspired an opposing trend. While the male masquerade remains a point of reference, a different trope seems at work in superhero narratives, especially since the 2000s. The figure of the hooded man, while being anything but new, has been reinscribed in several superhero vehicles and, more unexpectedly, in fictions that question the hero/normal man binary without strictly adhering to the superhero mythology.

Looking at literature first, and then film and TV, one cannot help but notice the number of caped and hooded characters. The hood is not always a supplement to the cape, as Superman clearly demonstrates. Brownie and Graydon remind us that it can often be seen as vital to show one's face as if to indicate the honesty and good faith of one's acts (2015, pp. 37–38). In this context, the hood plays as a middle-ground component between the act of wearing a mask (Spider-Man 2002) and the complete refusal to do so (Superman). Hoods on screen are initially connected with a medieval imaginary, from the various incarnations of Robin Hood to *The Name of the Rose* (Annaud 1986). Subsequently, the genre of fantasy has tapped into this reservoir of images provided by medieval iconography and has made extensive use of the hooded warrior figure: one can think of the frequently hooded Jedi characters in the *Star Wars* franchise. The examples of Aragorn in *The Lord of the Rings* (Jackson 2001) or of Tyrion Lannister in *Game of Thrones* (2011–2019) show that the hood functions not only as an element of generic convention but also as a plot device when both characters, using the garment to conceal their identities, end up dramatically revealing who they are—to the audience or to the characters in the narrative. The garment is also infused with a heavy set of connotations in popular and media culture, from its representations in the Unabomber portraits to its critical role in the killing of Trayvon Martin. These examples show that the hood-turned-hoodie carries dark overtones because of its association with famous villainous figures (The Unabomber, for example), which can in turn villainise people, especially people of colour (Lammy 2019). In the context of fiction, then, the hood can at once delay the apparition of a hero but also pepper the bland figure of the white male hero by tapping into race and class signifiers.

Unbreakable reworks the superhero figure by carving out all excessive traits attached to the hooded figure. In a sense, it operates the same erasure process on the hooded silhouette visual trope. Dunn's attire remains a simple raincoat, made to carry a richly layered set of former incarnations (Robin Hood, Zorro, medieval and fantasy warriors, etc.). Regardless of the rich semiotic process involved here, the hood still exists as a material, urban, contemporary piece of clothing. The same mechanism is at work in the TV series *Dexter* (2006–2013). Dexter Morgan is a forensics technician who is pathologically drawn to kill; using the code taught to him by his father, he only murders those who have themselves committed crimes, thus sublimating his urges into a vigilante's mission. In the second season of the series, the discovery of several of Dexter's victims and of their status as criminal offenders prompts some to create the 'Dark Defender' character, a media figure soon exploited in a comic book format. While Dexter has never intended to heroicise his own actions as a killer, he seems to subconsciously recreate a frame for such interpretation, sporting a hooded coat that contributes to the unwilling mythification of the Dark Defender. The hooded black silhouette functions visually in the same terms as Dunn's: it becomes a surface of inscription for fantasies and clichés, all removed from Dexter's reality. While the character is in no way a superhero, the trappings of the double identity (between serial killings and domestic life) force him to 'dance' repeatedly from one version of the self to the other. The two facets of Dexter are intricately intertwined, and no blank space safely enables the viewer to distinguish one from the other. In this framework, the hooded coat is just another signifier of Dexter's fluid identity, who no longer dances his identity, but smoothly binds one with the other.

Mr. Robot more recently reinvests the endless possibilities tied to the hood trope.[5] Elliot Alderson is a young tech engineer/hacker who, like Dexter, uses his professional skills to cover for his illegal activities. This double life requires the character to lie, hide and construct ways for himself to maintain both existences, although he, unlike Dexter, frequently considers giving up on one or the other activity. The hood is further emptied from previous connotations as it is materialised in the form of an average piece of unisex clothing, the hoodie. Unlike Kent's glasses, Dunn's raincoat or Dexter's hooded cape, this hoodie is never specifically focalised. It is associated with a range of clothes that are so average and plain-looking that they contribute to hypernormalise Elliot's appearance in all contexts: during his free time, Elliot always dons the same hyper-normal attire (black jeans, sneakers and said hoodie) while his work outfit (grey shirt, straight black pants) works as the epitome of the transparent working man's image. Elliot is frequently seen putting on his hood, especially when he sets himself on retrieving intel valuable to his hacking activities or when going out on a variety of missions. The hood comes flawlessly on and off in the same manner that Elliot evolves in various circles, from the high-end Evil Corp executives' lobbies to the underground space of the *fsociety* community. No longer a trigger for transformation or symbolic associations, the hood is just a hood: the ultimate sign of invisibility—one that does not get conjured by any superheroic alter ego. Here, male heroism seems to face a dead-end: while it is still possible to combine identities, even more so in the digital age, none of these personalities offer much stability. Elliot is damned to be a hooded figure: unlike Kal-El, he is not a nobody merged with a superhero; he is himself the blank space, no one and everyone. As movement is still key for characters like Dexter or Elliott, their geographies paradoxically appear to be without borders, as they do not include a space for change: they are, in themselves, change remapped as a masculine condition.

Conclusion: Dancing Without an Alter Ego

Let us return to what originally sparked this venture across masculinities: the spectacles. Interestingly, the glasses and the performance of taking them on and off stand for what *we* cannot see and what must remain unseen for the character to keep on existing. The figure of the superhero condenses far too many gazes: Superman's super look dominating the city, Kent's supposedly imperfect gaze, Lois's deficient gaze that cannot recognise Superman under the guise, and finally, our gaze, left with these identities to reconcile. Glasses, in the case of Superman, stand for a transition, a traversing of borders, that can otherwise not be represented. The transition from one identity to another then materialises as the site of several limits. First, the very technical means by which such change is achieved can come into consideration, but as of today, the development of CGI has not unveiled Superman's dark territory. The second limitation concerns the mapping of gender in Hollywood features: men cannot be shown dressing, at the risk of being feminised. What should appear on screen, then? It seems it is not so much about limitations as it is about borders, about the lines traced by the bodies as they move on screen and inhabit different skins. The most telling limit can be seen as a border, a philosophical one: to be dual, one has to accept discontinuity in terms of body and space. Superman thus comes to epitomise a schizophrenic split that spans beyond the psyche. To have a double personality, one must cope with a *double body*, itself a stand-in for a double space, and the blurry line that zigzags between the two. The space between the two bodily spaces is made as narrow as possible and must remain in place to deflate any potential gender uncertainty. Put another way, the *in-between* space that makes Superman stay heroic must remain blank, but for the transformation to exist, something must stand in its place. The removal of glasses thus triggers a discrete performance in that space, one that fills in for a greater one.

At the turn of the century, a slightly different paradigm seems to have slowly contaminated the superhero mythology on screen. I choose to say 'contaminated' because, unlike the glasses trope, which signals itself quite ostentatiously, the hood trope's very nature is to be discreet rather than discrete, thus making the masquerade less theatrical. Glasses are a part of Clark Kent's normal attire, but their normality is counterbalanced by their unique power to spark a transformative process. Donning a hood could suggest a transformation, but the gesture is of the most minimal kind, and it is the very nature of an otherwise unremarkable garment to invite frequent manipulations between *on* and *off* states. Furthermore, the on-and-off pattern does not reflect clear-cut personas anymore; if anything, it points to a fluid, ever-changing identity, as in the cases of *Dexter* of *Mr. Robot*. Dexter Morgan and Elliot Alderson exist on the base of several layered identities and go almost seamlessly from one to the other—situating their potential heroism in a blending of boundaries akin to the most recent masquerade of *Lupin* (2021–). Appropriated by Shyamalan as a primitive superheroic signifier or full of medieval connotations, the hood (and its contemporary form, the urban hoodie) is at once a blank space and a crowded semantic sign. Meanwhile, the colourful excesses of Superman and Captain America's costumes have been somehow tamed in more recent productions (*Man of Steel, Captain America: The Winter Soldier* (Russo and Russo 2014)), possibly indicating a wider process of erasure. While the superheroic visual legacy gets overwritten, *Mr. Robot* goes on to show that dualities endure, in a more complex and fluid manner, under the guise of a very simple, very ordinary hood. Elliot Alderson can put it on and off all he wants; there is no alter ego to turn (dance?) to.

NOTES

1. It is worth noting that two masquerades are, in fact, taking place in this scene, thus doubling the 'visible/not visible' dichotomy so central in Superman's on-screen mythology. While the identities of the superhero are shown flickering here, Lois's transition to a more formal attire happens off-screen.
2. By Doane's own admission, her concept of the 'masquerade' differs from Joan Riviere's seminal coining of the term in 1929.
3. Sometimes, the parody combines the play with glasses and the latent feminisation in male grooming, as in Woody Allen's *Take the Money and Run* (1970). We see the actor facing his mirror, getting ready for a date, trying to casually swing his glasses, then sliding them in his pockets. Eventually, he goes out of his apartment, only to come back a few seconds later. During the lengthy grooming process, he forgets to put his pants on, an omission that counters any masculinising effects his grooming could have had.
4. This shot is also a nod to Alfred Hitchcock's *Strangers on a Train* (1951). In this instance, the glasses also embody an absent look, the look of a woman being assaulted.

5. The use of a hood for disguising purposes is so frequent that it has been coined by the contributors of the TV Tropes website. The trope is derided as an unrealistic convention that sees heroes using hoods in combats where they need peripheral vision. See online the 'In the Hood' n.d. entry, https://tvtropes.org/pmwiki/pmwiki.php/Main/InTheHood.

WORKS CITED

Allen, Woody, Director. 1970. *Take the Money and Run*. Cinerama Releasing Corporation.

Annaud, Jean-Jacques, Director. 1986. *The Name of the Rose*. Twentieth Century Fox Film Corporation.

Baird, Stuart, Director. 1996. *Executive Decision*. Warner Bros.

Brownie, Barbara, and Danny Graydon. 2015. *The Superhero Costume: Identity and Disguise in Fact and Fiction*. London; New York: Bloomsbury Academic.

Bruno, Giuliana. 2002. *Atlas of Emotion: Journeys in Art, Architecture, and Film*. Brooklyn, NY: Verso.

Bukatman, Scott. 2003. *Matters of Gravity: Special Effects and Supermen in the 20th Century*. Durham, NC: Duke University Press.

Butler, Judith. 2014 [1993]. *Bodies That Matter: On the Discursive Limits of 'Sex'*. New York: Routledge.

Cavell, Stanley. 2005. *Philosophy the Day after Tomorrow*. Cambridge, MA: Belknap Press of Harvard University Press.

Chisholm, Ann. 2000. Missing Persons and Bodies of Evidence. *Camera Obscura* 15: 122.

Cohan, Steven. 1992. Cary Grant in the Fifties: Indiscretions of the Bachelor's Masquerade. *Screen* 33: 394–412.

Doane, Mary Ann. 1982. Film and the Masquerade: Theorising the Female Spectator. *Screen* 23: 74–88.

Donen, Stanley, Director, 1963. *Charade*. Universal Pictures.

Donner, Richard, Director 1978. *Superman*. Warner Bros.

Dyer, Richard. 1982. Don't Look Now. *Screen* 23: 61–73.

Dyer, Richard, and Paul McDonald. 1998. *Stars*. London: BFI Pub.

Engle, Gary D. 1987. What Makes Superman so Darned American? In *Superman at Fifty: The Persistence of a Legend*, ed. Dennis Dooley and Gary D. Engle, 88–95. Diane Pub Co.

Halberstam, Jack. 1998. *Female Masculinity*. Durham, NC: Duke University Press.

Hawks, Howard, Director. 1938. *Bringing Up Baby*. RKO Radio Pictures.

———, Director. 1946. *The Big Sleep*. Warner Bros.

Hitchcock, Alfred, Director. 1951. *Strangers on a Train*. Warner Bros.
Hoët, Sebastien. 2007. Le cristal et la trace, Portrait de Superman en messie impuissant. *Tausend Augen* 31: 23–26.
In the Hood. n.d. TV Tropes, *tvtropes.com*, online. http://tvtropes.org/pmwiki/pmwiki.php/Main/InTheHood
Iscove, Robert, Director. 1999. *She's All That*. Miramax.
Jackson, Peter, Director. 2001. *The Lord of the Rings: The Fellowship of the Ring*. New Line.
Kotcheff, Ted, Director. 1982. *First Blood*. Orion Pictures.
Lammy, David. 2019. Why There's Nothing Scary about a Black Man in a Hoodie. *The Guardian*, February 13. https://www.theguardian.com/world/2019/feb/13/david-lammy-on-why-theres-nothing-scary-about-a-black-man-in-a-hoodie.
Lester, Richard, Director. 1981. *Superman II*. Warner Bros.
Lester, Richard, Director. 1983. *Superman III*. Warner Bros.
Lichtenfeld, Eric. 2007. *Action Speaks Louder: Violence, Spectacle, and the American Action Movie*. Middletown, CT: Wesleyan University Press.
Mamoulian, Rouben, Director. 1931. *Dr. Jekyll and Mr. Hyde*. Paramount Pictures.
Mangold, James, Director. 2013. *Wolverine*. Twentieth Century Fox Film Corporation.
Manos, James, Jr. Developer and Writer. 2006–2013. *Dexter*. Netflix.
Mattern, Shannon. 2021. How to Map Nothing. *Places Journal*.
Minnelli, Vincente, Director. 1953. *The Band Wagon*. MGM.
Mulvey, Laura. 1975. Visual Pleasure and Narrative Cinema. *Screen* 16: 6–18.
Pandelakis, Saul. 2009. Petits arrangements avec la normalité. In *Du Héros Aux Super Héros: Mutations Cinématographiques*, ed. Claude Forest, 209–220. Paris: Presses Sorbonne Nouvelle.
Raimi, Sam, Director. 2002. *Spider-Man*. Columbia Pictures.
———, Director. 2004. *Spider-Man 2*. Columbia Pictures.
———, Director. 2007. *Spider-Man 3*. Columbia Pictures.
Rapper, Irving, Director. 1942. *Now, Voyager*. Warner Bros.
Riviere, Joan. 1929. Womanliness as a Masquerade. *International Journal of Psycho-Analysis* 9: 303–313.
Russell, Chuck, Director. 1994. *The Mask*. New Line Cinema.
Russo, Anthony, and Joe Russo, Director. 2014. *Captain America: The Winter Soldier*. Walt Disney Studios Motion Pictures.
Seaton, George, Director. 1958. *Teacher's Pet*. Paramount Pictures.
Shingler, Martin. 2008. Bette Davis Made over in Wartime: The Feminisation of an Androgynous Star in Now, Voyager (1942). *Film History* 20: 269–280.
Shyamalan, M. Night, Director. 2000. *Unbreakable*. Buena Vista Pictures.
Singer, Bryan, Director. 2006. *Superman Returns*. Warner Bros.
Snyder, Zack, Director. 2013. *Man of Steel*. Warner Bros.

Wachowski, Lana, and Lilly Wachowski, Directors. 1999. *The Matrix.* Warner Bros.
Wadlow, Jeff, Director. 2013. *Kick-Ass 2.* Universal Pictures.
Webb, Marc, Director. 2012. *The Amazing Spider-Man.* Columbia Pictures.
———, Director. 2014. *The Amazing Spider-Man 2.* Columbia Pictures.
Whedon, Joss, Director. 2015. *Avengers: Age of Ultron.* Walt Disney Studios Motion Pictures.

CHAPTER 10

Reconfiguring Masculinities: Generic Hybridisation, Postfeminist Fatherhood and Queer Readings in *Les Misérables*

Eleonora Sammartino

From page to screen, *Les Misérables* has established itself for its cultural importance and long-lasting popularity across different countries (Grossman and Stephens 2015, pp. 2–3, Behr 1989, pp. 140–142). After a gestation of over twenty years, the publication of the novel by Victor Hugo in 1862 was welcomed as an immediate international blockbuster owing to 'a carefully orchestrated promotional campaign' (Grossman and Stephens 2015, p. 1). Since then, *Les Misérables* has been transposed innumerable times onto a variety of media, from film to manga; among these, the 1985 stage musical remains the most celebrated adaptation (Grossman and Stephens 2015 p. 3). Originally conceived as a concept album in French by Alain Boublil and Claude-Michel Schönberg, this sung-through mega-musical was brought to London by producer Cameron Mackintosh and the Royal Shakespeare Company, with an English libretto by Herbert Kretzmer, and direction by Trevor Nunn and John Caird. Like the novel,

E. Sammartino (✉)
University of Southampton, Southampton, UK
e-mail: E.Sammartino@soton.ac.uk

© The Author(s), under exclusive license to Springer Nature Switzerland AG 2024
A. Thakkar et al. (eds.), *Border Masculinities*,
https://doi.org/10.1007/978-3-031-68050-2_10

191

the show was an instant success despite the critical panning (Nightingale and Palmer 2013, pp. 30–32). Hollywood's interest was piqued, but a screen adaptation concretised only in 2012. Co-produced by Mackintosh, Working Title, and Universal Pictures, the musical was directed by Tom Hooper, featuring an international cast. The film grossed more than $442 million worldwide and earned three Academy Awards and a large fanbase, mixed reviews notwithstanding (Box Office Mojo, n.d.).

While being an Anglo-American co-production mostly shot in Britain, *Les Misérables* firmly situates itself in the Hollywood musical tradition, adopting and adapting its conventions.[1] The musical genre has been inherently intertextual and self-referential since its origins, due to its reliance on pre-existing material and the recycling of its antecedents, as Jane Feuer (1993, p. 93) highlights. Michael Dunne (2004, p. 147) further cites allusions, parodies, and references to other texts at the level of sources, generic conventions, and style that audiences of the genre can recognise. Although already characterised by a degree of synergy and crossover in the studio and immediate post-studio period, the musical has been increasingly defined by the intensification of a multidirectional exchange between different media and industries since the 1980s (see Griffin 2018; Donnelly and Carroll 2018; Lobalzo Wright 2018; Kessler 2020; Lobalzo Wright and Shearer 2021). A great variety of sources is employed intertextually in adaptations from the stage such as *Evita* (Parker 1996) and *Chicago* (Marshall 2002) as well as in remakes of older musicals, such as *Fame* (Tancharoen 2009) and *Footloose* (Brewer 2011), or auteurist takes on the classics of the genre, like *La La Land* (Chazelle 2016), and jukebox musicals based on pop music hits, such as *Moulin Rouge!* (Luhrmann 2001), *Across the Universe* (Taymor 2007), *Mamma Mia!* (Lloyd 2008) and its sequel *Mamma Mia! Here We Go Again* (Parker 2018). Many contemporary musicals are further characterised by a more overt hybridisation, another process that draws from pre-existing material and conventions of different film genres on a semantic-syntactic level. *Les Misérables* exemplifies this trend, both as an adaptation, in its intertextual relations with its stratified sources, and as a hybrid between the musical and the recently revived historical epic (see Russell 2007; Santas 2007; Burgoyne 2011; Elliott 2014).[2]

I argue that intertextuality and hybridity are key to the understanding of the film in dialogue with its sources and the socio-cultural context in which it has been produced and consumed, with particular reference to a reconfiguration of masculinities in contemporary society. Whereas Hugo's work and other adaptations from the novel have been extensively explored, scholarship on this film is still emerging, mainly concentrating on the study of individual characters, the process of adaptation, or musicological aspects (Beaghton 2015; Gleizes 2015; Sapiro 2017). Yet, I maintain that the consideration of the film's location in the contemporary musical landscape and Hollywood conventions, and the specificity of the film medium are fundamental to the understanding of the inherently political value of this text in relation to gender discourses. In this analysis of *Les Misérables*, I will demonstrate how the adoption of the generic conventions of the historical epic informs the performance of an ideal masculinity in the musical, which is constructed through the prism of postfeminist fatherhood (Hamad 2014), and closely connected with discourses of nationhood and Christian self-sacrifice. This configuration of masculinity questions the borders between the public sphere, identified with active citizenship, and the private, conventionally associated with the feminine domestic, charging fatherhood with political meanings that resonate with a contemporary context. In the film, this ideal masculinity is articulated through the complementarity between the protagonist Jean Valjean (Hugh Jackman) and his antagonist Javert (Russell Crowe). This duality further negotiates the borders between heterosexual and queer masculinities, and hegemonic and alternative models, asserting gender through a performance that transcends heteronormative binaries. This emerges through the eroticisation of the hero's suffering body, which challenges bodily boundaries, and the gaze politics that inform the relationship between Valjean and Javert. My analysis of the formal elements of the musical, particularly the connections created by the score, the cinematography, and the performances of the actors, will also highlight how the power dynamic between the two characters is reshaped, gesturing towards a queer reading that is further supported by the film's reception, both in the press and among the fans.

Beginning in France in 1815, *Les Misérables* narrates the story of Jean Valjean, an ex-prisoner unjustly sentenced, abused by his warden, Javert, who obsessively chases him for nearly twenty years for escaping his parole and seeks to bring him to justice. Meanwhile, converted by the Bishop of Digne (Colm Wilkinson), Valjean has changed his name and become a wealthy man, raising Cosette (Amanda Seyfried), the daughter of Fantine (Anne Hathaway), one of his ex-employees-turned-prostitute, for whose ruin he feels responsible. Valjean and Javert face each other again in 1832, when their fates intertwine with those of a group of young revolutionaries. One of them, Marius (Eddie Redmayne), is the man Cosette has fallen in love with. Valjean risks his life and freedom to save him and ensure his daughter's happiness.

While the basic plot of the book is adapted in the film, both the play and the movie dispense with many of the minor characters and complex subplots of the novel, which amplify the main themes and characters. This was necessary to make the story accessible to an audience unfamiliar with it, according to John Caird, who identifies the core of the plot with Valjean's journey of redemption (Nightingale and Palmer 2013, p. 22).[3] For instance, Marius's father, Colonel Pontmercy, who sacrifices himself for his son, echoing Valjean's experience of fatherhood (Grossman 1994, p. 121), is expunged. Some of the other characters have been simplified. In particular, Thénardier is reduced to comic relief already on stage, with the elimination of his backstory in an attempt to present a straightforward plot (Behr 1989, p. 74). His role is further marginalised in the film, excluding the number 'Dog Eats Dog', and made even more grotesquely comic in Sacha Baron Cohen's performance.

However, the film also restores and extends some of the scenes between Valjean and Javert present in the book, such as their first meeting at the factory in Montreuil, which is omitted in the play, or Javert's plea to be discharged, more condensed on stage, where he never actually requests to be dismissed (Nunn and Caird 2004).[4] Thus, this different treatment of the story foregrounds the relationship between Valjean and Javert as the focal point of the film. This is further stressed by the publicity campaign. The image of young Cosette was widely used in posters of the film, establishing a para-textual connection between the movie and its sources through the artwork (Verevis 2006, pp. 130, 137; Nightingale and Palmer 2013, p. 33). Yet, in many international posters, such as the German and French ones, an alternative was employed, representing Javert and Valjean next to each other, towering over some of the other characters, who are reproduced in a smaller size (IMDb.com n.d.). The relationship between the antagonists is thus emphasised, further relying on the star power of both Jackman and Crowe.

The performance of masculinity as 'postfeminist fatherhood' unfolds in the film through this relationship. As Hannah Hamad (2014, p. 2) notes, this new model of fatherhood, which emerged in response to second wave feminism and its request for equality even in the private sphere, is framed as ideal masculinity in contemporary American culture and is characterised by emotional articulacy and a certain expertise in the domestic realm, especially with children (also see Rehling 2011, and Peberdy 2013).

Starting from the 1990s, postfeminist fatherhood has been normalised in films, bringing masculinity, often configured as heroic, back to the centre of the narrative (Hamad 2014, p. 14). This is further emphasised in post-9/11 films that negotiate the re-evaluation of traditional masculine models in mainstream discourses, potentially at odds with postfeminism, through fatherhood, which is posited as the defining trait of masculinity (Hamad 2014, pp. 48–49). The marginalisation of motherhood and the characterisation of the single father as victim, stressed by the adoption of a melodramatic cinematic mode, further contribute to this. While presenting an alternative to the nuclear family, patriarchal values are still asserted in a negotiation of hegemonic masculinity (Hamad 2014, pp. 21, 26–28). Michael Kimmel (2010, p. 24) highlights how this reshaping of fatherhood on screen reflects a similar change in American society, where this model has been adopted as a way to rearticulate manhood in the context of women's increased power in the public sphere. This entails a renegotiation of the separation between public and private spheres, which emerged as a result of the Enlightenment. The association between men and rationality marked the public sphere as the privileged locus where men could exercise their political life as citizens, while women were relegated to the domestic realm, characterised as the private sphere of emotions (Rose 1993, p. 35). Connell (1987, pp. 122, 126–129) analyses the persistence of this divide in contemporary society, identifying the ways in which the State, as a patriarchal institution, constructs and asserts hegemonic masculinity through the regulation of sex and gender, which further affects the gendered division of labour within the family. Kimmel (2010, p. 28) emphasises how this new model of fatherhood is increasingly embraced in the majority of American families, not as a politicised role, rather as a way to accept gender equality both in the public and private domains, and to make the experience of manhood more satisfying for men.

In contrast, groups like 'Men's Rights Inc.' in the USA or 'Fathers 4 Justice' in the UK advocate a politicised, anti-feminist approach to fatherhood in the public sphere (Kimmel 2010, p. 25; Hamad 2014, p. 51). Postfeminist fatherhood thus represents an alternative to the figure of the 'angry white man' that emerged in the past three decades, and which has become even more radicalised in a post-9/11 socio-cultural context. As analysed by Kimmel (2013), this kind of masculinity is also closely connected with the Great Recession (2007–2008), which has affected middle- and lower-middle-class men, and with immigration policies, thus inducing men to recuperate more traditional models of masculinity to counteract their sense of emasculation. As Susan Faludi (2007, p. 9) highlights, the 9/11 terrorist attacks have been also seen as an emasculation of the nation, of which women's independence is considered to be one of the main causes. Parallel to the recuperation of traditional role models like John Wayne was the immediate silencing of women in the media, whose presence on TV and newspapers dramatically dipped after the attacks (Faludi 2007, p. 7, 21).[5] Similarly, in the aftermath of the Great Recession, a performative rhetoric of 'masculinity in crisis', wherein men were implied to be the primary victims of the economic crash, has been amplified in popular culture, leading to the intensification of 'polarized gender norming', as Negra and Tasker (2014) assert. Thus, in a post-9/11 and post-Recessionary historical moment, in which men have been reframed as casualties of a process of emasculation, postfeminist fatherhood and the 'angry white man' emerge as two opposing facets in the recuperation of hegemonic masculinity.

Returning to the film, Valjean emerges as the hero of the Nation, a man who guarantees democracy through self-sacrifice, mainly motivated by his role as a father, further resonating with Christological symbolism. This portrayal, typical of the contemporary revival of the historical epic, best exemplified by *Gladiator* (Scott 2000), written by one of the screenwriters of *Les Misérables*, William Nicholson, and with Russell Crowe himself, is supported on a visual and narrative level, although the final face-off and the battles that characterise the epic genre become here duets sung by the two antagonists. The epic dimension, it should be noted, emerges already in the novel, as Grossman (1996, pp. 26–27) underlines, by presenting Valjean as an epic hero defined by physical strength and moral virtue, whose actions connect personal and collective destinies. The stage musical is meant to be equally epic in the creators' intentions, as the ambitious set design demonstrates (Behr 1989, p. 99).[6] But it is obviously the cinematic elements of the epic genre that contribute to the construction of masculinity in the film in relation to the socio-historical context. Burgoyne (2008, p. 75) notes the connection between historical setting in the epic genre and present-day America, taking *Gladiator* as an example, and compares the gloriousness and decadence of Rome to that of America at the end of the 1990s. This parallel between setting and context is also made by Kord and Krimmer (2011, p. 55), who see in the epic hero, especially as a father and private citizen, a symbolic figure that stands for the Nation and can save it through self-sacrifice, entering the public sphere. This resonates with the conflation of postfeminist fatherhood and nationhood, which appears to be depoliticised through the appeal to the affective sphere on screen, while actually holding political value in its process of negotiation of hegemonic masculinity (Hamad 2014, p. 31). Through the association between fatherhood and citizenship, as in Valjean's case, masculinity is reconfigured at the border between public and private spheres.

PUBLIC INTIMACIES: THE SPECTACLE OF THE SUFFERING BODY

The narrative of self-sacrifice is directly connected with the importance of the suffering body, particularly in scenes of violence, which abjectify the hero by threatening the distinction between subject and object positions through the lack of physical boundaries (Kristeva 1982). The hero can find empowerment in his ultimate sacrifice only by going through this process of abjection (Burgoyne 2008, p. 83), a position which feminises the hero as an erotic spectacle both for the audience and for a diegetic male gaze, and which therefore needs to be remasculinised in a hegemonic model (Fradley 2004, p. 239). Any threat of homosexual voyeurism is thus displaced by action involving violence (Hunt 1993, p. 69). The suffering hero is often also associated with the trope of crucifixion, particularly in the epic films of the 1950s–1960s, to which the emergence of a Christian discourse was central. As Hunt (1993, p. 73) argues, crucifixion shows control over one's body while demonstrating nobility through self-sacrifice, and avoiding eroticisation through transcendence, rather than through violent action. The film visually represents the metaphorical association with Christ's crucifixion through the martyrdom of Valjean, a trope which also characterises the literary work (Grossman 1994, p. 139). The insistence of the camera on Valjean's body recalls Christological iconography, while a staging that favours a collective performance and wider perspective precludes this direct connection for a theatre audience. The importance of the suffering body as a vehicle for Christian self-sacrifice in this way is particularly evident in three moments of the film, linking it with discourses of nationhood and postfeminist fatherhood through repetition and variation.

The opening sequence immediately connects the hero with the trope of self-sacrifice which is, in turn, linked with the discourse of Nation through symbolism. The film starts with muffled, distant noises off-screen, which gradually become distinguishable as the rhythmic sounds of drums, as the camera emerges from the deep bosom of the sea towards a ripped French flag, thus harnessing the power of symbolic emphasis on screen from the outset. Intertitles provide the necessary information to locate the setting (France, 1815), explaining that a king is again on the throne after the Revolution. When the camera gets to the surface, passing through the fabric of the flag with a continuous movement, an enormous, beached ship is shown, surrounded by tall waves and battering rain. The drums are now substituted by the non-diegetic sound of trumpets, playing the main phrase of 'Look Down'. The camera cranes up and approaches the ship while other instruments are added to the increasingly orchestral score. As the camera reaches the peak of the mast, a harbour is revealed behind it. The downward movement of the crane shot shows the convicts trying to bring the ship ashore. Thus, the opening already satisfies the expectations of spectacle through the CGI and the music, an example of hyperformalism typical of the genre, which is characterised by elements of formal excess such as a great number of extras, pervasive music, rich costumes, and grandiose visions (Sobchack 1990).

The crane movement ends on a high-angled medium close-up of a fatigued Valjean, who starts singing the song with all the other prisoners. Medium group shots that highlight the epic dimensions of the ship are intercut with close shots of Valjean, always looking up from the shadows, whilst a countershot presents Javert, who is controlling them from the top of the walls. Immediately setting him as the antagonist, he is framed in a very low-angled medium close-up, back-lit through a grey bright light, which gives him a menacing yet ethereal aura. His costume, a sky-blue coat, also clashes with the red hue of Valjean's clothes, in a colour palette that echoes the French flag (Lynn 2012) and which recurs throughout the film. With Javert looking down and wielding his power over Valjean, the score further underlines this opposition, setting the brilliant trumpet associated with Valjean against the deep brass sound that introduces Javert. As the song progresses, this dynamic of shots/countershots is repeated several times. The opening thus establishes the opposing masculinities represented by the antagonists, with a dialectic between wider and closer shots, which characterises the whole film and creates a link between the performance of masculinity in the public and private spheres respectively. The epic proportions of the wider shots emphasise the discourse of nationhood, in relation to the public sphere, symbolised by elements of the mise-en-scène like the flag and by the official role that Javert occupies. At the same time, the closer shots establish a private dialogue between Valjean and Javert, an example of the public intimacy that marks all their interactions.

After the tempest, Valjean and Javert face each other, as the inspector orders him to retrieve the flag, still attached to the broken mast ashore. Javert observes him as he complies. The repetition of the same musical phrase during this exchange creates tension and expectation, readying the audience for the spectacle about to happen. The trumpets blare triumphantly as Valjean nearly falls under the weight of the mast, and then succeeds in raising it onto his shoulder. His pained face as he pulls it is shown in a close-up. When he drops the mast at Javert's feet, the music stops without playing the last bars of the song, alluding to the fact that this is neither the last time that they will meet nor the last that Javert will see Valjean's vigour in action. This immediate identification of Valjean with physical strength, completely lacking in the staging of the play where he is just one of the other inmates, echoes the novel. The narrator describes Valjean as '[…] equal to four men. He would sometimes lift and carry enormous weights on his back and he would occasionally himself replace the tool known as cric […]' (Hugo 2009, p. 78), listing a series of extraordinary deeds he has performed. The mise-en-scène and the camerawork thus present Valjean's body as a spectacle of suffering, evoking Christological images as he drags the mast on his shoulder. Although abject, he shows the impressive control of the body Hunt talks about, avoiding passivity. In addition, this action hints at his carrying the weight of the nation later in the film. Nevertheless, Javert's insistent gaze heightens the eroticisation of Valjean, which the epic genre traditionally represses to preclude an association between masculinity and homosexuality (Neale 1983, pp. 14–15). Hark (1996) underlines a similar eroticisation of the male body in epic films, in which the male gaze of an often impotent master-like figure, thus empowered, objectifies the body of a man of a lower social standing, displacing gender difference onto class structures.

Therefore, Valjean's body stands for the negotiation of power between the two men. Javert's stillness and rigidity seem to indicate his impotent yet powerful position. He asserts his power by performing his official role in the State, conveyed through the gaze and the interpellation of Valjean as 'Prisoner no. 24601', which inscribes him as a criminal. Yet, his personal obsession undermines this. The frustration thus caused is reiterated in two other sequences that repeat this one on a visual and musical level. Valjean's activity and his reciprocated gaze repeatedly challenge him, although he always avoids the fight, responding only in self-defence, and mostly through singing, as in 'The Confrontation'. His control of the body, while also displaying his suffering, further re-centres his masculinity, in a narrative that performatively posits this masculinity in crisis, in relation to a reconfiguration of dominant models in contemporary society (Robinson 2000, pp. 9–11). When Javert recognises him again eight years later, precisely through the spectacle of his suffering body, Valjean—now in Montreuil—is known as Monsieur Madeleine, often being referred to with his title of mayor of the town as Monsieur le Maire. Both names are symbolically significant and allude to this reconfigured masculinity. The sound of *maire* is similar to that of *mère*, 'mother' in French, foreshadowing his role as a mother and father to Cosette, and further alluding to his role as parent to the townspeople. On the other hand, the biblical figure of Magdalene/Madeleine echoes his journey of redemption.

This self-naming represents another step towards a freedom which he has already started to achieve through the gifts of faith and silver from the Bishop of Digne. The silver allows Valjean to begin his ascent in the social system from being a member of the labouring class to entering the ranks of the bourgeoisie, denoted by the publicness of his role as Mayor and factory owner. Significantly, the period in which Hugo set the novel was characterised by the emergence of this bourgeoisie, which Price (1987, p. 131) attributes to a Christian ethic of hard work, thrift, and loyalty to family, all values embodied by Valjean. This socio-economic phenomenon runs parallel to the public/private dialectic already outlined, particularly owing to homosocial relations among men in the public sphere, which strengthened social hierarchies (Harrison 1999, p. 12). Yet, class boundaries were fluid and dependent upon a set of cultural and social practices, to which appearance was key (Price 1987, p. 121). Madeleine's successful performance of bourgeois masculinity relies precisely on his public persona as represented through costume, in a kind of class cross-dressing that reveals the fluid borders between classes (see Tasker 1998, p. 21). In contemporary society, such traversing of borders resonates with the myth of the self-made man, 'the single defining feature of American masculinity, over the course of American history', whose 'foundation has all but eroded' as a result of the Great Recession (Kimmel 2013, p. 14). At the same time, however, the reiteration of physical work in moments of public intimacy throughout the film serves as a continuous reminder of Valjean's labouring class roots. It is indeed 'the construction of the male blue-collar worker as the quintessential American man' that Banet-Weiser (2014, pp. 89–91) associates with the myth of the self-made man, demonstrating how this figure has been redeployed in the wake of the Recession as a symbol of nationhood and hope for economic recovery. Thus, the crossing of class boundaries, negotiated on the borders between public and private spaces, further establishes Valjean as the hero of the nation.

When a man becomes trapped under his cart, Valjean is called to help free him. Javert is shown in a close-up, looking at the events unravelling that seemingly confirm his suspicions regarding Madeleine's identity. A wider shot reveals Valjean raising up the cart as he had done with the mast. The repetition of the momentous act is further stressed by the reprise of 'Look Down'. The camera then moves closer to him, once again showing his suffering face. Close-ups of Javert are intercut with those of Valjean until he manages to free the man from under the cart. As Javert displays his incredulity and sings his doubts in an aside, Valjean challenges him to openly accuse him, but Javert remains silent. Once again, then, Valjean is made into an erotic spectacle under Javert's gaze, although the scene stresses the latter's passivity against Valjean's activity. The use of close-ups reveals the public intimacy of the moment, which emphasises the private nature of Javert's thoughts against the public setting. In turn, his suspicions endanger Madeleine's public persona, as Valjean's real identity threatens to surface.

This type of spectacle, heavily focused on suffering and the body, is reiterated for a third time in the last part of the film, set against the 1832 rebellion. His self-sacrifice is now closely tied with his role as a father and to the fate of the Nation. After learning that Cosette is in love with Marius and that he might die in the revolt, Valjean steals a uniform and infiltrates the barricades to protect him. Meanwhile, Javert has dressed as a rebel to spy on them, in a role reversal that echoes the previous class cross-dressing. Having been recognised, Javert is now a prisoner: on his knees, hands tied, a rope around his neck, and blood on his forehead. His spectacle of suffering is denoted by complete passivity, one that fails to model and perform a reconfigured hegemonic masculinity, as Valjean's had done. Nevertheless, Valjean refuses to wield his power over him, instead freeing him. A darker variation of 'Look Down' plays as Javert begins to unravel because of the other man's compassion.

The focus on suffering and the body is relentless. When Marius is shot during the battle, Valjean rescues him by hoisting him up onto his shoulders and dragging him to safety in the sewers. Close-ups of Valjean show again his pain, while 'Look Down' plays at a sped-up tempo to mark the urgency of the moment, as in the scene at the end of the second part in which Javert chases Valjean and Cosette. Valjean is confronted with Javert when he emerges on the surface. Smeared in dirt, Valjean is a show of abjection as he looks up at Javert, seen in a very low-angled shot, wearing his pristine uniform. The repetition of the music and the camerawork echo the opening sequence and signal another negotiation of power between the two, as private motivations play out in a public space. When Valjean begs for more time to bring Marius to safety, Javert ambiguously answers: 'I want you. I will not give in'. Yet, Javert ultimately lets him go, still affected by Valjean's previous gesture.

Valjean's descent into the sewers and his triumphant comeback is read as another Christological metaphor by Grossman (1996, p. 43), a transfiguration that brings Marius back to life, connecting his self-sacrifice with parenthood, both as a father and as a mother. While Grossman's (1994, pp. 165–166) interpretation of the novel sees this gradual transcendence as a further removal from history, I argue that Valjean becomes the hero of the Nation by saving Marius, as demonstrated in the very last scene of the film set in the afterlife. There, all those who have died in the narration glorify him by reprising 'Do You Hear the People Sing?'. The camera movement ends on a sea of waving French flags, significantly absent in the stage version, which links the ending with the very beginning. The contrast between the ripped flag dragged in the mud and this shot demonstrates how this rebirth of the nation has been possible only through Valjean's heroic journey, particularly as a father, by ensuring Cosette a future and the continuance of a new generation by saving Marius.

Body Politics: Nationhood and Complementary Masculinities

Whilst Grossman sees Valjean as an apolitical figure, she does recognise the novel as Hugo's political commentary on the present, in which the protagonist symbolises the ideal republican citizen, with his values of freedom, equality, and fraternity, in contrast with the second Empire. Thus, Valjean becomes the embodiment of a political utopia (Grossman 1994, pp. 199–200), linking the restoration of democracy with the epic hero's actions as a father, as theorised by Hamad (2014, p. 31), despite the fact that the political aspects of postfeminist fatherhood are often understated through the emphasis on affect. The lack of any historical background to the rebellion in the musical indeed amplifies the exceptionalism of Valjean's deeds in the public sphere, as Gleizes (2015, pp. 137–139) also observes. Valjean's rearticulation of masculinity through postfeminist fatherhood thus appropriates the private, 'feminine' realm of the domestic, while reasserting itself in the public sphere through association with a masculinist vision of nationhood.

Valjean's self-sacrifice is symbolic: a private citizen becomes a public hero for personal reasons. Death and the subsequent glorification also make him the Father on a Symbolic level, a name that represents 'the impossibility of the phallic masculine essence in its ultimate etherealisation' (Fradley 2004, p. 249). His transcendence at the end of the film is closely connected with a Christian discourse, made particularly evident in the mise-en-scène of his death scene at the convent. Surrounded by Marius, Cosette, and the spirit of Fantine, Valjean is immersed in a warm candlelight, which gives the space a heavenly quality. After he dies, his soul walks towards the Bishop of Digne, who is waiting for him in a triumph of golden light produced by many candles, which gradually engulfs Valjean as well. Thus, the presence of the Bishop, who initially converted him, brings his spiritual journey to a glorious end: by accepting the Bishop's bargain, freedom in exchange for a life dedicated to the Good, achieved through self-sacrifice, Valjean is now compensated with sainthood. Instead, on stage, Valjean is joined by Fantine and Éponine, while the Bishop appears only in the first act. On an intertextual level, the presence of Colm Wilkinson, who originally played the role of Valjean on stage, confers even more relevance on this relationship, symbolically ensuring the legacy of the story, and providing the film with a seal of approval. Finally, Valjean unites a traditional model of fatherhood, by giving away his daughter to Marius, with a contemporary sensibility, demonstrated through his singing, and compassion, which characterise a representation of postfeminist fatherhood in historical films (Hamad 2014, pp. 28–29). Thus, Valjean's performance of ideal masculinity as postfeminist fatherhood finds some continuance in the 'new man' Marius, who combines contrasting binaries, such as intellectual rebel/romantic hero, aristocrat/man of the people.

On the other hand, Javert gestures towards the figure of the 'angry white man', identified by Kimmel (2013, p. 38) with men from different classes who feel a sense of dispossession, blaming people in a lesser position than themselves for their crisis, rather than their inability to accept change. His failure to appropriately rearticulate his masculinity is demonstrated by 'Javert's Suicide', whose motif reprises 'Stars'. The differences between the two numbers highlight Javert's final emasculation. 'Stars', which appears at the end of the second part of the film, is an anthem of Javert's convictions, in which he fully identifies with the Law, both the State's and God's. After Valjean's second escape, Javert is on top of a building that offers a spectacular CGI view of Paris. The moon illuminates the scene, lending solemnity to it. He is often framed with an eagle statue behind him, its spread wings completely embracing his figure, a symbol of the Law and Javert's identification with it. Yet, the darker tones of the melody and the shots of his feet walking on the edge of the building anticipate his later suicide. In 'Javert's Suicide', the inspector is on the top of a dam after having failed to capture Valjean. The moon is now obscured by the clouds that put him in the shadows whereas the absence of the eagle behind him signals that even the Law has deserted him. The melody starts in an obsessive, darker tone, the same as that employed in 'Valjean's Soliloquy', while the lyrics almost repeat those of the previous number as Javert sings of his doubts. Yet, while the first song marked the start of Valjean's upward journey, this number signifies Javert's lowest point. His inability to change when confronted with Valjean's compassion, and different understanding of the Law, can lead only to this conclusion (Grossman 1994, p. 80).

This portrayal of Javert is enhanced by Crowe's vocal performance, similar to that of an angry rocker for its raw and raspy timbre, in stark contrast with Hugh Jackman's operatic singing, thus linking this character to the other angry epic heroes he had played before, such as Maximus (Fradley 2004, p. 235). At the same time, he brings humanity to Javert. This is particularly evident in a moment after the end of the battle, when he looks for Valjean among the dead bodies. While on stage he searches with ruthlessness and disrespect for the lives lost, here Javert is touched by Gavroche's death. On seeing the boy's body, he crouches beside him and pins his own medal on Gavroche's jacket, displaying his vulnerability through this gesture, which was improvised by Crowe on set (Beaghton 2015, p. 155). The inner complexity thus brought to the character by Crowe has been noted in reviews, such as Peter Bradshaw's (2013). However, unlike Valjean, Javert does not manage to reconcile his public role in the State with his private emotions. He thus represents the other side of contemporary masculinity vis-à-vis Valjean: the latter is a successful ideal of postfeminist masculinity while Javert is a failed attempt to become *that* ideal, inasmuch as that ideal marries public and private spheres. This dynamic is supported in the narrative by Javert's background, as he admits he was born and raised in jail, thus sharing a very similar experience to Valjean's. While drawing from the novel, both on stage and on screen, the musical dramatises this similarity by disclosing it in 'The Confrontation', in which Valjean and Javert sing in counterpoint.

This oppositional complementarity can be connected with the trend of the double-protagonist film, common in contemporary American cinema, as analysed by David Greven (2009, p. 125). In this type of film, both protagonist and antagonist are played by stars of the same calibre, and their characters can be seen as 'complementary halves' (Greven 2009, p. 129). For this reason, the main problem at the base of the narration is the negotiation of power between the two, which the opening scene of *Les Misérables* best exemplifies. Greven (2009, pp. 129, 140) highlights how this dynamic between characters often threatens the heterosexual binary, putting one of the two in a homosexual voyeuristic position that corresponds to masochism. Interpreting Javert as the one occupying this position against Valjean as an example of narcissism, their relationship opens up to a queer reading. This emerges through the adoption of the historical epic generic conventions in the musical, such as the hero's suffering body and gaze dynamics, as I have demonstrated.

Conclusion: Queer Readings

In a scorching review of the film, tellingly entitled 'Love Hurts', Anthony Lane (2013) proposes 'Would it be too fanciful to suggest that they have a thing for each other, to which they never confess? That would explain why Crowe and Jackman, both tough Australians, are made to sing at so agonized a pitch.' While facetious, the comment exposes this subtext. Fans fully embraced a queer reading of the Valjean/Javert dynamic. One of the most popular outlets of fandom, fanfiction provides a clear example of this. The database *Archive of Our Own* (n.d.) lists various 'Les Misérables' tags below the movie, book, and theatre directories, which are aggregated in 'Les Misérables – All Media Types'. Although there are fanfictions dated between 2005 and 2012, the production peaked after the release of the film in December 2012. In the tag, more than 1800 'slashfics' (i.e. fanfictions that focus on a same-sex relationship) are dedicated to Javert and Valjean, often explicitly identified with Jackman and Crowe. Most of these stories read their relationship as only sexual, featuring scenes of an adult nature, even though there are also many that imagine the two in a purely emotional romance. A common practice in fan cultures, slashfics provide multiple fantasies of identification for their writers and readers, mainly constituted by women, confronting dominant heteronormative representations on screen (Jenkins 2013, pp. 189–90, 198). Drawing from Eve Kosofsky Sedgwick's (1985) conceptualisation of the 'homosocial' as a form of social bonding between people of the same sex, Jenkins emphasises that slash fiction works on the subtexts of popular media and 'throws conventional notions of masculinity into crisis by removing the barriers blocking the realization of homosocial desire; slash unmasks the erotics of male friendship' (2013, p. 205). A comparable response can be seen on other social platforms, such as Tumblr, where posts and blogs are dedicated to them, such as 'FYValvert' (n.d.), a portmanteau of their names. The blog aggregates posts on the relationship between the two characters, which mainly featured material from the film or inspired by it in the months following its release. Therefore, the audience reception brings into relief forms of desire between the two characters, supporting a queer reading of their relationship that privileges the private sphere of intimacy and emotions over political ramifications.

Such a response further demonstrates the fluidity of the borders, therefore, that characterise the construction of masculinity in the film. Situating itself in the contemporary musical landscape, *Les Misérables* proposes a model of ideal masculinity that emerges through the hybridisation of the generic conventions of this genre with those of the historical epic. Cinematic elements of the latter genre construct Valjean as an epic hero. Camerawork and mise-en-scène emphasise his suffering body, abjected and yet in control, echoing Christian discourses of freedom and salvation through its iconography. This position also eroticises his body for a diegetic male gaze, creating a queered power dynamic between Valjean and Javert, which is enacted in moments of public intimacy that further resonate with the reception of the film. Yet, Valjean is remasculinised through the prism of postfeminist fatherhood. Motivated by his paternal affection, he crosses over the borders between private and public spheres, acting as a private citizen to save the Nation and restore a democratic utopia. This performance of masculinity, further characterised by fluid class borders, thus establishes itself as ideal, in a reconfiguration of hegemonic masculinity that resonates with the post-9/11 and post-Recessionary contexts, both marked by a rhetoric of 'masculinity in crisis' due to a sense of emasculation of the nation. In response to a political-economic crisis, cultural discourses have thus emphasised the necessity of a reconfiguration of hegemonic masculinity through the recuperation of traditional models paired with a renewed affective sensibility. On the other hand, Javert fails to negotiate his masculinity across borders as an example of the 'angry white man', demonstrating the necessity of Valjean's rearticulation. As much as Hugo's novel spoke to the socio-cultural shifts of his age, from the emergence of the bourgeoisie to the persistence of Republican values, the film negotiates tension arising in contemporary society vis-à-vis changes in gender discourses and socio-economic milieu. From adaptation to adaptation, *Les Misérables* affirms itself as a compass for the present, reinforcing its popularity while confirming the inherent political value of popular culture.

Notes

1. The film was recognised as a British feature by BAFTA due to the significant involvement of British creatives. However, Universal's financial backing should be noted alongside its lead in the publicity campaign, which pushed the film particularly on the American market through special trailers, targeted promos on broadcast television, industry screenings, and an official release before the UK and other markets (Galloway 2012). The association with Hollywood is further reinforced by the presence of international stars who have established themselves in blockbuster films.

2. *Gladiator* (Scott 2000) is considered the catalyst for a new cycle of epic films in all of them, although both Russell (2007) and Santas (2007) trace a revival of the genre back to 1993.

3. Wolf (2012) notes that the streamlining of the complex plot in the stage musical often comes at the expense of the female characters, who have much more weight in the novel. Such a marginalisation of women is explained by Wolf through the 1980s backlash against feminism. This further resonates with the marginalisation of women in media noted by Faludi (2007) in a post-9/11 context and exemplified by the foregrounding of the father-son relationship between Valjean and Marius in the second part of the film at the detriment of the bond between Valjean and Cosette.

4. All further mentions to the stage musical refer to this recorded performance.

5. When appearing in media, women were usually depicted as victims, mostly identified as middle-class housewives or young girls caught in the threat posed by terrorism, as Faludi (2007) examines.

6. The observation refers to the stage design prior to the revamp of the West End production in 2021, when the revolving stage, central in the barricade scenes in particular, was removed.

WORKS CITED

Banet-Weiser, Sarah. 2014. 'We are all workers': Economic Crisis, Masculinity, and the American Working Class. In *Gendering the Recession: Media Culture in the Age of Austerity*, ed. Diane Negra and Yvonne Tasker, 81–106. Durham: Duke University Press.

Beaghton, Andrea. 2015. The Many Faces of Javert in Anglophone Adaptation. In *Les Misérables and its Afterlives: Between Page, Stage, and Screen*, ed. Kathryn M. Grossman and Bradley Stephens, 143–157. Farnham: Ashgate.

Behr, Edward. 1989. *'Les Misérables': History in the Making*. London: Cape.

Bradshaw, Peter. 2013. Les Misérables – Review. *The Guardian*, 10 January. http://www.theguardian.com/film/2013/jan/10/miserables-review. Accessed 5 September 2022.

Brewer, Craig, Director. 2011. *Footloose*. USA: Paramount Pictures. DVD.

Burgoyne, Robert. 2008. *The Hollywood Historical Film*. Oxford: Blackwell.

———. 2011. Introduction. In *The Epic Film in World Culture*, ed. Robert Burgoyne, 1–16. New York; London: Routledge.

Chazelle, Damien, Director. 2016. *La La Land*. Lionsgate. DVD.

Connell, R.W. 1987. *Gender and Power: Society, the Person and Sexual Politics*. Cambridge: Polity in association with Blackwell.

Donnelly, K.J., and Beth Carroll. 2018. Introduction: Reimagining the Contemporary Musical in the Twenty-First Century. In *Contemporary Musical Film*, ed. K.J. Donnelly and Beth Carroll, 1–10. Edinburgh: Edinburgh University Press.

Dunne, Michael. 2004. *American Musical Themes and Forms*. Jefferson: McFarland.

Elliott, Andrew B.R. 2014. *The Return of the Epic Film: Genre, Aesthetics and History of the 21st Century*. Edinburgh: Edinburgh University Press.

Faludi, Susan. 2007. *The Terror Dream: Fear and Fantasy in Post-9/11 America*. New York: Metropolitan Books.

Feuer, Jane. 1993. *The Hollywood Musical*. 2nd ed. Basingstoke: Macmillan.

Fradley, Martin. 2004. Maximus Melodramaticus: Masculinity, Masochism and White Male Paranoia in Contemporary Hollywood Cinema. In *Action and Adventure Cinema*, ed. Yvonne Tasker, 235–251. London, New York: Routledge.

FYValvert. n.d. Tumblr. http://fuckyeahvalvert.tumblr.com/. Accessed 5 September 2022.

Galloway, Stephen. 2012. Inside the Fight to Bring "Les Mis" to the Screen. *The Hollywood Reporter*, 5 May. https://www.hollywoodreporter.com/news/les-miserables-anne-hathaway-russell-398099?page=2. Accessed 4 September 2022.

Gleizes, Delphine. 2015. Adapting *Les Misérables* for the Screen: Transatlantic Debates and Rivalries. In *Les Misérables and its Afterlives: Between Page, Stage, and Screen*, ed. Kathryn M. Grossman and Bradley Stephens, 129–142. Farnham: Ashgate.

Greven, David. 2009. *Manhood in Hollywood from Bush to Bush*. Austin: University of Texas Press.

Griffin, Sean. 2018. *Free and Easy? A Defining History of the Film Musical Genre*. Chichester: Wiley-Blackwell.

Grossman, Kathryn M. 1994. *Figuring Transcendence in 'Les Misérables': Hugo's Romantic Sublime*. Carbondale: Southern Illinois University Press.

———. 1996. *'Les Misérables': Conversion, Revolution, Redemption*. New York: Twayne Publishers; London: Prentice Hall International.

Grossman, Kathryn M., and Bradley Stephens. 2015. Introduction. In *Les Misérables and its Afterlives: Between Page, Stage, and Screen*, ed. Kathryn M. Grossman and Bradley Stephens, 1–16. Farnham: Ashgate.

Hamad, Hannah. 2014. *Postfeminism and Paternity in Contemporary U.S. Film: Framing Fatherhood*. New York; London: Routledge.

Hark, Ina Rae. 1996. Animals or Romans: Looking at Masculinity in Spartacus. In *Screening the Male: Exploring Masculinities in Hollywood Cinema*, ed. Steven Cohan and Ina Rae Hark, 2nd ed., 151–172. London, New York: Routledge.

Harrison, Carol E. 1999. *The Bourgeois Citizen in Nineteenth-Century France: Gender, Sociability, and the Uses of Emulation*. Oxford: Oxford University Press.

Hooper, Tom, Director. 2012. *Les Misérables*. UK, USA: Universal Pictures.

Hugo, Victor. 2009. *Les Misérables*. Trans. Julie Rose. London: Vintage.

Hunt, Leon. 1993. What are Big Boys Made of?: *Spartacus*, *El Cid* and the Male Epic. In *You Tarzan: Masculinity, Movies and Men*, ed. Pat Kirkham and Janet Thumim, 65–83. London: Lawrence & Wishart.

Jenkins, Henry. 2013. *Textual Poachers: Television Fans and Participatory Culture*. 20th anniversary ed. New York; London: Routledge.

Kessler, Kelly. 2020. *Broadway in the Box: Television's Lasting Love Affair with the Musical*. Oxford: Oxford University Press.

Kimmel, Michael. 2010. *Misframing Men: The Politics of Contemporary Masculinity*. New Brunswick: Rutgers University Press.

———. 2013. *Angry White Men: American Masculinity at the End of an Era*. New York: Nation Books. EBook Library.

Kord, Susanne, and Elizabeth Krimmer. 2011. *Contemporary Hollywood Masculinities: Gender, Genre, and Politics*. Basingstoke: Palgrave Macmillan.

Kristeva, Julia. 1982. *Powers of Horror: An Essay on Abjection*. New York; Guildford: Columbia University Press.

Lane, Anthony. 2013. Love Hurts. *The New Yorker*, 7 January. http://www.newyorker.com/magazine/2013/01/07/love-hurts-2. Accessed 4 September 2022.

210 E. SAMMARTINO

Les Misérables. n.d. Box Office Mojo. https://www.boxofficemojo.com/release/rl1952351745/. Accessed 7 September 2022.

Les Misérables – All Media Types. n.d. Archive of Our Own. https://archiveofourown.org/tags/Les%20Mis%C3%A9rables%20-%20All%20Media%20Types/works. Accessed 7 September 2022.

Les Misérables (2012) Photo Gallery. n.d. IMDb.com. https://www.imdb.com/title/tt1707386/mediaindex?page=1&ref_=ttmi_mi_sm. Accessed 6 September 2022.

Lloyd, Phyllida, Director. 2008. *Mamma Mia!* Germany, UK, USA: Universal Pictures. DVD.

Lobalzo Wright, Julie. 2018. *Crossover Stardom: Popular Male Music Stars in American Cinema*. London: Bloomsbury Academic.

Lobalzo Wright, Julie, and Martha Shearer, eds. 2021. *Musicals at the Margins: Genre, Boundaries, Canons*. London: Bloomsbury Academic.

Luhrmann, Baz, Director. 2001. *Moulin Rouge!* Australia, USA: 20th Century Fox. DVD.

Lynn, Cary. 2012. Oscars: Striving for "factual realism" in "Les Misérables" Production Design. *Deadline.com*, 29 December. https://deadline.com/2012/12/oscars-striving-for-factual-realism-in-les-miserables-production-design-393793/. Accessed 5 September 2022.

Marshall, Rob, Director. 2002. *Chicago*. USA: Miramax Film. DVD.

Neale, Stephen. 1983. Masculinity as Spectacle. Reflections on Men and Mainstream Cinema. *Screen* 24 (6): 2–17. https://doi.org/10.1093/screen/24.6.2.

Negra, Diane, and Yvonne Tasker. 2014. Introduction. Gender and Recessionary Culture. In *Gendering the Recession: Media Culture in the Age of Austerity*, ed. Diane Negra and Yvonne Tasker, 1–30. Durham: Duke University Press.

Nightingale, Benedict, and Martyn Palmer. 2013. *Les Misérables: From Page to Screen*. London: Carlton.

Nunn, Trevor, and John Caird, Directors. 2004. *Les Misérables*. London: Victoria and Albert Museum Theatre Collections.

Parker, Alan, Director. 1996. *Evita*. USA: Buena Vista Pictures. DVD.

Parker, Ol, Director. 2018. *Mamma Mia!: Here We Go Again*. UK, USA: Universal Pictures. DVD.

Peberdy, Donna. 2013. *Masculinity and Film Performance: Male Angst in Contemporary American Cinema*. Basingstoke: Palgrave Macmillan.

Price, Roger. 1987. *A Social History of Nineteenth-Century France*. New York: Holmes and Meyer.

Rehling, Nicola. 2011. *Extra-ordinary Men. White Heterosexual Masculinity in Contemporary Popular Cinema*. Lanham: Lexington Books.

Robinson, Sally. 2000. *Marked Men: White Masculinity in Crisis*. New York: Columbia University Press.

Rose, Gillian. 1993. *Feminism and Geography: The Limits of Geographical Knowledge*. Cambridge: Polity.

Russell, James. 2007. *The Historical Epic and Contemporary Hollywood: From Dances with the Wolves to Gladiator*. New York: Continuum.

Santas, Constantine. 2007. *The Epic Film: From Myth to Blockbuster*. Lanham: Rowman and Littlefield.

Sapiro, Ian. 2017. Beyond the Barricade: Adapting *Les Misérables* for the Cinema. In *Contemporary Musical Film*, ed. K.J. Donnelly and Beth Carroll, 123–139. Edinburgh: Edinburgh University Press.

Scott, Ridley, Director. 2000. *Gladiator*. USA, UK: DreamWorks Distribution LLC, Universal International Pictures. DVD.

Sedgwick, Eve Kosofsky. 1985. *Between Men: English Literature and Male Homosocial Desire*. New York: Columbia University Press.

Sobchack, Vivian. 1990. 'Surge and Splendor': A Phenomenology of the Historical Epic. *Representations* 29: 24–49. https://doi.org/10.2307/2928417.

Tancharoen, Kevin, Director. 2009. *Fame*. USA: MGM Distribution Co. DVD.

Tasker, Yvonne. 1998. *Working Girls: Gender and Sexuality in Popular Cinema*. London; New York: Routledge.

Taymor, Julie, Director. 2007. *Across the Universe*. USA, UK: Sony Pictures Releasing. DVD.

Verevis, Constantine. 2006. *Film Remakes*. Edinburgh: Edinburgh University Press.

Wolf, Stacy. 2012. Why We Love 'Les Miserables', Despite its Miserable Gender Stereotypes. *The Washington Post*, 28 December. https://www.washington-post.com/opinions/why-we-love-les-miserables-despite-its-miserable-gender-stereotypes/2012/12/28/bc8ef17e-4f84-11e2-839d-d54cc6e49b63_story.html. Accessed 7 September 2022.

CHAPTER 11

Feminicidal Masculinities: Cultural Contestations of Gender Violence in Ciudad Juárez

Joey Whitfield

In 2013 a woman wearing a blonde wig entered a bus on the outskirts of Ciudad Juárez and shot the driver dead. Two days later the same woman entered another bus and killed a second driver. Shortly afterwards, the following statement was sent to various local news websites:

> You think that because we are women we are weak, and that may be true but only up to a point, because even though we have nobody to defend us and we have to work long hours until late into the night to earn a living for our families we can no longer be silent in the face of these acts that enrage us. We were victims of sexual violence from bus drivers working the *maquila* [large assembly plant] night shifts here in Juárez, and although a lot of people know about the things we've suffered, nobody defends us nor does anything to protect us. That's why I am an instrument that will take revenge for many women. For we are seen as weak, but in reality we are not. We are brave. And if we don't get respect, we will earn that respect with our own

J. Whitfield (✉)
Cardiff University, Cardiff, UK
e-mail: WhitfieldJ1@cardiff.ac.uk

© The Author(s), under exclusive license to Springer Nature Switzerland AG 2024
A. Thakkar et al. (eds.), *Border Masculinities*,
https://doi.org/10.1007/978-3-031-68050-2_11

213

hands. We the women of Juárez are strong. 'Diana la cazadora de chóferes'. (trans. Herrera 2013)

It is not clear whether or not Diana's acts of vengeance were targeted at these particular drivers for any specific wrongdoings on their part, or indeed whether the statement was even written by her. It clearly is intended to create a fear in the men of the city equivalent to that felt by the women of the city which has, because of the numbers of sexually mutilated bodies of women discovered in and around the city, become synonymous with femicide and indeed *feminicide*. The distinction between these terms has been developed by feminist activists to emphasise not only the role of individual perpetrators (emphasised by the former) but also the political and structural causes of the misogynistic killing of women (emphasised by the latter). In the case of Diana, public prosecutors stated that the email had been sent from a computer in El Paso and that its style did not seem to be characteristic of someone capable of carrying out such killings. Despite admitting that both murders took place, they therefore questioned Diana's existence (*Diario* 2013). Nevertheless, in an investigation into the story, the journalist and now internationally well-known author Yuri Herrera interviewed surviving bus drivers after the attacks and heard of the fear they felt (2013). Whether she was mythical or not, what makes the idea of Diana compelling in a city associated with violent misogyny is her reversal of the usual order of things. As the exception to the rule, she underscores that murderous violence is an intensely gendered phenomenon.

However, despite the overwhelming monopolies on crime held by cisgender men, theorists of masculinities and crime James Messerschmidt and Stephen Tomsen caution against concluding that crime is inherently a male phenomenon or that gender necessarily implies criminal behaviour:

Male crime is gendered crime; yet when commentators on the masculinity-crime nexus cannot acknowledge the link between the bulk of male offending and such other factors as social class and race, they risk inadvertently naturalizing male offending. This shortsighted view reinforces a widespread public belief in a commonsense opinion of masculinity as a force inevitably leading millions of men to involvement in crime and violence. (2011, p. 182)

They go on to expand that 'there is scant progressive gain in simple essentialist understandings of male offending, a denial of human agency, or a cynical dismissal of substantial efforts to educate and promote diverse and non-violent masculinities' (2011, p. 183). Masculinity perceived as a singularity is, in this border context, unavoidably associated with certain kinds of violent criminality just as femininity is associated with victimhood and subjugation. If, as Jill Radford and Diana Russell put it, femicide is at the extreme end of ordinary anti-female terror, then the crimes in Juárez evidence a city at the extreme end of the extreme end. However, the strength of this logic paradoxically makes the attempts to denaturalise or *delink* masculinity from violent and sexual crime all the more important. In a sense it is precisely what Diana's desperate actions were designed to achieve.

This chapter looks at two pieces of detective fiction which explore border masculinities, but feature violent women protagonists: Alicia Gaspar de Alba's detective novel *Desert Blood: The Juárez Murders* (2005) and Sabina Berman and Carlos Carrera's film *Backyard* (*El Traspatio*) (2010). Both *Desert Blood* and *Backyard* cross borders of aesthetic and gender norms for their genre. They are both examples of what Sarah Gillman calls 'creative theorising' (2014, p. 12), interdisciplinary palimpsests, informed by a huge amount of research on their subject matter. Their purpose was not to entertain but rather to spark meaningful, responsible debate and, crucially, *action* on the femicides. In order to achieve their goals, however, they go beyond anything achievable in theoretical discourse. Their use of generic conventions of the thriller and detective story produce emotional effects in readers and viewers that I characterise here, building on Gilmann, as *affective theorising*. Since the so-called affective turn, *affect* has often been defined, after Brian Massumi, as both distinct from emotion and as a pre-cognitive response (1995). Jo Labanyi (2010), for example, defines affect as 'the body's response to stimuli at a precognitive and prelinguistic level' (p. 224). The idea that affects might be pre-linguistic presents an obvious problem for literary scholarship and may seem also antithetical to *theory*. Recent work on affect and literature by Alex Houen has pushed against a dichotomy between 'noncognitivist' and 'cognitivist' accounts, arguing instead for an approach to affect in theory and in literature that is neither strictly cognitivist nor noncognitivist, and that is open to considering literary affect in terms of fusions of content and form' (p. 5). It is my contention that these works work precisely to combine content (theorising) together with form, here understood as readers' and viewers' embodied understandings of the violence of the border, or indeed border*less* masculinities, with which both novel and film are concerned. In suggesting that Gaspar de Alba, Sabina Berman and Carlos Carrera engage in

216   J. WHITFIELD

affective theorising, I do not mean the theorising of affects, but rather the use of affective stimuli and theoretically informed plotting together in order to achieve the political goals of these texts.

Desert Blood was published in 2005 and won the Lambda award for best lesbian mystery. It is an unusual detective story because its protagonist Ivon Villa is not, as Irene Mata puts it, a 'typical private dick' (Mata 2010: 24). Not only is she an assistant literature professor who uses the skills of cultural studies to help her to track down her sister's kidnappers, she is also a butch gay woman. In the hyper-machista worlds through which the story takes her, she brings to bear not only the skills of the culturally literate, feminist academic (her PhD thesis is on toilet graffiti) but also the epistemic privilege of understanding the situation from the point of view of a multiply marginalised subject. Like Gaspar de Alba herself, Ivon is a native of the border, although both author and protagonist grew up on the El Paso side. Indeed, Ivon's positionality as an embodiment of Gloria Anzaldúa's border-crossing 'new mestiza' is ultimately key to her ability to make sense of the murders. The story concerns Ivon and her wife's attempt to adopt a baby from a pregnant fifteen-year-old *maquiladora* worker from Juárez. On arrival in El Paso, however, she discovers that the mother and unborn baby have been brutally murdered. Shortly afterwards, Ivon's sixteen-year-old 'kid sister' Irene is abducted while visiting a fair in Juárez. Ivon is forced to turn detective in order to try to save her sister, while simultaneously arranging another adoption and, as it turns out, avenging the murdered child she never got to parent. *Backyard* (2009) has a very similar agenda to *Desert Blood*. Written and produced by the playwright and public intellectual Sabina Berman and directed by Carlos Carrera, the film won several Ariels (the awards of the Mexican Academy of Film). It is a police procedural with a woman in the lead role that predates the international boom in feminist Scandinavian noir, the plot line involving colonel Blanca Brava (Ana de la Reguera), who is sent to Juárez to investigate the femicide crimes. Despite making immediate headway, she finds herself thwarted by the corruption within the police force itself and within local politics and economic elites. Parallel to Blanca's pursuit of the wealthy perpetrator, Mickey Santos (Jimmy Smits), is the tragic story of Juana (Asur Zagada), a young Tsotsil speaker from Chiapas who has moved to Juárez to work in the *Maquila* industry and to live with her cousin, and who gets romantically involved with another young southerner, Cutberto (Iván Cortes).

Rather than focusing on the women victims in these works, this chapter looks at six masculine characters that are central to Gaspar de Alba and Berman and Carrera's efforts to interpret the multiple factors which are responsible for the femicides. All perform border masculinities of one kind or another, crossing not only physical borders between nations but also the boundaries of a widely accepted hegemonic masculinity. In what follows, I begin by outlining some of the most prescient ideas from theories of masculinities. I go on to explore the representation of monstrous feminicidal masculinities embodied in the characters of JW and Mickey Santos, who I argue are used not only to explain the structural underpinnings of the crimes but also act as the emotional, affective, conduits for those structures. Analysis of the characters of Ivon and 'Oaxaca' explores how they express more contradictory and complex accounts of the relationship between violence and individual expressions of structurally constituted masculinity. Finally, I turn to two further characters, Jorgito and Pete McCuts, and consider the extent to which, by crossing generic borders, i.e. those between academic feminist theorising, political calls to arms and entertainment, these cultural products are able—paradoxically, perhaps, but necessarily—to imagine and affectively communicate alternative forms of non-violent or even anti-feminicidal masculinity.

STRUCTURES OF MONSTROSITY

The strikingly gendered nature of crime in general has given rise to much academic discussion of criminal masculinities. The starting point is often Raewyn Connell's deliberately 'sparse' taxonomy around 'hegemonic masculinity' ([1995] 2005, p. 81). In Connell's definition, 'hegemonic masculinity' is defined as the 'currently most honored way of being a man' (2005, p. 832). It is always relational and contingent, existing in contradistinction to its feminine obverse, 'emphasised femininity', which is so named in order to point out its inherently subordinate position relative to masculinity (Connell and Messerschmidt 2005, p. 848), and to other forms of masculinity that Connell loosely labels 'subordinate' (often in terms of sexuality) and 'marginalised' (those who play a 'symbolic role for white gender construction' ([1995] 2005, p. 80)) and 'complicit'. 'Complicit masculinity' is the broadest category, describing the majority of men who fail to conform precisely to the archetype of hegemonic masculinity but nevertheless do nothing to disturb its dominance. Along with all men, of course, such men do benefit from patriarchy and 'draw the patriarchal dividend' (2005, p. 79). An important sub-category of marginal masculinity in Connel's taxonomy, often associated with criminalised practices, is 'protest masculinity': characteristic of men in a marginal social location with the masculine claim on power 'contradicted by economic and social weakness':

> Protest masculinity may be reflected in hypermasculine aggressive display, as well as in anti-social, violent, and criminal behavior. Frequently, it exhibits a juxtaposition of overt misogyny, compulsory heterosexuality, and homophobia. (Messerschmidt and Tomsen 2007: 174)

In the case of violent crimes against women, research has often also 'stressed the relationship between offending and everyday, often legitimized constructions of manhood' (Messerschmidt and Tomsen 2011, p. 173). In the case of femicide, feminists have long argued that there is a strong link between relatively minor, commonplace forms of sexism and misogyny and femicide. In the most well-known definition of the term, Diana E. H. Russell defined femicide as the 'misogynous killing of women' (1992, p. 3). Jane Caputi argued that such violence was therefore inseparable from everyday misogyny: '[f]emicide is on the extreme end of a continuum of anti-female terror' (1992, p. 15). What we might term 'femicidal masculinity'—the masculinity of men who murder women—exists at this extreme end.

But the principal debates around the femicides in Juárez have rarely held masculinities alone to be responsible. The crimes have been explained by the nefarious confluence of intersecting, hierarchical relations of unequal privilege, along lines of economic power, gender, national citizenship, race and age. Blame is often placed on the economic and social upheavals resulting from the intensification of the *maquiladora* industry in the wake of the 1993 North Atlantic Free Trade Agreement (NAFTA). González Rodríguez's *Huesos en el desierto* (*Bones in the Desert*) pointed the finger at the white slave trade, which was linked to the *maquiladora* industry, local drug trafficking gangs, porn rings and serial killers (2002). Marxist feminists have tended to view the crimes as the result of the intersection of capital and patriarchy (e.g. Fregoso and Bejarano 2009) and critics of liberalism have emphasised the failures of the liberal state (Rodríguez 2009). Indeed, many scholars and activists prefer the term 'feminicide', derived from the Spanish translation of femicide, because it has come to emphasise the structural and intersectional forces behind the killings and the ultimate responsibility of the state (Lagarde y de los Rios 2009). Cynthia Bejarano and Rosa-Linda Fregoso prefer feminicide because of its capacity to bridge the gap between

> the "private" and "public" distinction by incorporating into its definition both systematic and systemic or structural violence sanctioned (or commissioned) by state actors (public) and violence committed by individuals or groups (private), since most of the violence suffered by women happens to be at the hands of private actors. (2009, p. 8)

Arguably the most significant gender theorist to have emerged in Mexico in recent years is Sayak Valencia whose work builds on both Connell and Sergio González Rodríguez's notion of the 'femicide machine' (2012). Valencia describes the violent masculine subject as a *sujeto endriago*. The term is a reference to the medieval romance *Amadís de Gaula*, in which Endriago is monstrous hybrid of man, hydra and dragon. The activities Valencia associates with such a subject are defined as follows: 'These endriago subjectivities use crime and overt violence as tools for meeting the demands of hyperconsumerist society and its processes of capitalist subjectification' (2018, p. 134). Valencia proposes the development of practices and discourses, *transfeminismo*, as the only solution to the destructive ultra-violence meted out by the *endriagos*. The *sujeto endriago* is, for Valencia, a product of a hyper-consumerist context in which physical violence is a means of rapidly gaining financial capital. It is no accident that it becomes particularly visible in border contexts in which the relationship between patriarchal violence and the nation-state—or, as Valencia would have it, the 'nation-market'—becomes particularly clear (2018, p. 45).

In both novel and film, the principal perpetrators of the crimes turn out to be ultra-violent, powerful border crossers whose masculinity we might call, after Lagarde, feminicidal. In *Desert Blood* the crimes are the responsibility of a paedophile snuff film ring headed by Jeremy Wilcox or JW, a Chief Detention Enforcement Officer with the US Border Patrol. The reader first encounters him in the second chapter, when he sits next to Ivon on the plane ride from LA to El Paso. He appears to conform to several hegemonic masculine archetypes. He wears a cowboy hat and drinks whisky but these superficial trappings also seem inauthentic to Ivon who observes that he looks, '[m]ore like a golfer than a cowboy, or maybe a surfer on steroids' (2005, p. 4). His casual sexism and racism are immediately revealed when he tells her, 'You don't look Mexican' then justifying that this is because she does not 'have an accent or anything' (2005, p. 6). He mocks her butch appearance by betting he can guess her profession before asking whether she is a model or works in the movie business. He then apologises in a gentlemanly fashion and, having lost his bet, attempts to give her a roll of pennies, which, we later learn, he forces his victims to swallow. The opening encounter with JW, relatively standard though his comments are, is sinister and constitutes what I am terming the *affective theorisation* of the continuum of misogyny that links everyday microaggressions to the rape and murder of women. JW is not encountered again until much later in the narrative, but it is not hard for the reader to identify him as a likely culprit, not least because Gaspar de Alba flags up the significance of the pennies in her introductory 'disclaimer' a few pages earlier. Readerly suspicions are thus immediately raised about JW, and his culpability is confirmed long before Ivon realises he is one of the ringleaders. This subversion of the usual puzzle-solving *raison d'etre* of the detective novel for readers means that the narrative tension is instead created through the question of whether Ivon will manage to negotiate the state institutions that protect him and facilitate his crimes.

JW's feminicidal masculinity operates as a kind of 'structural pathology', facilitated by his enjoyment of intersecting privileges: as a white officer of the US state agency who can operate on both sides of the border, he is able to kidnap women on the Juárez side and take them to the 'studio' in El Paso with impunity. When Ivon next encounters him it is as she is attempting to cross back into El Paso. In his role as border guard he stops her car and tells her that she will not be allowed into the US because of her sexuality, asking if she is not aware 'that gays and lesbians are a threat to national security?' and adding: 'All psychopaths and sexual deviants are supposed to be excluded' (2005, p. 277). The border itself is thus shown to be the instrument of homophobic masculinity, mimetically masquerading as a shield. After JW's death at the end of the novel, *El Paso Times* reports that he and another police officer who operates as his accomplice were killed as part of a sting operation and, with phrasing that strains to restore homophobic masculinity as the guardian of impermeable barriers, describes how they died 'in the line of duty, holding the line' (2005, p. 326). That the same corrupt state apparatus that protected him in life protects him in death illustrates how the patriarchal institutional structures that protect the nation are also culpable for its crimes.

The roots of JW's feminicidal masculinity are not examined. He arrives in the novel a fully formed torturer, in a way that pathologises but does not explain the excessive form of hegemonic masculinity he embodies. Although he directly participates in the commercialisation of torture and death, his privileges mean that he does not fit with the definition of Valencia's *endriago*, as he is not motivated by economic necessity to participate in the market in murder. Rather it makes him more akin to what Nicholas Groth's taxonomy of rapists describes as a 'sadistic rapist'—a perpetrator of 'ritualistic and potentially lethal' violence who is blatantly psychotic but is 'usually able to conceal these darker impulses from others' (2013, p. 46). The motivations of the relatively rare sadistic rapists have less to do with social contexts and more to do with perverseness as they are 'sexually excited by the pain and fear they cause their victims' (Robertiello and Terry 2007, p. 510).[1] Thus, the social structures and institutions around JW facilitate his actions and protect him but are not in and of themselves the sole source of his violence.

The question of individual vs structural culpability is also at the heart of *Backyard*. Like *Desert Blood*, the film involves a feminist take on traditionally male-centred crime thrillers. It opens with a collage of overtly border-related items—fences, wires, signs, police cordons. The first image is of a clump of long hair, caught on a barbed wire fence, blowing slightly in the wind, associating the crossing of borders with the violation of bodies. The camera pans right across the police cordon, then close-ups and a crane shot seem to foreground the land itself. Within a colour pallet imbued with yellow, mounted police officers and other uniformed men move across the *mise-en-scène*, recalling cowboy films. The slightly unexpected appearance of Blanca, a woman investigator who seems to be in charge, subverts our expectations of a border patriarchy implied by the earlier shots. JW's equivalent in *Backyard*, Mickey Santos, is a privileged border crosser whose power emanates from what Valencia calls, as mentioned above, the nation-market, or *mercado nación*. A Chicano entrepreneur, he is also identified as a perpetrator early in the plot. His accomplice 'El Sultán' (Sayed Badreya), an Egyptian based on the historical figure of Omar Sharif Latif, is arrested and held in custody. The real Sharif Latif was a chemist who was convicted of femicide in 1996 and sentenced to thirty years imprisonment. The crimes continued after his incarceration, however, and after he died in prison in 2006 (*El Universal* 2006). In *Backyard*, Blanca immediately raises suspicions against Santos because he is known to have met El Sultán when both were imprisoned in El Paso for sexual crimes. In Santos' home, we see how—on the surface—he too conforms to an ideal of hegemonic masculinity: he is married to a glamorous woman, father to a young daughter, dresses well and possesses a large, beautifully maintained home in El Paso. He crosses the border regularly, to work but also to commit crimes under the protection of the corrupt chief of police. Thanks to his economic power and connections, Santos is able to confound Blanca's efforts and undermine her investigation. Santos is eventually only brought to justice after Blanca (in a scene I analyse below) is forced to 'go rogue' in order to end his crimes.

With both JW and Santos, the plot device of revealing their identities early on makes the political point that in cultures of impunity, the identification of the perpetrators is not enough. In terms of a conventional narrative structure, then, neither novel nor film adheres to the convention Todorov attributes to SS Van Dine, that detective fiction should reveal information about the plot according to the homology 'author: reader = criminal: detective', in other words the criminal and author share knowledge of the crime and the reader discovers the truth at the same time as the detective (1977, p. 27). The deviation from this norm means that, rather than the traditional insecurity about the identity of the killer, the narrative tension depends on whether the women detectives will be able to overcome the duplicitous structural obstacles ranged against them by the combination of the forces of state, gender, organised crime, capital and the border. Both characters thus serve an important function not only in terms of narrative direction but also because they demonstrate the culpability of the intersecting factors which constitute their power.

Feminicidal masculinity, as an extreme form of misogynist killing, does not conform to the hegemonic archetype because it grotesquely exceeds it: the current hegemonic standard of masculinity, patriarchal and exploitative as it might be, does not condone misogynistic killing. It is nonetheless significant that Santos and JW exceed the hegemonic ideal: their positions of privilege mean their violence cannot be made sense of as a form of 'protest masculinity' as, in its sadism, it even exceeds the excesses of the economically-motivated *sujeto endriago*. Their purpose in these stories is to demonstrate that structural complicity with feminicidal masculinity is more active than the complicity of individual men who passively draw the patriarchal dividend. Because both men appear in the narratives fully formed, already at the height of their powers, occupying positions of intersectional privilege, while neither experiences any character progression and their crimes are resolvable only through their violent deaths, they reveal something of a paradox in constructionist thinking on feminicides: a focus on how the fact that multiple, structural factors demonstrably work to *protect* feminicidal men does not necessarily explain how those same structures work to *produce* multiply privileged, feminicidal individuals in the first place.

Violent Complexes

More complex and arguably more significant for the way they affectively communicate the misogyny/feminicide continuum are the narrative trajectories of Cutberto and Ivon. In *Backyard*, Cutberto, also known as 'Oaxaca', is a would-be boyfriend of Juana. Insofar as he is a poor, indigenous man, in terms of Connell's typology, Cutberto occupies a marginalised masculinity. The nickname is indicative of this marginalised status as Oaxaca is a state with a large indigenous population but is not Chiapas, where Tsotsil speakers come from. It acts to erase important cultural differences and demonstrates the racism of his friends. At the beginning of the story we learn that Juana had previously lived in poverty with her father, for whom she had to clean and cook. Despite the poor wages and working conditions, life in Juárez is liberating for her as she is freed from the paternal yoke. Her cousin, Márgara teaches her to do her hair and dress in a style that is distinct from her indigenous past. While out clubbing she is approached by the timid southerner, who asks her to dance. They speak to each other in Tsotsil and begin dating. After their first date he takes her to see where he lives and she confidently begins to seduce him. He is shy and reluctant, telling her, 'We should talk to your father first' (translations taken from the subtitles). In retrospect the fact that his reticence is expressed through an appeal to patriarchal authority is a red flag. When Juana soon tires of Cutberto and begins socialising with other men, he is heartbroken. He tells her that all he wanted was for them to belong to each other, again revealing an understanding of relationships in terms of possession. He does not insist or attempt to stop her when she humiliates him by abandoning him for an older man who does not appear to be indigenous, in front of a group of his friends, surrendering to a patriarchal regime based on age as well as race.

Nevertheless, Oaxaca seems to intuitively understand the femicides better than almost any other character. He does still articulate the nonsense of victim-blaming when the embattled regional governor bows to public pressure to respond to the femicides by putting on self-defence classes for women, in which Juana is one of the best pupils, easily dispatching the instructor. The perverse logic of training women to avoid their own murders in this way is encapsulated by Cutberto, who points out that 'If they were armed at least they'd have a chance'. Later on, at night, when Juana rejects him, though, he demonstrates a keen political (not to say feminist) understanding of the femicides. As his friends are discussing the killings, stating that the attention given to the women is unjust given the far larger numbers of men who are murdered, it is Cutberto who answers their charge of reverse sexism, explaining:

> But the dead men are always armed. They're mostly dealers, right? And they get shot in the crossfire. But not the dead women. They take them so they can screw them [...] You know a man by how he treats women and children.

Their reply is that this is precisely the attitude that led Juana to humiliate him. They tell him he has a choice, 'Either you forgive her and keep moaning, or you don't forgive shit and quit being such a fag'. He is persuaded that he should drug Juana and abduct her for sex, without realising that the other men also plan to rape her. The sinister logic of his earlier chivalry is revealed as he perceives nothing wrong with the first of the rapes, his own of her, seeing it as consistent with his earlier declarations of love. Cutberto is thus capable of simultaneously recognising the horror of the femicides while remaining blind to the link between them and what he considers to be the justified date rape of a woman he believes to belong to him. This continuity is only brought home to him when he realises that his friends have further, even worse plans for Juana.

Unlike Mickey Santos and JW, Cutberto is not a monster, but just a kid with standard chivalrous values who is, in a sense, also a victim of circumstance. His journey from a naive male *ingenue* to conspiring rapist demonstrates the complex confluence of marginalised, hegemonic and feminicidal masculinities. Cutberto's marginal masculinity, his expressiveness, and even his later descent into murderous violence are shown to be the result of his own vulnerability at the hands of older, larger, whiter men. Cutberto's violence recalls Rita Laura Segato's work on violent masculinity. She points out that respectable masculinity is a quality which it is possible to 'lose'. Segato (2004) argues that the crimes in Juárez can be explained as the actions of men under pressure to maintain or demonstrate their masculinity in front of their peers. Pointing out that rape is a form of violation of the sovereignty of the individual, Segato draws a link between the loss of traditional masculine economic activities and the violations of Mexican sovereignty represented by the mainly US-owned *maquiladoras*, ultimately suggesting that the murdered women are bearing the brunt of a masculinity which is protesting the loss of its 'sovereignty' (2005). Certainly Cutberto's actions are explicable as part of a 'protest' against the loss of his symbolic sovereignty inflicted by his humiliation at the hands of his companions and Juana's defiance of his sense of ownership over her. The fact that he is, in this sequence, the focaliser of the action draws viewers intimately and horrifyingly into an affective experience of his transformation into a monstrous, feminicidal *sujeto endriago*.

Even more complex than Cutberto is Ivon, a character who has been central to many laudatory critical responses to *Desert Blood*. Her position as a queer, butch, Chicana detective is almost single-handedly responsible for the positive academic reception of the novel. Mata, for example, sees Ivon as a personification of Chela Sandoval's 'methodology of the oppressed' whose 'marginalised position [allows her to develop] a consciousness that allows her to see beneath the surface and draw connections not easily recognised' (2005, p. 24). In the scene where she first meets JW it is clear how her subject position grants her a certain epistemic privilege to identify a possible suspect. Erica Haggerty and Marieta Messmer have similarly positive readings of the character (2012; 2012). This enthusiastic reaction to Ivon bears out Judith Kegan Gardiner's point that '[o]ne paradox of female masculinity discourses is that instead of being considered derivative, female masculinity may be celebrated as superior to masculinity in men' (2012, p. 599). This resonates with a point Jack Halberstam makes in *Female Masculinity*, namely that '[i]f what we call "dominant masculinity" appears to be a naturalized relation between maleness and power, then it makes little sense to examine men for the contours of that masculinity's social construction', and that women's masculinities shine a brighter light on the construction of masculinity than those of men (or AMAB people) (1998, p. 13). Halberstam argues that female masculinity has subversive power within both hetero- and even in many homonormative contexts. It represents a structural threat to male masculinity because it reveals its fragile and constructed nature.

Ivon represents a threat to established patriarchal forms of masculinity in several ways. She sports a tattoo of a labrys (a double-headed axe, symbol of lesbian identity) on her neck. Her mother considers the tattoo to have been responsible for the death of her father, who died after a drunken fall on Father's Day, supposedly having become inebriated because of his shock at seeing it. This (non-symbolic) killing of the father (although Ivon's mother is a far from reliable source) foreshadows the later killing of

JW. But, aside from allegedly directly causing the death of her father, Ivon's gender non-conformity also makes visible the extent of patriarchal masculinity as her masculine appearance alone constantly provokes all manner of prejudiced responses. As we have seen, some of these come from the very same men who turn out to be rapists and murderers or at least complicit in those crimes. Her masculinity also provokes women within her own family, most notably her mother, Lydia, who is relentless in her homophobic persecution of her daughter. She constantly attempts to police gender norms and abusively calls her '*¡Manflora! ¡Marimacha. ¡Sin vergüenza¡*' ('Shemale! Dyke! Shameless!') (2005, p. 67). Lydia's abusive behaviour towards her is revealed, however, to be patriarchal in origin. It is the result of resentment towards her deceased, unfaithful husband. She also abuses Ivon for being a *mujeriega* (a womaniser) like her father, who Ivon also physically resembles. Viewed through the lens of her own personal relationships, Ivon's masculinity is even more complex than this. Rather than merely exemplifying a positive image that necessarily performs the task of 'undermining' hetero-normativity, there are more awkward aspects to her subjectivity, mainly related to the fact that she is far from immune from expressing elements of patriarchal behaviour herself. Her violence and rage, while entirely justifiable in the circumstances, are frequently turned against those who love her most. In anger she gets into bar fights and punches her former lover Raquel.

Ivon's relationship with Raquel is another way in which Gaspar de Alba subverts tropes of hardboiled noir. Raquel is one of the novel's queer *femmes fatales*—a seductive, untrustworthy woman. Raquel is eleven years older than Ivon and originally seduced her when the latter was still in high school. In keeping with this trope, when Ivon remembers Raquel it is in ways that make her the passive subject of Ivon's male gaze: 'her black eyes and full red lips, the *suavecito* movement of her hips on the checkered dance floor of the Memories bar' (2005, p. 13). Ivon had previously imputed to Raquel an almost supernaturally dangerous sexuality ('Once, Ivon had believed Raquel put a spell on her with those black eyes' (2005, p. 73)) and disbelieves her claim that she is married: 'she's not even wearing a ring. Same old Raquel, always lying about something' (2005, p. 78). Even more in keeping with the hypocritical machismo of the hardboiled detective, Raquel is assaulted by Ivon, who also cheats on her wife Brigit with Raquel. Raquel's reaction to being assaulted is to question how much she provoked the attack:

Maybe I asked for it, she thought. Maybe she just wanted to lure Ivon back using the same infallible trick she had always used before. Stir up her rage. If the way to some people's hearts is through their stomachs, to get to Ivon's you have to go through her rage ... But afterward, after the rage settled, there was love and tenderness and so much passion. (p. 192)

Ivon's relationship with her wife Brigit (whose own name recalls Mary Astor's Brigid O'Shaughnessy in *The Maltese Falcon* (1941)) also casts her in a role that evokes the machismo of the private hardboiled detective. She responds to Brigit's attempts to be emotionally accommodating with cruel comments about how she 'hates it when [she] get[s] all co-dependent' (2005, p. 328).

In a nuanced analysis of Ivon's character, Sarah Gillman reads Ivon's behaviour towards Raquel as the result of 'suppressed rage of [her] internalised coloniality' (2014, p. 18). As she points out it is her inability to deal with her own violence that drives Ivon to leave El Paso. Gaspar de Alba's novel is thus significant in its laying-out of the ways in which abusive hierarchies of gender can manifest themselves in almost all of the characters. The hyper-self-aware feminist literary critic Ivon's gendered and occasionally violent behaviour does not mean she is in any sense as bad as the murderers, but according to Caputi and Russel's continuum of misogyny, her actions cannot be considered to be entirely unrelated. In terms of the novel as affective theorising, Ivon militates against overly simplistic uses of Connell's four-part model, demonstrating how elements of marginality and subordination and complicity can coexist in the same body. Gaspar de Alba uses Ivon's behaviour to reveal the culpability of patriarchal practices even as she simultaneously denaturalises gender crime as masculine by practising a further iteration of protest masculinity. Far from representing an ideal archetype of a transgressive alternative masculinity, Ivon demonstrates the enormous difficulties of fully overcoming internalised patterns of structural violence. Her female masculinity simultaneously performs three functions: it reveals the sexism of others; it shows the extent to which patriarchal tendencies can leave the male body; and it highlights the functioning of epistemic privilege. Ivon demonstrates the need to both de-essentialise toxic masculine traits as inherently male and remain vigilant about its capacity to corrupt.

ANTI-FEMINICIDAL MASCULINITIES

Both film and novel attempt to explain and expose the persistence of masculinities that allow for the violence of femicide to continue. In terms of the taxonomies of masculinity outlined by Connell, the feminicidal characters of Mickey Santos and JW demonstrate how individuals with the economic capital, gender privilege, border-crossing abilities and the ability to corrupt the state are able to create an environment of impunity around them. The psychopathic nature of these two figures places them well outside normative definitions of hegemonic patriarchal masculinity. At the same time they show that complicit masculinity goes far beyond the passive gaining of a patriarchal dividend and that pre-existing structural factors are at play in the creation of such complicit masculinities in the first place. Where film and novel differ is that ultimately *Backyard* is, on the face of it, very pessimistic about the potential for masculinity to evolve except in negative directions. Blanca's final lethal shooting of Santos is, for Nina Namaste, evidence that she too has succumbed to the logic of patriarchal violence: 'in using unethical methods she perpetuates the highly patriarchal, ineffectual, and gender-biased behaviours of her profession' (2012: 486–7). The sequence that leads to Santos's death is worth examining in more detail. Santos receives a phone call from the Juárez police commander (Alejandro Calva) who is showing his successor Fierro (Marco Pérez) what kinds of corruption the role entails. The commander tells him to 'proceder sin problemas' ('proceed smoothly') and wishes him a good night. Blanca and Fierro then track Santos, however, and interrupt him in the act of kidnapping a schoolgirl. On exiting his car, Santos is left standing between Fierro and Blanca, facing Blanca. The girl flees into the night and he observes: 'She is more scared of the cops than me. On the other hand, I turn myself in knowing that I'll get a fair trial from the authorities, a fair trial and fair sentence.' As he speaks, Santos turns briefly to look at Fierro, who represents the future of the Juárez police. As Santos throws his gun to the ground, the handheld camera dips, indicating that the perspective is Blanca's. There is a reverse close-up of Blanca aiming the gun then a shot from over her shoulder showing the entire scene with Fierro, out of focus, behind Santos. The sense that Blanca and Fierro represent two very different ways out of the situation is underlined when he asks 'So, what do I do, cop? Which way? Here? [indicating Fierro] There? [gesturing towards her]'. Blanca requests him to place his hands up and then shoots him repeatedly in the chest. The way the scene is shot implies her action is based on a lack of faith in there being any other way to prevent more women from being killed by him. Like Diana la Cazadora de Chóferes, she no longer believes in the possibility of any kind of anti-feminicidal—that is to say state-based—justice.

On the other hand, the consideration of *Desert Blood* as a form of creative theorising begs the final question as to which of the many competing theories about the crimes it confirms, and whether there is space for a more positive outlook. After the novel's bloody climax, Ivon goes and sits on a hill overlooking the twin cities in order to reflect on all that she has learned. After weighing the many influences and possibilities, she concludes that beyond the crime ring she has uncovered, the most significant reason for the murders of the women is economic, linked to the control of their reproductive cycles, designed to ensure their *productive* power by limiting their *re-productive* power. The murders represent a 'cost effective way of disposing of non-productive/reproductive surplus labour while simultaneously protecting the border from infiltration by brown bodies' (2005, p. 333). Despite this realisation and the fact that Pete McCutts, the detective she cooperated with, has new leads in the case, Ivon decides to go home, finish writing her dissertation and get tenure which in turn will mean she is able to buy a house for Brigit and their newly adopted son. Although turning away from detection and moving towards family, Ivon is not totally abandoning concerns around the crimes.

Earlier in the novel, Ivon, who had previously resisted Brigit's desire for a baby, sees a cute, lonely boy in a bookstore and is overcome with an inexplicable desire to have a son. When the baby they had planned to adopt is murdered, her social worker and activist cousin, Ximena, takes Ivon to meet a toddler Jorgito, whose mother is fatally ill. Jorgito is probably the biological son of Amen Hakim Hassan, the Egyptian chemist and rapist who is the only person in prison for the murders (he is also based on the historical figure of Omar Sharif Latif). Hassan had been fraudulently operating as a doctor, in the *maquilas* where, in a reflection of a real widespread practice, his role was to administer contraceptives to prevent the women workers becoming unproductive to their employers through pregnancy. He abused this position by sexually assaulting and conducting medical experiments on the workers. When Ivon learns of Jorgito's provenance, she is furious with Ximena ('you knew the kid you were asking me to adopt came from the sperm of a pervert and possible serial killer' (2005, p. 97)) and thinks, incorrectly as it transpires, that 'Brigit would never accept Jorgito under these circumstances' (2005, p. 97). By overcoming

230   J. WHITFIELD

these initial reactions and adopting the son of the serial rapist, Ivon makes the ultimate reconciliatory gesture. This extraordinary act of compassion and acceptance flies in the face of any instinctive/affective response that the reader might have to reject a child of such provenance. Once again, Gaspar de Alba uses plot to emotionally model the journey of a border(less) masculinity: that of Jorgito. Here, however, through her acceptance of the boy into her family, Gaspar de Alba symbolically places her faith in the healing power of the queer family to break the patriarchal relations that also blighted Ivon's own childhood. Gaspar de Alba finally posits queer, interracial and intercultural parenting as a way to overcome cycles of historical violence by producing new masculinities.

There is also an adult character in *Desert Blood* who is the product of such a queer family and represents the possibility of a non-patriarchal or at least significantly revised masculinity: El Paso detective, Pete McCutts. Despite his gringo name he is a Chicano whose parents are a good-hearted El Paso Judge Anacleto or 'Cleto' and a butch lesbian car mechanic named Bernie. Judge Anacleto is first mentioned because he regularly expunges the record of Ivon's lawbreaking activist cousin Ximena (2005, p. 34). McCutts explains the circumstances of his conception as a reversal of the norms of gendered seduction. He tells his colleagues: 'Bernie came over one day with a jar of her famous spiked *limonada* and just straight up proposed to my dad' (2005, p. 155). The judge responds by protesting he is too old:

> 'I'm not a young macho, any more, you know. I can't just impregnate on command.' Always Cleto's military training crept into his speech, but in the end, it was Bernie who took command—she could fix anything, that Bernie. (2005: 157)

Cleto's condition is that he gets to give the child the unconventional name which is an acrostic of the nine Greek muses plus Sor Juana (2005, p. 157).[2] Bernie accepts, in spite of its gringo sound, saying, 'Okay, *viejo*, you wanna name your son after ten women, *pues*, it's fine with me, but don't go blaming my ass if your kid turns out funny. *Nada de que* like mother like son, eh?' (2005, p. 158). McCutt's name and parentage mean that he is also a border crosser, straddling Chicano and European identity, and the product of a relationship that transcends the nuclear family. In an Oedipal manner, McCutts is strongly attracted to dominant masculine women, especially Ivon. He is the only policeman to take the case seriously and his pursuit of the trail in defiance of his superiors is the only reason it is finally resolved. His role in the climax of the novel confounds expectations around the hero policeman. In a moment of symbolic castration he is immediately shot and wounded before handing his gun to Ivon and calling for help. McCutts is an unlikely character, but he represents an important vision of non-violent masculinity which is reconciled with the state, although crucially this involves failing to follow orders. Together with Cleto, McCuts comes to demonstrate a way of being a man that could be described as *anti-feminicidal*, a kind of queering or subverting of the masculinist institutions of the police force and the legal system, and hence embodies the possibility of a functional legal system for a future Juárez/El Paso.

Through the carefully plotted emotional trajectories of their characters, Berman and Carerra and Gaspar de Alba give viewers and readers disarmingly complex theoretical understandings, not only of masculinities along the 'continuum of anti-female terror' but also of the shifting, constructed, contingent and potential hopeful nature of masculinity when it becomes unbound, (or unbordered) by the essentialism of hetero-patriarchal normativity. The specific mechanisms, as I have described here, function through affective impacts and theoretical explanations that work in concert to deepen the message of both novel and film.

Notes

1. The other, more common, 'types' have been categorised as 'power reassurance rapists (compensatory); power assertive rapists (power, impulsive) and anger retaliation rapists (power, control)' (Robertiello and Terry 2007, p. 510).
2. '"Polyhymnia, muse of the Song; Euterpe, muse of Lyric Poetry; Thalia, muse of Comedy; Erato, muse of Love Poetry […] There's Melpomene, the muse of Tragedy; Clio, the muse of History; Calliope, muse of Epic Poetry; Urania, muse of Astronomy; Terpsichore, muse of the Dance; and Sor Juana Inés de la Cruz, the tenth muse of Mexico"' (2005, p. 125).

WORKS CITED

Caputi, Jane, and Diana E.H. Russell. 1992. Femicide: Sexist Terrorism Against Women. In *Femicide: The Politics of Woman Killing*, 13–24. New York: Twayne.

Carrera González, Carlos, Director. 2010. *El Traspatio [Backyard]*. Maya Entertainment.

Connell, Raewyn. [1995] 2005. *Masculinities*. Berkeley: University of California.

Connell, Raewyn, and James W. Messerschmidt. 2005. Hegemonic Masculinity Rethinking the Concept. *Gender & Society* 19 (6): 829–859.

Diario. 2013. Fiscalía Duda de Existencia de 'Diana La Cazadora'; Especialistas Critican Manejo de Investigación. http://diario.mx/Local/2013-09-07_c3a9657c/fiscalia-duda-de-existencia-de-diana-la-cazadora-especialistas-critican-manejo-de-investigacion-/. Accessed 25 March 2016.

El Universal. 2006. Muere feminicida egipcio de infarto en Chihuahua. http://archivo.eluniversal.com.mx/estados/61426.html. Accessed 30 March 2016.

Fregoso, Rosa-Linda, and Cynthia Bejarano. 2009. *Terrorizing Women: Feminicide in the Americas*. Durham: Duke University Press.

Gardiner, Judith Kegan. 2012. Female Masculinity and Phallic Women—Unruly Concepts. *Feminist Studies* 38 (3): 597–624.

Gaspar de Alba, Alicia. 2005. *Desert Blood: The Juárez Murders*. Houston, TX: Arte Público Press.

Gillman, Laura. 2014. Queering Decoloniality: Epistemic Politics in Alicia Gaspar de Alba's Desert Blood. In *Identities on the Move: Contemporary Representations of New Sexualities and Gender Identities*, ed. Silvia Pilar Castro-Borrego and Maria Isabel Romero-Ruiz, 11–26. Lanham: Lexington.

González Rodríguez, Sergio. 2002. *Huesos en el desierto*. Barcelona: Anagrama.

———. 2012. *The Femicide Machine*. Los Angeles: Semiotext(e)).

Groth, A. Nicholas, and H. Jean Birnbaum. 2013. *Men Who Rape: The Psychology of the Offender*. New York: Springer.

Haggerty, Erica. 2012. Desert Blood: A Powerful Synthesis of Narrative Strategies. *UCB Comparative Literature Undergraduate Journal*. http://ucb-cluj.org/announcing-clujs-fall-2011-issue/vol-22-spring-2012-special-issue/2621-2/. Accessed 4 September 2014.

Halberstam, Judith. 1998. *Female Masculinity*. Durham: Duke University Press.

Herrera, Yuri. 2013. Diana, Hunter of Bus Drivers. www.thisamericanlife.org. http://www.thisamericanlife.org/diana-hunter-of-bus-drivers/. Accessed 24 March 2016.

Labanyi, Jo. 2010. Doing Things: Emotion, Affect, and Materiality. *Journal of Spanish Cultural Studies* 11 (3–4): 223–233.

Lagarde y do los Rios, Marcela. 2009. Feminist Keys for Understanding Femicide: Theoretical, Political and Legal Construction. In *Terrorizing Women:*

Feminicide in the Americas, ed. Rosa-Linda Fregoso and Cynthia Bejarano, xi–xxvi. Durham: Duke University Press.

Mata, Irene. 2010. Writing on the Walls: Deciphering Violence and Industrialization in Alicia Gaspar de Alba's Desert Blood. *Multi-Ethnic Literature of the U.S.* 35 (3): 15–40.

Messerschmidt, James, and Stephen Tomsen. 2011. Masculinities. In *Handbook of Critical Criminology*, ed. Walter S. DeKeseredy and Molly Dragiewicz. London: Routledge.

Messmer, Marieta. 2012. Transfrontera Crimes: Representations of the Juárez Femicides in Recent Fictional and Non-Fictional Accounts. *American Studies Journal* 57. http://www.asjournal.org/archive/57/202.html.

Namaste, Nina. 2012. Not Just a Ciudad Juárez Problem: Extreme Capitalism, Masculinity, and Impunity in Sabina Berman's Backyard. *Contemporary Theatre Review* 22 (4): 485–498.

Radford, Jill, and Diana E.H. Russell. 1992. *Femicide: The Politics of Woman Killing*. New York: Twayne.

Robertiello, Gina, and Karen J. Terry. 2007. 'Can We Profile Sex Offenders? A Review of Sex Offender Typologies', Aggression and Violent Behavior. *Crime Classification and Offender Typologies* 12 (5): 508–518.

Rodríguez, Ileana. 2009. *Liberalism at its Limits: Crime and Terror in the Latin American Cultural Text*. Pittsburgh: University of Pittsburgh Press.

Segato, Rita Laura. 2004. Territorio soberanía y crímenes de segundo estado. *Labrys* 6. http://mujeresdeguatemala.org/wp-content/uploads/2014/06/Territorio-soberani%CC%81a-y-cri%CC%81menes-de-segundo-estado.pdf. Accessed 12 January 2016.

Todorov, Tzvetan. 1977. *The Poetics of Prose*. Ithaca: Cornell University Press.

Valencia, Sayak. 2018. *Gore Capitalism*. Boston: MIT Press.

Index[1]

A
Affect, 4, 49, 51, 97, 136, 160, 174, 195, 202, 215, 216
Affective theorising, 16, 215, 216, 227
Amilhat Szary, Anne-Laure, 2
Anzaldúa, Gloria, 4, 5, 9, 10, 45–52, 55, 56, 58, 60–62, 125, 216
Auster, Paul, 12, 109–127

B
Beasley, Christine, 8, 14, 26, 154, 155, 164
Biopolitics, 9, 23, 157
Borders
  borderity, 2
  borderlessness, 4, 5, 17, 159
  borderscape, 2, 18n2
  borders (gender), 163, 165
  borders (general), 10
  borders (spatial), 3–5, 7, 16–18
  borders (temporal), 152
  flux, 4

masculinities, 1–18, 18n2, 122, 138, 215, 217
  as method (Sandro Mezzadra and Brett Neilsen), 1, 4, 17
  studies, 2, 8
Bourdieu, Pierre, 14, 158, 160, 163, 165
Brown, Wendy, 2, 7

C
Caciquismo, 5, 13, 149–169
Capancioni, Claudia, 3, 5, 150
Carrera, Carlos, 16, 215–216
Cartographies, 3
Chen, Ying, 10, 28, 45–63
Class, 4, 5, 7, 22, 24–27, 33–38, 69, 76, 94, 151, 158, 162, 164, 165, 184, 199–201, 203, 206, 214, 223
Climate, 16, 30, 96
Coetzee, J.M., 11, 87–102, 103n5
Concetta Costantini, Maria, 3

---

[1] Note: Page numbers followed by 'n' refer to notes.

© The Author(s), under exclusive license to Springer Nature Switzerland AG 2024
A. Thakkar et al. (eds.), *Border Masculinities*,
https://doi.org/10.1007/978-3-031-68050-2

235

236 INDEX

Condé, Maryse, 13, 129–143,
  145n12, 145n13,
  145n15, 145n16
Confucianism, 8
Connell, Raewyn, 7–9, 12, 16, 22, 23,
  27, 30, 32, 36, 46, 53, 56, 89,
  92, 103n7, 139, 151, 154, 162,
  168, 195, 217, 219, 223,
  227, 228
Costantini, Mariaconcetta, 3

D
Devi, Ananda, 10, 45–63
Diaspora, 48, 70–74
Digital technologies, 84
Disabilities, 6, 11, 87–102, 103n7

E
Eagleton, Terry, 3, 4
Epistemologies, 3–5, 17
Ethnicity, 7, 28, 69

F
Facultad (Gloria Anzaldúa),
  10, 51, 60
Femicide/feminicide, 5, 15,
  214–219, 221, 223,
  224, 228
Feminism, 89, 194, 207n3
Foucault, Michel, 9, 22, 23, 157

G
Gaspar de Alba, Alicia, 16, 215–217,
  220, 226, 227, 230, 231
Giraut, Frédéric, 2
Globalisation, 16, 62
Goch, Dylan, 80, 81

H
Hamad, Hannah, 15, 193–195, 197,
  202, 203
Haywood, Chris, 5
Hird, Derek, 4, 22, 27–29
Hooper, Tom, 15, 191–207
Hybridities/hybridisation, 11, 52, 81,
  83–85, 141, 191–207
Hypermasculinities, 26
Hyphen/hyphenation, 2, 7, 8

K
Kimmel, Michael, 15, 50, 69, 163,
  195, 200, 203

L
Liminality, 8, 11, 47, 90, 91, 97, 100

M
Maalouf, Amin, 10, 47, 49, 50, 53,
  58, 61, 62, 63n7
Mac an Ghaill, Máirtín, 5
MacInnes, John, 6
Marginalisation, 9, 31, 80,
  195, 207n3
Masculinities
  complicit, 7, 16, 89, 154, 217, 222,
    226, 228
  female, 6, 7, 16, 225, 227
  hegemonic, 8, 9, 25, 27, 94–96,
    100, 103n7, 139, 151–154,
    164, 168, 195–197, 201, 206,
    207, 217, 221
  marginalised, 89, 154, 223
  patriarchal, 8, 23, 63n5, 228
  protest, 218, 222, 227
  queer, 193
  resistant, 8

INDEX   237

sub-hegemonic, 5, 8, 27, 30, 34,
  37, 154, 155
subordinate, 16, 164
Mattoscio, Mara, 3, 117
Mezzadra, Sandro, 1
Mignolo, Walter, 1
Migration, 2, 3, 13, 29, 47, 52, 53,
  55, 56, 60, 63n9, 69–73, 80, 83,
  84, 88, 131, 133, 143, 145n13
Mobility/mobilities, 2, 3, 5, 7, 11, 16,
  29, 47, 62, 67–85, 130
Mozley, Fiona, 13, 91, 149–168
Mulvey, Laura, 14, 174–176
Music, 5, 11, 68, 70, 82–85, 96, 100,
  192, 198, 199, 202

N
Nationalism, 28, 68
Nature, 3, 7, 8, 14, 16, 80, 88, 90,
  100, 112, 118, 135, 141,
  145n18, 156, 158, 159, 163,
  186, 201, 205, 217, 225,
  228, 231
Négritude (Aimé Césaire), 13,
  135, 140–143
Neilsen, Brett, 1
Novel (detective), 5, 6, 16, 118, 122,
  124, 215, 220
Novel (epistolary), 5, 59

P
Patriarchy, 9, 26, 35, 38, 111, 217,
  218, 221
Pérez Firmat, Gustavo, 2
Planetarity (Gayatri Chakravorty
  Spivak), 8, 16–18, 155
Postfeminism, 195
Postmodernism, 12, 111, 114, 115,
  117, 125

Private/public, 4, 9, 11, 14,
  15, 23, 27, 36, 40n9, 76,
  79, 93, 96, 97, 99, 114, 122,
  150, 155–157, 159, 167,
  193–204, 206, 214, 216, 219,
  223, 227

R
Race, 4, 5, 45, 46, 74, 132, 133, 141,
  142, 184, 214, 218, 223
Relation (Édouard Glissant), 13, 130
Reproductive arena (Raewyn Connell),
  9, 23, 27, 32, 89
Rhys, Gruff, 11, 68, 70–72,
  74–76, 79–85
Rulfo, Juan, 13, 122, 151, 152,
  154, 159

S
Schwalbe, Michael, 11, 89
Sedgwick, Eve Kosofsky, 15, 33, 206
Self/Other, 4, 5, 26, 31, 59
Shen, Haofang, 9
Shyamalan, M. Night, 14, 182,
  183, 187
Song, Geng, 4, 22, 24, 25, 27–29
Space/spatial, 1–18, 26, 33, 36,
  46, 47, 50, 52, 54, 72, 76, 79,
  82, 84, 85, 90, 93, 96–98,
  102, 120, 125, 130, 132–135,
  138, 142, 143, 150, 158, 159,
  165, 167, 171–187,
  201–203, 229
Spivak, Gayatri Chakravorty, 8, 14,
  16–18, 155
Subjectivity, 2–4, 7–9, 18n1, 23, 24,
  31, 33, 52, 69, 85, 89, 90, 120,
  138, 167, 219, 226
Superheroes, 6, 14, 171–187

T

Transitions, 9–11, 25, 45, 46, 76, 90–92, 97, 125, 173, 178, 180, 186, 187

V

Vigilantes, 5, 6, 184

Violences
physical, 149, 167, 168, 219
psychological, 48–53
structural, 219, 227

W

Williams, Raymond, 10, 74, 76–79